A DEVIL'S DICTIONARY OF BUSINESS

A DEVIL'S DICTIONARY OF BUSINESS;

Monkey Business; High Finance and Low;

Money, the Making, Losing, and Printing Thereof;

Commerce; Trade; Clever Tricks; Tours de Force;

Globalism and Globaloney; Industry; Invention;

the Stock Market; Marvelous Explanations

and Clarifications; All Presented

with Wit and Attitude . . .

NICHOLAS VON HOFFMAN

NATION BOOKS
NEW YORK

A DEVIL'S DICTIONARY OF BUSINESS;
MONKEY BUSINESS; HIGH FINANCE AND LOW; MONEY, THE MAKING,
LOSING, AND PRINTING THEREOF; COMMERCE; TRADE; CLEVER TRICKS; TOURS
DE FORCE; GLOBALISM AND GLOBALONEY; INDUSTRY; INVENTION; THE STOCK
MARKET; MARVELOUS EXPLANATIONS AND CLARIFICATIONS; ALL PRESENTED WITH
WIT AND ATTITUDE

Published by
Nation Books
An Imprint of Avalon Publishing Group
245 West 17th St., 11th Floor
New York, NY 10011

Nation Books is a co-publishing venture of the Nation Institute and
Avalon Publishing Group Incorporated.

AVALON
publishing group incorporated

Library of Congress Cataloging-in-Publication Data is available.

ISBN 1-56025-712-1

9 8 7 6 5 4 3 2 1

Book design by Maria E. Torres

Printed in the United States
Distributed by Publishers Group West

To my son
Constantine

INTRODUCTION

Don't go to an angel if you want to know what's happening. Angels are optimists. Go to the devil. A good devil, if there be such a thing, knows everything an angel knows because he started out as one. Then he got bored and bad and found out things that angels never learn.

This book is full of diabolic stuff about business. Angelic stuff, too, and that will inspire you, give you hope and enlightenment of almost celestial quality; the diabolic stuff will make you gnash a tooth or two and provide enlightenment of almost hellish quality. A person needs both and if, by perusing this dictionary you were to get rich, be promoted or otherwise succeed in business, please remember to give this devil his due.

It pays to heed the devil because business is an unknown land even to the tens of millions who live in it. They may have knowledge of their own particular field, but once they move outside their own domains they are lost. That is why few people who make a success in one industry are able to repeat the feat in another.

Despite his reputation for inflicting pain, the reigning imp in this book is disposed to grant mercy to his readers and therefore has no room in his dictionary for economics, government, grand theories, sweeping statements, patriotic exhortations, high level abstractions, dogmatics, proven truths, wonky expositions or immutable doctrines, regardless of how well founded and meticulously researched. This devil is strictly business. But not business as usual. The infernal author of this work has included many little known, brain boggling business facts, fantasies and fallacies.

A Devil's Dictionary, with short, clear explanations of business terms and practices, is intended as a guide to the humdrum yet strange world of business, which for over two centuries has been as powerful an influence in the molding of American society, American culture and American character as religion or politics. It was neither church nor state which put an end to the time-honored practice of the shared family meal. It was not free thinking agnosticism which changed Sundays in America from days of quiet prayer into the shopping and recreational carnivals they are now. It was business.

As much as the 19th-century suffragettes and the 20th-century women's libbers, it was business which changed the social roles of women. It was business which weakened parental authority over children, changed the nation's courtship patterns, undermined slavery and made it possible for African Americans to escape the peonage in which they were trapped in the post Civil War South.

It is business which has been responsible for the gigantic cross border outpouring of Hispanic people with consequences nobody can foresee. It was business which, for better or worse, defined and made practical what politicians call The American Dream. Certainly it has been American business which gave Americans the highest material standard of living in the world, although that particular boast may no longer hold true.

Not that business intended to do any or many of these things. Business just does business. It takes countless shapes according to countless circumstances, without a thought for the abstractions of the classroom or political debate. Business is the most deliberate activity in the world and the most mindless. It is the most calculating of the consequences of what it does and the least conscious of its own side effects.

Like everything else, today's business arises out of yesterday's. Wal-Mart didn't just pop up out of the Arkansas soil like a new volcano coming up out of the ocean. It was the logical extension of practices which go back to the Federalist days of the door-to-door Yankee peddler. How it arose is encrusted in the fossil record called history. Although no entry in this book is more than five hundred words long, many of them provide a glimpse at that record.

Lacking a higher organizing principle I have fallen back on the alphabet—business from alpha to omega with a few stops in between. Other than a certain diabolic eccentricity the criteria for inclusion were a degree of usefulness in daily life, things which would give an inkling of how a society of material want and scarcity was transformed, primarily by business people, into one of abundance and even excess.

The transformation was not done through an automatic process, a doctrine, a theory, the laws of history or egomaniacal politicians. It was not done by evolution or nature or by talking television heads but by extraordinary men and women. You can say they were in it for the money, but that's not all they did it for. It absolutely is not.

abacus An energy-efficient office calculator. The first piece of office equipment we have knowledge of, if you don't count the clay tablet. It may have been invented by the ancient Lebanese or Phoenicians and used by Chinese and Roman businesspersons thousands of years ago, before most of us were born. After that the office equipment industry went on prolonged holiday, only to wake up in the last quarter of the nineteenth century when, one after another, there came tumbling out into the nation's offices the filing cabinet, the typewriter, the cash register, the loose-leaf ledger, the office scales, the time clock, the adding machine, the mimeograph machine, and the Rolodex. These tools helped business become the multilayered, bureaucratic organization the children of the twenty-first century abominate.

absolute auction Good for the buyer, bad for the seller. In an absolute auction the highest bid, which can be pathetically low, gets the goodies. In this it differs from a nonabsolute auction, in which the winning bid must meet a preset minimum or reserved or upset price. *Nota bene* that while the grand majority of auctions are straight—at least we hope they are—auctions offer more opportunities for cheating than three-card monte. But, be not discouraged; civil magistrates since Roman times have labored to keep business games honest, and occasionally, when not themselves bribed, they've enjoyed a degree of success.

accountant Men, and a few women, wearing green eyeshades and sporting elastic bands around their shirt sleeves, began sitting on high stools and acting as accountants from the 1850s onward. As business grew bigger, accounting grew more complicated and training was to be had only through proprietary colleges of commerce, the most famous of which was the Packard Business College. The school, founded by Silas S. Packard (1826–1898), played a major role in introducing women to office work, teaching them stenography and how to operate the recently introduced typewriter machine.

Instruction in the abstruse and ever changing art of accounting didn't migrate from for-profit commerce colleges to the high-status precincts of academia until after 1881, when Joseph Wharton (1826–1909), the founder of the zinc industry in the United States, gave the University of Pennsylvania $100,000 to start a school that would impart "a liberal education in all matters concerning Finance and Economics." (See **business schools**.)

accounting Without accounting there would be no business. In its various manifestations, and there are many of them, it not only displays the condition a business is in but is indispensable in managing every enterprise of any size and complexity. In the seventeenth century, this included itemizing the locks, the chains, and the irons used to make the jails holding the Salem witchcraft prisoners "witch tight." Accounting records of the same period, or "books of accompts," were sometimes balanced in wampum, legal tender in certain parts of North America until somebody set up a wampum factory, which, of course, brought on a wampum inflation. This led to the beads being outlawed in 1800 and replaced by dollars, which have been more or less OK except whenever the government sets up its dollar factory and wampum begins to look good again.

Over the centuries accounting has picked up a reputation as a less-than-a-laugh-a-minute occupation. In the early years of the twenty-first century, accounting got unfunnier still when it came out that outside auditors or accountants had colluded with their corporate customers to lure the innocent into buying vastly overpriced stock. Other than destroying the future happiness and the present comfort of about fifty million people, little damage was done. Even with its nil entertainment rating, accounting is the single most important business activity. For specific aspects of accounting, see **fixed costs, depreciation, Generally Accepted Accounting Principles,** and **Public Company Accounting Oversight Board**.

accrual An accounting word that usually means "counting money that isn't there," as in pretending customers who haven't paid yet really have paid. The CFO (chief financial officer) may have good and sufficient reasons to use accrual accounting, but it can open the door to misrepresentation of a company's financial position or even to . . . but we shall not use the ugly word *fraud,* since there has been entirely too much of it lately. Companies that don't use accrual keep their books on a cash basis. This sounds good, but you can cheat that way, too.

acid test Dropping a coin in acid to see if it really is gold. By extension, testing to see if a deal is as good as it looks, which it seldom is.

acquisitions See **mergers**.

actually buying a bond Bonds are recommended by the stuffy, the timid, and the prudent as safer and more dependable than stocks. Which is true, but there is a hitch. Try to buy a bond or sell one. With the exception of United States government bonds, which can be bought with ease at any bank, the bond business is not set up for individuals but for wholesale traders. Walk-in business isn't solicited. It's easier to find your way out of a coal mine without a flashlight than to discover the current price of most bonds, much less where and how you might buy one. Selling them can be a pain, also. Thus most people buy shares in bond funds (see **mutual funds**), which are more expensive and less remunerative, but also less troublesome.

From time to time a few corporations that issue bonds have tried to eliminate the layers of middlemen and sell them directly to individuals, only to have the wrath of God—or, more precisely, the bond dealers' cartel—land on them.

ADR (American Depository Receipts) ADRs are devices of convenience for those who purchase stocks in foreign corporations. Although they don't actually get to hold the shares, owners of ADRs get the dividends, capital gains, and so forth, of a person owning the stock directly. ADRs are not for amateurs, who ought not to be dabbling in the shares of companies based thousands of miles away. It is difficult enough to pull back the veil of obfuscation, not to mention chicanery, practiced by domestic corporations, but doing the same for foreign companies is best left to people who at least think they are expert at it. Furthermore, it is a known fact—known in the United States at least—that foreigners are less honest than Americans.

advertising A prurient, maddening, socially subversive, vulgar, exploitive, manipulative, coarse, honey-fugling necessity for the business society. Advertising didn't exist when men wore three-corner hats and every female knew what a distaff is, because there was nothing to advertise. Staples were sold in bulk, unbranded, unpackaged, and undifferentiatable. Most people made their own clothes from the fibers they raised, spun, and wove. What was made for sale was made locally by silver-, clock-, lock- and other kinds of smiths, whose products were known to potential buyers and needed no advertising.

Comes the revolution—the industrial one—and a tub of lard was no longer just a tub of lard. It was an ingredient in a bar of sweet-smelling, nicely colored soap, manufactured hundreds of miles away by a maker who had to let people know what he had for sale. In the decades after the Civil War, that's all that many ads did—announce the product and display pictures of the factory, the owner, and the owner's family.

But as goods and services proliferated, it became necessary not only to announce the product but to entice the buyer. These increasingly elaborate inducements have made advertising the folk art of the business society. Every accusation made against it is true, but if business can't sell, business can't exist.

African-Americans Slave traders who took black people from their native lands did not extinguish the spirit of business enterprise that existed in the African cultures. We know that slaves found ways to engage in business as far back as the eighteenth century, but no slave entrepreneur was more astonishing than Free Frank (1777–1854). Born in South Carolina, he was able both to satisfy the demands of his owner and build up a business mining and processing saltpeter, the main constituent for making gunpowder, and selling it to white people. With his profits, Free Frank was able to buy his wife and children's freedom and then, lastly, his own.

Prior to emancipation, freedmen and freedwomen were engaged in a variety of businesses, such as catering, restaurants, and dressmaking, as well as a number of other trades that served a white clientele. After the Civil War, despite the black codes in the South which kept African-Americans out of many businesses, thousands found ways to own land and go into farming.

Until the second emancipation brought about by the civil rights movement, black business activities operated much as those of foreign-language immigrant groups, who were also blocked from entering the larger business arena; they centered on enterprises that served the needs and tastes of their own ethnic markets. In 1899 North Carolina Mutual Insurance Company, the largest

African-American company of its kind, was started in much the same way as Poles, Germans, and Italians used their ethnic base to build up savings and loan associations, banks, and myriad companies serving their own communities.

air conditioning A term coined in 1906 by Stuart Cramer, a North Carolina engineer, who was dehumidifying air to prevent yarn from breaking in the wet, hot atmosphere of a Southern textile mill. Although Cramer invented the term, he did not invent the machine. Nobody did, though among the procession of businesspeople and engineers who helped develop and spread the technology, the best known is Willis Carrier (1876–1950). In 1928 he made what many would consider a serious mistake by air-conditioning the United States Capitol, thereby making it more comfortable for legislators to remain on their feet bloviating through Washington's intolerable summers.

Air conditioning first made an impression on the broad public when silent movie operators began putting the first, by no means perfected, systems in the movie palaces they erected after the First World War. By the 1930s the industry had split in two, with some companies backing window units and others, led by Carrier, promoting centralized air conditioning. The latter was preferred by architects, since it did away with the need for windows for ventilation and allowed them to design tower buildings whose curtain walls contained glass but no windows that opened. Central air conditioning also changed domestic design; attics with their fans gave way to flat-roofed houses without cross ventilation. In 1952 tract house developments with central air conditioning were built in Falls Church, Virginia, and Dallas, Texas. Air conditioning had made the sun states of the South and Southwest livable, changing the distribution of population and, therefore, the balance of political power in the United States.

airlines and aviation News of the Wright brothers' invention was disbelieved for five years, because the world wouldn't accept that people could fly. Such early skepticism probably accounts for the doubt as to the first company that might be called an airline. It's possible that in 1913 someone was providing scheduled flights across the bay separating San Francisco and Oakland. But for sure, the next year, the Tampa-St. Petersburg Airboat company was flying passengers across that bay.

Aviation, like the dot-coms, could not support itself unaided; early on, it learned to lean on the government. In the 1920s, World War I planes were the mainstays of an industry that depended on airmail contracts for survival. In 1934, C. R. Smith (1899–1990), the head of American Airlines, which wasn't much to brag about in those days, went to the federal government's Reconstruction Finance Corporation for a loan to finance Douglas Aircraft Company's development of the DC-3 passenger plane. The capacity and comfort of the DC-3 attracted enough customers to make an airline profitable, and it became the aircraft of choice of every airline in the world.

The airlines, like the railroads before them, have gone through exaggerated boom and bust cycles because of recurring overcapacity. In 1938 the industry was stabilized by the creation of the Civil Aeronautics Board, which prevented the airlines from competing themselves into extinction by controlling airfares and routes, basically the same kind of government regulation that kept the railroad and trucking industries from killing themselves off.

Though the industry fought it fang and claw, by the late 1970s deregulation and unfettered competition were the hot new idea in political economy, and we entered the present period of airline competitive turbulence, the remedy to which is, as of this writing, bankruptcies, mergers, government loans, and subsidies. Some people never learn to swim without a life jacket.

Alger, Horatio, Jr. (1832–1899) The real Horatio Alger was no Horatio Alger. A Harvard graduate and a Unitarian minister, the author of countless inspirational books for boys undertook the writing career that gave his name an enduring fame after he was forced to resign his pulpit in the wake of accusations of pederasty with adolescent males in his congregation.

The boy heroes of Alger's books, which sold hundreds of thousands of copies, were Protestant-ethic lads, whose hard work, loyalty, initiative, and energy took them from poverty into the comfortable regions of the middle class, not to enormous wealth. Nevertheless, Horatio Alger means "rags to riches," which has happened and still does, but not as often as people would like to believe.

aliases The best guess as to why corporations put themselves under the perpetrator's protection program and adopt aliases is that they are hiding from enraged customers and infuriated stockholders. Why else would Southern Bell, Bell Atlantic, New England Bell, and New York Bell huddle together under the name Verizon? Supposedly a conflation of *veritas*—truth—with horizon,

what Verizon really seems to mean is the remonopoliza-
tion of local phone service in the eastern third of the
United States. Also hiding under aliases are Cincinnati
Bell, now known as Broadwing, and Woolworth, one of
the oldest and best-known trade names in the United
States, which has renamed itself Venator. A *venator*, for
those not up on rare English words, is a hunter. Is Woolworth switching from hair combs to hare? Some years
ago the mighty U.S. Steel Corporation, a landmark company name if there ever was one, bought Marathon Oil
and vanished by changing its name to USX. There is also
CSX, which was once a railroad with a recognizable
name. Texas Industries rebaptized itself TXI Corp. Corporate America, like the Black Muslims, seems to have a
thing about the letter X.

The alphabet names are the most useful for causing
mass befuddlement. How do you know what you're being
billed for when the credit card charges you $47.22 from
ZBARF, Inc.?

Adopting an alias can cost millions, and that's not
counting all the new stationery and signage, but a thousand or more companies do it every year. The *Wall Street
Journal* did a quickie survey of what happened to the
price of the stock after a company changed its name.
More often than not, it fell.

American Dream No slogan moves inventory better.

Americanization American citizens living in fear that a
human, polyglot seiche of huge dimension is obliterating
English-speaking society can rest easy. The American
business culture sets all styles, declares all norms, and
prescribes all values. Its promise of the ideal life as

crafted by advertising agencies is irresistible, and, around the globe, people of every hue, faith, and background are trying to learn American English. The danger is not that Americanisms will vanish but that every other culture, language, and tradition will. Diversity doesn't stand a chance.

American Stock Exchange See **Curb Exchange**.

American System (Not to be confused with Senator Henry Clay's program of the same name for protective tariff and massive infrastructure improvements. For which see **Clay, Henry**.) The manufacturing method put on display by Yankee businessmen at the 1851 Crystal Palace Exhibition in London was such a leap ahead it was named the "American System." The heart of the system consisted of using interchangeable parts, instead of having master craftsmen measure, fit, buff, and refit each item. With the introduction of identical parts, guns, clocks, and locks, particularly, could be rapidly put together by unskilled workers.

The credit for the system, the basis for all mass production ever since, has been given to Eli Whitney (1765–1825), more famous as the inventor of the cotton gin, and to Samuel Colt (1814–1862), who is also more famous for something else—the invention of the revolver and the repeating rifle.

amortization (see also **depreciation**) Paying off a debt, such as a mortgage, according to a schedule and not helter-skelter as some people handle their credit card bills, making minimum payments some months and larger amounts other months.

analyst A human steam calliope employed by stockbrokers to tout securities the brokerage owns (or has a hidden financial interest in) and wants to unload onto the naive and ever hopeful. For years they swarmed on the financial cable channels, hawking their companies' wares. Analysts were presented by brokerages as nonpartisan experts who studied companies with detached expertise, after which they made their buy, sell, or hold recommendations. A few independents fulfilled that definition, but most said "buy, buy" all the time, with an occasional "hold," which was code for, "Sell that puppy as fast as you can snap open your mobile phone."

The sorry, all but pauperized, small investor millions were shocked, in the course of the stock market scandals of the early 2000s, to be told that analysts were ordered by their bosses to wax ecstatic over the worthless stock their companies intended to sell to the innocent and the innocently greedy. Wall Streeters referred to this kind of touting of worthless securities as "painting the corpse" or "putting lipstick on the pig."

Andersen, Arthur Edward (1885–1947) Founder of the company that bore his name and eventually achieved, in connection with the great Enron scandal of 2002, worldwide recognition of a kind not every accountant hopes for. The cupidity cum stupidity of Andersen's successors culminated in the firm's conviction in federal court for criminal misdeeds in connection with Enron. The company fell to pieces and vanished amidst the ruination of thousands of lives. Nevertheless, its conviction was an accomplishment of sorts for the people who ran it. They had done the undoable. Large, well-connected American business enterprises do not get convicted of anything.

Andersen himself was anything but scandalous. The son of Norwegian immigrants, he started his business career as an office boy and learned his profession at night school. Before he was finished, he taught his trade at Northwestern University, wrote a much-used textbook on accounting, and may have been the first person to get accountants into tax advice and general business consulting. In the wake of the Enron scandal, consulting and tax strategy work was denounced as a conflict of interest, and the firm to which Andersen gave his name was forced out of it even as the law was being changed to make it illegal. All this indignation may have been hasty, since accountants, with their exacting breakdown of a corporation's parts and their interrelationships, are ideally suited to give advice. In business there are so many potential conflicts of interest that, if there were a rule prohibiting possibly suspect situations, nothing would get done. In the end business depends on men and women who, out of good character or fear of being caught, do their work with a modicum of honesty.

annual reports In the 1870s, as the number, size, and complexity of manufacturing companies grew, teams of stockholders often descended on a corporation's headquarters to study the books and learn what was going on with their investment. This arrangement left something to be desired, so corporations began preparing reports summarizing the organization's state of financial health. The annual report was born and with it the never settled question of whether these documents reveal, conceal, or confuse. Some, issued in the latter part of the 1990s, have been nominated for a Pulitzer prize as examples of finely achieved magical realism.

annuity   A pension that you buy for yourself or that someone else buys for you. You set up an annuity by handing over a lump of money to an insurance company; in return, it pays you so much per month for the rest of your life. The insurance company is betting that you will die before it begins to lose money on the deal. An annuity can come with all kinds of side bets, such as a life insurance clause or anything else the good folks over at You Bet Your Life Mutual can come up with to befuddle and bemuse. The insurance industry is nonpareil when it comes to customer befuddlement. Nevertheless, annuities can be useful to both seller and buyer, but the buyer had better be sure the seller is solvent. How is solvency determined? The devil only knows.

Anthony, Susan B. (1820–1906)   Ms. Anthony, pioneer feminist, was accorded a kind of secular canonization when her likeness was embossed on the dollar coin. The Anthony dollar flopped, but it is safe to say that without her efforts women would have far less spending money, regardless of whose image may be on it.

antitrust   As in "antitrust laws" or "antitrust suit." Although it once had a very specific meaning, today it's a generic term, loosely used to cover the laws, prosecutions, and government agency actions intended to prevent or punish monopolists, oligopolists, price riggers, market fixers, and all plots to prevent free, fair, and open competition (haha!).

The first of the antitrust laws was passed in 1890 and, since then, not an hour has passed without controversy about them. Sometimes businesspeople hate them, and sometimes they love them, as in the recent antitrust suit against Microsoft, which divided the computer industry.

Suits against conspiracies to charge higher prices are much more popular. Recent jailings of the top people at companies such as Christie's and Archer Daniels Midland for cooperating when they should have been competing caused few sympathetic sobs, even among the crustier proponents of private enterprise.

APR or **annual percentage rate** APR, a child of the 1968 Consumer Protection Act, is the interest a consumer pays, and it must be printed in easy-to-read type on the sales contract. Consumer Protection Act or no, it's anybody's guess as to whether customers take advantage of the protection, or if they view it as one more government-mandated line to fill out.

arbitrage 1. The exploitation of a difference in price for the same thing sold in different places by different people at the same time. In what passes for high finance, people bending over computers in London are able to see a variation of one-hundredth of a cent between the price of a security in Tokyo and in Frankfurt, and leap to buy at the infinitesimally lower price or sell at the infinitesimally higher one. If you can do this in large quantities you can make money, but it's not much fun. Some economists insist that this form of passing your time is helping to make the world's financial markets run more efficiently, but as a productive activity it is akin to using a piece of gum on the end of a string to fish quarters out of the bottom of a grated well. Something like arbitrage is committed twenty-four hours a day on e-Bay, where people seem to have a lot more fun. **2.** Buying stock in a company in anticipation that a bid will soon be made to buy the company, thus pushing up the price of its stock.

Hence the term *arbitrageur,* one who, of course, sells his or her stock on the rise in price. The word is of distinctly French origin and therefore mildly suspect.

Armstrong, Edwin Howard (1890–1954) Driven crackers by large corporations infringing on his patents and the resulting lawsuits by which the big guys aimed to rob him of the fruits of his genius, Armstrong ended his travail by jumping out of a New York City apartment house window. Armstrong was the inventor of a string of electronic devices that made modern broadcasting possible, the most famous being FM radio.

Around 1930 Armstrong perfected what was then called "staticless" radio. Even today FM is far superior to AM radio broadcasting, but seventy years ago the quality gap was enormous, and it scared the pants off commercial AM broadcasters, who feared that if FM caught on, they would only be able to sell their AM equipment for junk. Using their influence with the Federal Communications Commission, they managed to prevent FM's coming into common use for more than a generation.

Arnaz, Desi (born Desiderio Alberto Arnaz y de Acha III) (1917–1986) Pioneer television executive and one of the countless immigrants who have played significant parts in American business. Arnaz was born of a wealthy family in Santiago de Cuba who were chased off the island by Fulgencio Batista, the right-wing dictator who preceded the left-wing dictator Fidel Castro. Although Arnaz achieved considerable success as a musician and yet greater fame as comedienne Lucille Ball's husband, his most lasting accomplishments were off-camera. Desi reorganized television production methods, moved the center of the industry from New York City to Los Angeles, and invented the rerun syndication system, which holds the industry together to this day. In 1955 he bought the RKO studio with its twenty-five sound stages and, using a variety of cost-cutting methods, turned what had been an expensive handcrafted business into today's mass production industry, which cranks out the staple programming for the world.

asset **1.** Euphemism for a spy or saboteur. **2.** Coy name for a military or naval unit, as in statements such as "Our agreement with the emir allows us to station our assets at Gaping Wound Airbase in Bloodybloody Land." **3.** Any object, piece of paper, or property that can be sold or traded for something of value, such as money. The variety of forms assets come in is seen in the number of combinations used with the word, such as fixed assets, capital assets, nonrecurring assets, goodwill assets. Strange to say, in the world of banking, loans are carried on the books as assets, but then again, loans can be and are bought, sold, traded, and diddled with like many another thing of value.

With assets, care is in order, for there have been regrettable instances in the history of business when it turned out that the assets claimed by individuals and companies didn't exist or had much less value than advertised in the annual report. Happy surprises such as the discovery of hidden assets do occur sometimes, or at least occasionally . . . well, it has been known to happen.

asset-backed security A bond or loan, the interest and repayment of which are not based on some airy-fairy promise but on a particular asset's ability to generate money. When the highway commission sells bonds whose income derives from the Great River Gorge Bridge, it is selling an asset-backed security. If the commission defaults on its payments, the bond owners can come and take the bridge, or so they tell us.

The variety of asset-backed securities expands as rapidly as the lupine imaginations of investment bankers can come up with new wrinkles. For example, your credit card debt, for which you may be paying anywhere from 8 to 18 percent interest, is used as the basis of an asset-backed security referred to as plastic bonds in the trade. (See **securitization**.)

associate The new name for salesclerk. The spirit of the times demands of twenty-first-century management that it appear egalitarian, while at the same time preserving hierarchical authority. Endowing low-status jobs with high-status titles is one of the ways this sleight of hand trick is realized.

AT&T At one time AT&T, or American Telephone and Telegraph, was the epitome of a blue-collar stock, the widows' and orphans' stock. It paid its dividend without fail, quarter after quarter, decade after decade. The simple but lordly letter T was the company's stock exchange symbol, and it stood for respectability and predictability. AT&T's reliability depended in no small measure on its having been informally and illegally granted an exemption from the antitrust laws. (See **Vail, Theodore Newton**.) For many years Ma Bell, as the corporation encouraged people to call it, gave telephone subscribers across the nation a quality of service that earned it a position that was close to sacrosanct, but a monopoly is a monopoly and in due course AT&T's bureaucratic ways and resistance to overdue change cost popular support. When, in 1982, a federal court decreed that Ma Bell would have to be drawn and quartered, the weeping and gnashing of teeth were all but inaudible. Faced with the sneaky games characteristic of the modern telephone company, some persons old enough to have jumped for joy back then are gnashing a tooth or two for Old Ma Bell now.

Although the corporation's renowned Bell Labs brought forth inventions without which the e-age would not have come into existence, the company as a whole remained in its heart not a twenty-first-century electronics company, but an early twentieth-century electromechanical one. From 1982 onward, it flipped and flopped, buying companies, selling companies, dividing, and reorganizing while it spent multi-oodles on a variety of endeavors it never seemed to be able to manage. Then in December 2000, with debts of over $62 billion and expenses mounting, AT&T announced it was cutting the dividend for the first time in more than a century. With this news, the world was reminded that nothing lasts forever except the Roman Catholic Church. Maybe.

auction market or **double auction** or **two-sided market** An auction in which many people are buying and selling the same thing, preeminently stocks. Stock exchanges are an endless double auction conducted under very exact rules to preclude cheating, swindling, and other breaches of etiquette. They have so many rules that the people in the stock market have to take examinations. It doesn't follow that because a person knows the rules, a person will obey them. It does follow that a person who knows the rules well, knows well how to get around them.

audit Ideally a full and complete statement of the condition of a company prepared by a certified public accountant. That's ideally, but ideally is expensive, so some audits are less than full, and some auditors are lazy idiots who fail to look where they should, and some auditors take bribes from their auditees, so sometimes it pays to audit the audit.

Babbage, Charles (1792–1871) British mathematician generally given credit for having invented the computer. Poor Babbage, who also invented the cowcatcher and the speedometer, was denied the satisfaction of ever running his hands up and down his computer, much less using it, because the necessary technology to build it did not yet exist. Few inventions stand alone, able to be put into service without inventions and complementary institutional arrangements. (See **Eastman, George** for other inventions needing help to exist.)

back-end or rear-end load Although the term sounds like something pertaining to a construction site, it has to do with investments such as mutual funds. It means: if we don't get you coming in, we'll get you going out. The back-end load, which also goes by such names as exit fee or redemption charge, is levied on someone selling or withdrawing his or her shares. Customarily, the fee drops with each year the shares are held. There's nothing objectionable about back-end loading, as long as the customer is clearly given to understand the charge. One of the besetting vices of financial institutions is hiding its fees and charges from its smaller, retail customers. Whether the industry's silence is owing to laudable shame at the enormity of its profits or fear of what the customers might do if they realized how much of their investment's earnings are consumed by fees and commissions, the devil leaves for you to decide.

bailout The dropping of dough by the government or a private party into a company, or otherwise aiding a distressed corporation nearing bankruptcy. There are countless ways to slip some dying organization money without its being noticed. Sometimes bailouts pay off, as when, some years ago, the government helped the Chrysler Corporation survive a near-death experience. On that occasion the government made a profit. But some bailouts merely keep half-dead organizations half-alive. When there are jobs being lost, the political and sentimental pressure to keep companies on life support is often irresistible. (See **too big to fail**.) Whole nations such as Brazil and Mexico have been bailed out, not for charitable reasons, but because if they defaulted on their debts the big American banks would suffer.

baksheesh A tip, a commission, a kickback, or a bribe. The word is often used in international trade, although the practice is illegal under American law. A U.S. businessperson risks a fine or the slammer for injudiciously baksheeshing foreign business associates. Why the United States should have a law forbidding its citizens to bribe foreign citizens on foreign soil is beyond understanding, save as a misplaced exercise in Calvinism. If other countries don't want Americans bribing their business executives, they can pass laws forbidding the practice and then enforce them if they can.

balloon framing or **platform framing** The name for the nearly universal framing system used in American home construction, the most familiar part of which is the two-by-four wooden studs. Balloon framing replaced the post and beam, which required huge pieces of hard-to-transport lumber fastened together on-site by highly skilled joiners, using the mortise and tenon method. Faster, cheaper, and needing less-skilled craftsmen, the balloon system arrived sometime in the 1830s in the American Midwest, made possible by the steam-powered rotary saw and the manufacture of cheap nails.

Balloon construction made possible the vernacular housing design and real estate development in which most of the American population now lives. It was the first of a long train of improvements, inventions, and improvisations by which, decade after decade, business has been able to lower the cost and raise the quality of housing available to an ever-growing proportion of the population.

Some of the changes involved the introduction of new materials in building. The coming of the railroads, for example, made it possible to use woods such as ash, oak, and maple, which don't float and could not, therefore, be moved from forest to market via the river drives. The changes continue to this day, with copper piping replaced by more efficient plastics, and nails and screws by glues with greater strength.

By standardizing design, business has been able to manufacture more houses off-site in mill and factory. This has produced the monotonous and oppressive ticky-tacky associated with dreary suburbia, but even the most depressing housing developments eventually take on the individual stamp of the owners. Whatever its failings, and they are legion, without the housing industry's successes, half the population of the United States would be living in the streets, or in hovels so ghastly they might wish they were.

balloon payment The last payment on a loan, but it can be a doozy. The balloon is the unpaid balance of an expired loan. Some loans are written so that only the interest is paid during their duration; the principal, the amount borrowed, has to be paid when the loan expires.

bank "Banking consists of facilitating the movement of money from Point A, where it is, to point B, where it is needed," sayeth Victor, Lord Rothschild (1910–1990) of the famous banking family. The old boy got it right. That is the nub of what a bank is and does. At bottom, people give banks the use of their money, for which banks pay the lenders or depositors.

Now comes the magic or the wickedness, depending on your point of view. Since all the depositors will not withdraw their money at the same time (unless there is a panic, in which case all bets are off), the bank is free to lend out more money than it has on deposit. This is not naughty or even illegal, but helpful in making sure that businesses and individuals have the money they need.

Most of the time the system works, but every so often the bankers go crazy with greed, stupidity, corruption, or just the frenzy of boomer enthusiasm. Then they make bad loans that cannot be repaid, and if they make too many of them, all hell breaks out in bankruptcies, unemployment, swooning prices, and various degrees and kinds of misery.

Incidentally, banking, which was already old when Adam Smith (1723–1790) was writing how necessary it is to business prosperity, may be the first true multinational industry. By the beginning of the Renaissance, bankers in one country had offices in others. A hundred years ago, National City Bank, now Citigroup, had firmly placed its tentacles in South America, Russia, and China.

bankrupt, bankruptcy A word of Italian origin, which is not surprising, since banking and finance began with the descendants of Romulus and Remus, and not, despite the stereotype, with the Jews. The early bankers/moneychangers of northern Italy customarily did their business seated on benches, and, when one of them committed the unpardonable sin of being unable to pay his obligations, a committee of his confreres seized his bench (the *banco*) and broke it (Medieval Latin *ruptus,* "broken"). "Broke" and "busted" are still with us, meaning without pecuniary resources, but that is not exactly the same as bankrupt. People may be insolvent, meaning without funds or owing more than they own, but they are only bankrupt when their creditors fall on them and demand payment they can't come up with.

The Romans, from whom we derive some of our ideas of commercial law, were said at one period in their long history to hack a bankrupt debtor into pieces, each of which was given to one of his creditors. At a later date, they took to selling the bankrupt into slavery, and in the English-speaking world imprisonment for debt was common into the middle of the nineteenth century (as described in the works of Dickens and Thackeray). This practice has recently been revived in the United States, where husbands who fail in their child support payments are carted off in chains. Getting one's bench broken seems mild by comparison.

bar code In June 1974 at Marsh's Supermarket in Troy, Ohio, a package of Wrigley's gum went through a checkout scanner. It was the first appearance of the bar code, which is now in use all over the world in countless fields of endeavor.

The bar code system was called forth by a committee of businessmen in the grocery industry—trade association executives, food-manufacturing companies such as Heinz and General Foods, and big retailers such as Kroger and A&P. They had the idea for it, and they found the technical people to make it for them. Instead of using competing, incompatible systems, the two industries agreed on a standardized, symbolic language with an infinite capacity to grow, specialize, and adapt to unforeseen needs and uses. The money saved and the productivity gained in retail, manufacturing, and transportation are beyond calculation. There would be no just-in-time delivery systems without the ubiquitous little black and white stripes. Without the Universal Product Code, by the end of the twentieth century—with literacy becoming as rare as it was before Gutenberg—there would not have been enough clerks to handle half the nation's business.

The bar code is a heaven-sent aid for illiterate personnel, the oafs and oaflettes cranked out by the high schools and community colleges.

From the start, the new system was in the hands of the big guys, and, though the bar code might have been used differently, the big guys used it to get bigger. In 1960 decent-sized supermarkets carried about six thousand different items; they now carry ten times that number.

As the size of the stores has grown, so has the dominance of the big retailers, snuffing out many thousands of small, owner-operated shops, which cannot compete with the fast-as-a-flash, cheap-as-dirt distribution systems of companies such as Staples and Home Depot. When a bottle of Procter & Gamble's shampoo is rung up on the register at Wal-Mart, this fact is simultaneously sent to Procter & Gamble's computers, so that without having to place an order, Wal-Mart keeps its shelves stocked.

For cost there's never been anything like it. On the days when you want some item, it's there for you. On other days you have to wonder if all this hasn't stuffed our homes and lives with crap.

barons Long before newspaper proprietors were ennobled by being dubbed press barons, there were newspapers in America. The first was published on September 25th, 1690, by one Benjamin Harris. Its less than snappy moniker was *Publick Occurrences Both Foreign and Domestick.* It announced it was to be "furnished once a moneth (or if any Glut of Occurrences happen, oftner)." Had the policy of publishing only when there was news persisted, it would be a different world, but you can't make money by selling people only what they need.

The most baronial of American press lords was William Randolph Hearst (1863–1951), the willful, arrogant, and quixotic son of an immensely rich father, whose money from mining made all things possible for his son. Hearst built up a chain of more than one hundred garishly shrill newspapers, which, in policy, ranged over the years from embracing a soft form of socialism and animal rights, to promoting reactionary positions and a craziness that led his paper to suggest that someone put a bullet into President William McKinley. Guess what? Somebody did. For decades Hearst was a large presence on the American scene, but as a businessman he was no great shakes. His chain of newspapers was, for a time, the largest, but it wasn't the first and it was certainly not the most profitable.

Far more deserving of a baronage was Henry Robinson Luce (1898–1967), who founded *Time, Life, Fortune,* and *Sports Illustrated* magazines, all aimed at a new, college-trained generation of pre-TV Americans. The influence of his publications can only be described as prodigious and cannot be judged by the wilted, insipid, and directionless publications that still bear their names but not their influence. Media with a powerful punch cannot be directed by corporate management, and certainly not by the lumbering, civil servant–like timeservers at AOL Time Warner, who are, in stately fashion, guiding themselves and the Luce publications toward extinction.

DeWitt Wallace (1889–1981) and Lila Bell Acheson (1889–1984), his wife and business partner, might have been a baron and baroness save for their being such retiring people. Nevertheless, they brought the *Reader's Digest* into the world and directed it to a circulation of thirty million around the globe, a figure never remotely approximated by any other publication. Many another copied the *Digest* format but none succeeded as the Wallaces did.

Probably more mad mogul than baron, Robert Edward (Ted) Turner (1938–) did what Luce and the Wallaces had done earlier. Ted Turner came up with a new thing—CNN, the Cable News Network. Prior to CNN, Turner had cut more then one ingenious, profitable dido, but, for impact in the industry and outside of it, nothing compared to his all-news-all-the-time formula. Although the wallop delivered in the 1840s by the coming of the telegraph—the first form of instant communication—has no equal, Turner's CNN gave the world a bit of a shake. (See also **robber baron**.)

basis point One-hundredth of one percent. For the thick of tongue and the impatient, it is better to say "eleven basis points" than "eleven-hundredths of one percent." Basis points are commonly used when talking about bond yields and such.

Batten, Barton, Durstine and Osborn The best-known advertising agency in the inter-war period, BBD&O, as it was always called, gave the nation Betty Crocker. The agency achieved its fame in part because it was fun to chant its name or initials and in part because of the fame of Bruce Barton (1886–1967), one of the founding partners. In 1925 Barton published *The Man Nobody Knows,* in which he conflated religion and business so thoroughly they have yet to be disentangled. His book, which stayed on the bestseller list for years, revealed Jesus Christ to have been "the World's Greatest Salesman," a management genius "who picked up twelve men from the bottom ranks of business and forged them into an organization that conquered the world." The influence of Barton's muscular Christianity, as it has been called, on pinheaded Protestantism was and is immense.

bean counter   Term of contumely applied to bookkeepers, accountants, and CPAs by persons who cannot get it through their heads that bean counters are more important to the organization than they are.

bear   Any furry, plantigrade quadruped of the genus Ursus, of which the most fearsome are *Ursus horribilis* (grizzly bear) and *Ursus wallstreetianus* (short seller bear).

bearer or **bearer bond** or **bearer paper**   A bond or any other kind of financial instrument that can be instantly converted to cash by whoever has it in his or her physical possession. Bearer bonds are as good as gold, but pretty much a thing of the past.

bear market   A prolonged period characterized by *Ursus horribilis* prowling around the stock exchanges gobbling up people's savings. Bear markets are thought to be caused by interest rates, lack of interest rates, faulty stellar alignments, irritable bowel syndrome in high places, and bull markets.

beer   The elixir of life for the prime male demographic group. Beer, ale, porter, or stout is made and drunk in countless cultures, but the American beer industry came with the mid-nineteenth-century immigrants. German brewers brought with them the knowledge of how to make a honey-colored beer (Pilsner or lager) that looked ever so much nicer than the dark, thick, slightly bitter brews, which had been all that was available. (The lager brewers got a big assist from the glass industry, which drove ceramic bottles and beer steins into the antique shops.)

And then came Bud! Named after Ceské Budejovice or Budweis (its German name), a town in Bohemia, this somewhat sweeter beer was the perfect brewski for the American palate. Eberhard Anheuser, whose company makes it, started out in life as a soap manufacturer, but the genius behind the company was his son-in-law, Adolphus Busch (1831–1913), a fella who knew how to move inventory.

Although alcohol is not recommended during physical exertion, beer and sports got married more than a century ago. Brewers bought professional baseball teams in their tireless merchandising efforts, which also included the famous free lunch, offered in saloons everywhere to those who ordered a five-cent glass of beer. These days there's no free lunch. All you get is a bowl of those awful fish things or a couple of miniature pretzels.

below par A stock or a bond with a hangover or a wasting disease.

Bell, as in **The Bell** The Bell is The Buzzer on some stock exchanges, but bell or buzzer, the sounding of either marks the beginning and end of the working day. It is accounted a signal honor to ring The Bell, placed on a little balcony overlooking the New York Stock Exchange's trading floor, which multimillionaires, swindlers of international stature, celebrities of the month, wolfish politicians, and prostitutes of the better sort sound with violent joy.

beny, benies Not to be confused with bennies, as in Benzedrine or other amphetamines used by overworked subordinates to meet a demanding boss's expectations. A beny, slang for fringe benefit, is a perk for the lower echelons such as health insurance, a pension, paid sick days, flextime, and so forth.

big boo-boos The deals you didn't make and some of the deals you did. In 1941 Thomas Watson, Sr., the founder of IBM spurned a sales pitch from Chester Carlson, an inventor, who trotted off with his patents to found the Xerox Corporation. Time Warner would have had a much happier financial history had it only done to AOL what Watson did to what was to become Xerox.

Bilderbergers See **sinister doings**.

blind trust The very name should inspire skepticism. A blind trust is property, usually investments, held in trust for a public official who does not know the contents of the trust and therefore avoids a conflict of interest; for example, Mr. Golden Loan In The Pants is appointed Secretary of the Treasury and hands billions over to a trustee—it could be a bank or it could be his pal, Harry—who is supposed to invest the money secretly without telling Loan In The Pants. Only a blindly trusting public could take this bit of kabuki seriously.

blue chip As in "blue chip stock." The stock in a high-class corporation, which usually means an outfit with a famous name and the profits to match. In the old days, whenever they were, the name was associated with words such as *reliable, old line, high dividends, prudent management, sound,* and the like. How many fit that definition now is a matter for close scrutiny. Corporations with illustrious names can rot out in a remarkably short time. Others with nondescript pedigrees may be off in a corner performing like a blue chip champion without too many people noticing.

boarding house In the mid-nineteenth century, half or more of the families in some American cities took in at least one roomer, and until just after World War II, a sizable portion of the population got room and often board from establishments whose proprietors were more often than not women. The lodging industry was an early port of entry for women into the business world, and phrases like "star boarder" and "boarding house reach," now archaic, were commonly used figures of speech. Some catered to specific groups—theatrical boarding houses and those providing rooms for people from certain areas—some were comfortably middle class, and others were anything but, as in this description of lodgings on New York's Lower East Side: "A star boarder slept on a folding bed. . . . I knew a printer who every night unscrewed a door (and) put it on two chairs; he couldn't pay as much as the one who had the bed."

bond Most of the money that governments and private organizations raise for big projects comes from selling bonds, but in a stock market culture, bonds are the glitzless securities, looked down on as stodgy, old-fogy stuff. The boring things pay their promised interest quarter after quarter, year after routine year. Bonds do fluctuate in value, going up when interest rates go down, and going down when interest rates go up, and some bonds have interest rates that move up and down. Hence, they can be as much of a crap shoot as stocks, but these often complicated pieces of paper have little attraction for amateur investors.

The bond is simply an IOU, and they were once written in embossed letters on heavyweight paper with a gold seal, issued by a public body, such as the Bayou City Sewer District or the United States Treasury, or by a company or a corporation. Bonds of such impressive aspect went out of existence generations ago, but the idea remains that a loan of this kind binds—hence the name—the borrower to repay exactly according to its terms, and no ifs, ands, or buts about it.

Bonds come in bewildering varieties. The length of their maturities can vary from short-term loans to those that are never meant to be paid back. The latter you buy for the interest alone. Callable bonds can be paid off before their maturity, whenever the issuer wants, an irritating feature if you bought them hoping to enjoy the nice, fat interest rate for many years. Some bonds are based on collateral, a specific property that is forfeit if there is a default; some bonds, called debentures, are based on nothing more than a solemn promise; other bonds are called convertibles, because the bondholder may convert them into stock in the company issuing the bond.

This doesn't come close to describing all the different kinds of bonds the men and women of high finance have thought up and sold over the years. It's anybody's opinion whether this is a help for the efficient distribution of money, or whether it's flummery calculated to extract the largest fees and charges for those in the bond business.

bond ratings His word is as good as his bond, but some bonds are a helluva lot better than others (see **toxic waste**). The absolute best are the ones with the triple A (AAA) rating, which, generically, refers to any rock-solid, absolutely safe, sleep-through-the-night bond. (When all three are capitalized—AAA—the designation has been awarded by Standard & Poor's, an investment advisory service. When only the first A is a capital—Aaa—the rating is by Moody's Investors Service.) The ratings are as reliable as the raters, who can, on occasion, be fooled or swayed or intimidated by grand old corporate names, prestigious reputations, crooked auditors, and their own stupidity. Nevertheless, whatever their shortcomings, the rating services, of which there are many, are all that nonprofessionals have to rely on in making investment decisions.

brand In the 1850s, Singer Sewing Machine and McCormick Reaper, mass producers of the most complicated objects yet to be sold to the general public, put their company names on their products. By the 1880s, the National Biscuit Company, Wrigley chewing gum, Procter & Gamble and others were building brand consciousness to persuade women not to make things but to buy them, and not to buy them in bulk from a barrel or a bin, but in a brand-name package.

Nobody but nobody was more relentlessly ingenious at building a national brand consciousness than Mr. 57 Varieties, Henry Heinz (1844–1919). He put concrete letters on hillsides all over America, reading "Heinz 57." New York's first electric billboard, with 1,200 bulbs costing ninety dollars a day to operate, went up in 1900 declaring "Heinz 57 GOOD THINGS FOR THE TABLE," and if he had had his way, no one would have gotten to the graveyard without wearing one of Henry's pickle pins. Before there was a federal Food and Drug Administration or public inspection, Henry Heinz made his last name synonymous with quality.

No such branding would have been possible without breakthrough inventions in continuous flow manufacturing, in packaging and containers. Heinz brought all the elements together and, after making his company a byword in America, set out to do the same around the world. Nobody told him about the global economy, yet in 1886 he concluded an agreement to supply condiments to Fortnum & Mason. By 1910 he was exporting to twenty-five countries, including South Africa, India, and New Zealand. "Mountains and oceans," he told his diary, "do not furnish any impossible barrier to the extension of trade. . . . Our market is the world."

breakfast In pre-business society, it was the first meal of the day taken by the family together. Now, like the evening meal, it is increasingly restricted to weekends and high holidays. For five thousand years the Jewish, Moslem, and Christian faiths incorporated some form of familial eating together in their worship, be it only saying grace before meals. The business society induced, albeit unintentionally, the junking of these immemorially old social rituals in hardly more than a century.

Middle-class family cohesion has been broken apart by the schedules, work demands, and priorities of a business society. Instead of family members gathered around a table, there is "dashboard dining," that is, eating commercially prepared food designed to be consumed in bumper-to-bumper traffic on the way to work on I-19.

Although many Americans associate "family values"

with the presumed social conservatism of the business society, business institutions and business power have as much to do with the formation of the twenty-first-century family as left-wing permissiveness and liberal moral relativism.

Bretton Woods agreement of 1944 Signed by forty-four nations, the agreement bumped the British pound off its throne as the currency by which other currencies were measured and replaced it with the dollar. The agreement, which also gave birth to the International Monetary Fund, set a fixed exchange rate between a gold-based dollar and other currencies, an arrangement which did fairly well until inflation in the United States made it unworkable. The inflation was caused by the American government cheapening the dollar by madly printing too many of them in the basement, to pay for the Vietnam War and the rising price of oil.

The old gold-based dollar was a dollar backed by the enormous American gold hoard at Fort Knox, Kentucky; that is, a fixed number of dollars were minted per ounce of gold. Individuals were not allowed to trade in their dollars for gold but foreign governments could, although they did not until the American inflation made them choose the yellow stuff over the green. At that point the U.S. Treasury was literally pulling the gold out of Fort Knox, shipping it to New York, and putting it on freighters heading east to Europe. There was only so long that circus could go on. Washington closed the gold window, and the first steps were taken to establish the present system, in which the value of any currency is determined by what somebody is willing to pay for it in another currency.

bubble A subjective term for a stratospheric rise in the price of something, far beyond its previous value.

The first famous bubble was the tulipmania episode of 1634–1637, when immutable legend has it that, possibly as a result of an attack of the bubonic plague, all sense deserted the theretofore sober burghers of Holland, who staked their fortunes on a wild tulip bulb speculation, with prices mounting until a bulb named the Semper Augustus is supposed to have been bought for tens of thousands of dollars. To this day tulipmania is synonymous with greed-crazed people bidding up a market to ridiculous levels, only to get crushed when the roof falls in.

In actuality bubbles aren't a species of infectious disease that unaccountably sweeps through whole populations of investors. The solid Dutch businessmen had nothing to do with tulipmania, which was mainly a wacky form of gambling carried on in the taverns of seventeenth-century Amsterdam. Yet the quasi-fictitious tale of tulipmania lives on in Wall Street as a cautionary story for the gullible and the overenthusiastic, neither of whom will ever pay it heed.

Quick rises in the prices of intrinsically worthless objects may come about through the fickleness of fashion, as when millions of the numbskull mothers and daughters of America collected Cabbage Patch dolls for a few years. In the late 1990s, tulipmania took hold of investors in dot-coms, who drove share prices up to laughable levels. Some bought the stock believing they could get in and out with a profit prior to the pop. Some few did.

bucket shop A satisfactorily derisory term for a brokerage house (also **bucket shop operator**). Bucket shops flourished from about the 1870s to the end of the 1920s and were places where people who couldn't afford to buy stocks could go and place bets on the stocks' price movements. Bucket shops were reputed to be dens of dishonesty, but whether the proprietors of these gaming places were less honest than those whose higher-status brokerages actually sold securities is an open question. From its wee beginnings at the end of the eighteenth century till now, the securities business has not been able to escape accusations of one kind of cheating or another.

build a better mousetrap and the world will beat a path to your door Like hell it will.

One man who built a better mousetrap was Isaac Singer (1811–1875), a wandering actor of uncertain ability but with a genius for things mechanical and procreational. He sired twenty-four children with five women, some of whom he was married to, and he perfected the sewing machine. The Singer sewing machine was the best of its kind, but sales were impeded by a legal snarl over patents.

In 1851 he went into partnership with Edward Clark (1811–1882),a business genius who started a network of agencies where machines were sold and repaired and where women were taught their use and care. An adjunct to the sales blitz was the first consumer easy-payment program—five dollars down and five dollars a month. The sewing machine was the first mass-produced, labor-saving appliance sold to American women.

Clark may or may not have invented the modern multinational corporation, but the Singer Company was in the vanguard. He must be credited with the development of important corporate internal controls and communications systems, without which the company could not have carried off its groundbreaking feats in international trade. In 1882 the company opened a large factory in Scotland, as it discovered what the Japanese car manufacturers learned a century later: when the export business hits a certain volume, it makes business sense to build a factory abroad.

In 1904, Singer's St. Petersburg headquarters on the Nevski Prospekt became the first steel-girder building erected in Russia, where the company already had a manufacturing plant pouring out hundreds of thousands of machines. The company's indefatigable sales organization sold them to illiterate serfs across the tzar's immense empire. In 1907 a Singer executive, writing from Siberia about their nomadic Kirzhiz customers, said, "so they are irregular payers, without being bad or unworthy of credit . . . our agent can hardly avoid trading or bartering here, as our buyers have no cash at disposal, but for their goods, i.e. cattle, pelts or fish." If Singer and the other corporations moving into Russia had not been stopped by the Bolsheviki, we can only wonder at what might have been.

bull Variously: **1.** Male bovine excreta. **2.** A letter from the Pope. **3.** A policeman. **4.** An optimist.

bull market A prolonged period characterized by the thunder of ungulate hooves and happy hordes of human Morris dancers in the nation's stock exchanges. Bull market periods are thought to be accompanied by a rise in the consumption of costly French wines and a drop in sexual harassment cases.

business cycle (See also **Kondratieff wave** and **cyclical stock**.) The periodic expansions and contractions of business activity are as old as business itself. Whenever business begins to sag, there is a squabble over whether or not the economy is in recession, with all kinds of statistical definitions being flung about—but checking your wallet works just as well. The causes of the business cycle have been definitively explained by every major economist and every stockbroker blabbing on cable TV. All their explanations are correct, and if they contradict each other, well, they just do. While you wait for the business cycle problem to be disposed of, it may help to recall what the fabled investment banker J. P. Morgan is supposed to have said when asked whither the price of securities: "They will fluctuate." And so life goes, up and down, in and out, back and forth.

business schools Don't look for the business school on prestigious, liberal arts campuses. It is never placed on the quad. The bee school is to be found off-campus in a geographic and status penumbra, its faculty members looked down on by the academic panjandrums. Bee school professors may take comfort in making a lot more money and having a lot finer digs than their higher-status colleagues, who read the *New York Review of Books* and sneer that a master's in business administration represents featherheaded fads and mumbo jumbo akin to the twaddle taught in schools of education and social work.

The crypto-collectivist, closet Luddites who hold forth loudest where the ivy grows the thickest dis vocational education in general, but really have it in for business and engineering schools. Nevertheless by the end of the nineteenth century a distinct body of knowledge and technique for the management of large enterprises was there to be imparted in some organized fashion, and Dartmouth College opened the Amos Tuck School of Administration and Finance in the autumn of 1900. Edward Tuck (1842–1938), who put up the money, was an expatriate living in Paris, of no great distinction in business history, who'd married rich and got much richer successfully investing his wife's money. His one big idea was the business school, and, of course, ultimately, the ubiquitous MBA, which was so self-evidently useful that in less than ten years Harvard copied the idea and opened a school of its own, which—need it be said?—is located well away from Harvard Square and all those nice old Georgian buildings.

Buttonwood Agreement Noteworthy as the first of endless efforts to clean up shady practices in the stock market business, even before there were any stocks to buy and sell. The agreement was so named because it was concluded under the limbs of a buttonwood tree at 68 Wall Street in the year of our Lord 1792, after the first of what has turned out to be an infinite number of subsequent Wall Street scandals. To work up a scandal was no easy feat, given that the only things these dealers had to trade were a few government bonds. Like the periodic cleanups of crooked police departments, this one only lasted twenty years before another scandal erupted. The Buttonwood Agreement contained the first of many arrangements to prevent price competition by fixing brokerage fees. The direct descendant of Buttonwood is the New York Stock Exchange.

call, callable, call risk, call premium, etc. Whenever you see the word *call* in finance, you know that it has something to do with somebody having to cough up something immediately. A call loan is one in which the lender can demand repayment of principal and interest; a bond with a call proviso is one that can be paid off or "called away," bought back from the bond's owner by the bond issuer; a call option on a stock gives the buyer of the option the right to call away the stock from its owner at a stated strike or exercise price within a stated period of time. Buyers of calls hope that the market price of the stock in question will go higher than the price they've optioned, so that they can call in the stock and sell it for more.

camel "And again I say unto you, it is easier for a camel to go through the eye of a needle, than for a rich man to enter the kingdom of God." (Matthew 19:24) Jesus wrote this verse on the back of a Chinese fortune cookie slip and snuck it into the Bible, where it has been a source of difficulty ever since. As a result of this heedless scribble by the Christian divinity, every weekend camel traffic jams clog the highways leading to the Hamptons and the other watering places of the wealthy. (Use of the word *rich* is discouraged these days.) In addition, several newly minted billionaires have ordered their foundations to fund the design and construction of gigantic sewing needles with ramps leading up to their eyes. This is but one of many attempts to solve the Matthew 19:24 problem. (See **purgatory** and **CEO**.)

capital The name of that portion, should it exist, of your money that you do not need to live on and can invest, in hopes that you will make a profit. Hence the money set aside to pay for the groceries or the kids' soccer fees is not capital; the money in your retirement account, assuming you have not been swindled out of it by a lying stockbroker or a knavish investment adviser, is your capital. By extension, any moneys free to be used for investment. (See also **working capital**.)

capital gains The profit on real estate, stocks, bonds, factories—the big solid stuff—after it has been held six months or more. Although capital gains are taxed at a lower rate than that of ordinary income tax, which the drones must pay, the moneyed classes are in a state of perpetual apoplexy over this tax. They say that it prevents owners from selling their property, particularly if they have owned it for a long time, as some of what appears to be capital gains profit is actually no more than a nominal rise owing to years of inflation. They are correct, of course, but, outside of Social Security recipients and certain government employees, few people are reimbursed for losses caused by inflation. Capital gains tax haters argue that if the law were changed, people would realize their pent-up profits, which they would invest in new business, and everybody would be the gainer. Looking back on the investment boo-boos of the 1990s, you might argue that we don't need more capital to invest but more brains for investing what we already have.

capitalism The name of a religion based on the worship of money.

capitalist Technically, anybody with a buck to invest, but in ordinary usage the word is only applied to major moneybag types. When applied to an ordinary person, the implication is that said person is an impecunious jackass putting on plutocratic airs.

capitalization or **market capitalization** The number of a company's shares multiplied by the stock market price of a single share. The result is what the company is supposed to be worth, and, in theory, it is what it's worth on any given day—but every given day is different, so that a small company can get bigger or smaller overnight. It is altogether too possible for companies that have never taken in a dime to have a market capitalization of a billion dollars. Other and perhaps better ways of judging the size of a company are its sales, its profits, its return on investment (ROI), and so forth. There are many yardsticks, no one of which will tell the full truth about what manner of corporate beast you may be contemplating.

Carnegie, Andrew Morrison (1835–1919) When his name comes up it is usually in connection with his immense benefactions, although Carnegie, a man of his times, played the robber baron part with the ruthlessness it demands. He was the person most responsible for the Homestead steel strike of 1892, one of the most violent and bitter in American history, but, nonetheless, Carnegie's business accomplishments were seminal.

Among them was the introduction of cost accounting into manufacturing. Until Carnegie, such businesses did "lump" accounting; that is, all costs were lumped together and then at the end of the week the owner looked to see if the lump going out of the till was smaller than the lump of money coming into it from the customers. Cost accounting breaks down every operation and procedure in the plant into the smallest of parts and assigns a cost to each, so that, one by one and bit by bit, Carnegie was able to drive down his costs. He was monomaniacal on the subject of costs and able to use his obsession to underprice his competitors into a panicky state of near bankruptcy. Dull stuff unless you have a yearning to don the green eyeshade, but those of us attached to our pleasant little material conveniences and modest luxuries might give Carnegie a nod of gratitude, because cost accounting is the sine qua non of modern management and therefore of modern high productivity and low prices.

A businessman, not a technician, the son of a crofter family whose poverty drove it to emigrate from Scotland, Carnegie put up a steel plant in 1875 that was the precursor of assembly line mass production forty years later (see **Ford, Henry I**). Carnegie led the way toward the vertical integration of industrial corporations and the use of scientifically trained specialists, even as he scandalized conservative business practice by junking old equipment that still worked in favor of new equipment that worked better. At one juncture Carnegie ordered the destruction of a three-month-old rolling mill because he was told of a new, more productive design. (See also **technology transfer**.)

Carnegie sold his business to J. P. Morgan who used it in the formation of the U.S. Steel Corporation, a gigantic agglomeration of steel and iron makers and fabricators, whose inefficiencies and high costs made the company the antithesis of what Carnegie stood for.

cartel An agreement by a group of companies or countries to manipulate prices by controlling production. The word is customarily used in connection with international combinations, such as the dreaded and feared Organization of Petroleum Exporting Countries (OPEC). The word has a stinky odor to it and is almost never used with approval. (See **pools**.)

cash money, moola, do-re-me, lettuce, spondulicks, coin, dough, bread, skins, groat, long green, shekel, smackeroo, pelf, buck, cowrie-shell, the root of all evil, viaticum, specie, big ones, farthing, scratch, fish, cabbage, talent, lucre, assignat, boodle, ducat, simoleon, currency, dinero, what makes the world go 'round, gelt, jack, smacker, store of value and medium of exchange, wampum. If the number of words for the same object is indicative of its importance to a society, draw your own conclusions.

cash cow The gentle lowing of these aureate bovines is beloved by philargyrists everywhere. The animal can be defined as a regular milker, one which, because of the loyalty of its customers or its unique position in its business segment, has a long record of paying off nicely and regularly.

cash flow Bearing in mind that accountants get to play with definitions, the term generally means the money coming into a firm on a regular basis, minus the cash that's going out. Taken alone it may be a deceptive measure of a corporation's health, since a large cash flow is not the same as large profits. A company with an anemic cash flow may nevertheless be quite valuable, thanks to inventions it owns that haven't yet been brought to market, or to possible oil strikes. Investors have been known to be attracted to companies with brisk cash flows because they hope and believe that the tinkle of coin betokens future profits and because, where there is cash, regardless of profit, there are games to be played, dividends to be declared, loans to be made, and favors to be granted from the company exchequer.

cash register The cash register made its debut among small retailers in the waning years of the nineteenth century. At first it was sold as a "thief-catcher," designed to keep hands out of the till. When this approach inflamed the likes of retail clerks and bartenders, National Cash Register substituted advertising pitches such as "The grocer who tries to keep his business in his head can't keep ahead in business," a reference to the fact that as late as the 1920s small store owners often kept no written records save the names of those to whom they owed credit.

cashier's check Sometimes called a treasurer's or official check, a cashier's check is what you demand by the way of payment if you suspect foul play, because, once issued, a cashier's check cannot be stopped, recalled, or prevented from being cashed. (See **certified check**.)

catalogue merchandising In 1872 Aaron Montgomery Ward (1844-1913) started the first mail-order catalogue store, introducing the consumer society into the sparse lives of farm families, who made up a majority of the population. The Montgomery Ward catalogues, popularly called "dream books," brought not only farm equipment but china, pianos, and new fashions into the drab, isolated prairie homes described by Willa Cather.

By the turn of the century, local merchants had gone to war against mail-order houses like Ward's and Sears, Roebuck. William Allen White, the quintessential small-town newspaper editor, wrote in the Emporia, Kansas, *Gazette* that "There is such a thing as 'tainted dry goods,' 'tainted groceries,' and 'tainted furniture.' All such that are not bought at home, of men who befriended you, of men to whom you owe a living, are 'tainted' because they come unfairly." The catalogue companies fought back with satisfaction guarantees and a variety and depth of merchandise at prices no country store could match. Nevertheless, Sears had to send packages to their customers wrapped in plain brown paper.

Ultimately, the once great Montgomery Ward was forced to close its doors. Sears first combined mail-order catalogues with chain stores, then, under a succession of idiot CEOs, dropped the catalogues, growing smaller as the years and the times passed it by. Merchandise by mail, however, continues to thrive as catalogue companies like L.L. Bean, Harry & David, and Williams-Sonoma do a land-office business.

CEO (chief executive officer) The president of a corporation and also often the chairman of the board of directors. As a class these men—and they are, in overwhelming numbers, male—vaguely correspond in modern American life to the nineteenth-century English squirearchy or the knight merchant class in Republican Rome. Not only are they given special deference and respect, but they seem to be men apart, seldom seen godlets who move about in private airplanes and limousines with smoky windows, occasionally glimpsed, but never approached save only by their fellow CEOs. Be they wise men or ignorant, hairy-handed, grasping brutes, their opinions are solicited on every topic from the cure of cancer and the secret of happy marriage to the likelihood of a meteor obliterating Phoenix, Arizona. In a society where all are addressed by their first names, CEOs are called Mister, a title otherwise reserved in the pages of the *New York Times* for murderers on death row.

A CEO's authority over his corporation is roughly equal to that of a carpet-eating despot of a small, unnamed country. Although his domain is smaller and he regrettably lacks the power to put people to death, the American CEO is as famous for his temper tantrums, his demands for lebensraum (market share), and his arbitrary, stupid, and costly decisions as many a bushleague fascist. With appetites as omnivorous as those of a Tiberius Caesar, the more egregious of contemporary corporate CEOs must have mansions, artworks, luxury apartments, hunting lodges, ski chalets, beach houses, yachts, staffs, and retinues in a dozen cities around the world. These are ten-kowtow guys who must not be told bad news and must always be agreed with. However, unlike movie stars and professional baseball players, who make it a point to boast about how much money they make, the CEO, fearful of the reaction should people find out, hides the amount his servile board of directors has agreed to pay him. With CEOs the controlling dictum is, "Ask not what I can do for the company, but what the company can do for me . . . and then double it." A CEO's level of compensation (the word *pay* is infra dig) is arrived at by equaling the level of compensation of rival CEOs in an infinitely rising, golden corkscrew.

certified check An unbounceable check for which the bank certifies that there is sufficient money in the writer's account. A certified check can be stopped. (See **cashier's check**.)

certified public accountant (CPA) By the last decade of the nineteenth century, so many segments of business had come to depend on accountants that, even if they had not wanted it, which they did, legal recognition of the occupation was necessary. Hence in 1896 the New York State legislature created the title of CPA, granted only after the candidate had passed an examination. Other states followed in short order.

chain store The chain store era began in the 1860s with the Great Atlantic & Pacific Tea Company, which started out selling coffee and tea. Over the next thirty years, A&P added stores and product lines, peaking in 1930 with over 17,000 outlets. By systematizing the work so that low-paid, poorly educated clerks, particularly women, took the place of more skilled personnel; by eliminating the middleman; by knowing how to increase turnover; and by pressuring discounts out of manufacturers, the chains—Woolworth, United Drug, Kresge—took business away from local retailers, who fought back as best they could. "Trade-at-home" campaigns were organized throughout the country. A former pharmacist told a Senate committee that, "When a man with a business investment of three thousand dollars is told to compete with a man having a business investment of three million dollars—he is told to do the impossible. Unrestricted competition in its broadest sense is nothing short of a cruel joke."

The dominant retail chains of seventy-five years ago have gone out of business or shrunk to insignificance, having had no better luck at escaping the aging process than people do. Complacency, sloth, and brain-dead management led to the financial infarction of many and their replacement by modern chains such as Wal-Mart, Starbuck's, and the Gap.

channel stuffing Pushing products out to wholesalers and into the distribution stream, then entering them on the books as though they're already sold, when they're not. (See **receivables**.) Channel stuffing makes the next quarterly figures look fat for the analysts, but in due course the facts come out and the company looks worse than it would have, had it come clean about its sales. Channel stuffing may or may not be illegal, depending on whether cute misdirection has been used, or the books have been flat-out cooked.

Chapter 7 Shorthand for death-sentence bankruptcy. The name is taken from the federal Bankruptcy Act and is invoked when a company's debts have mounted past all hope of repayment. At that point, either the management declares bankruptcy or its creditors force it to do so by going to court. Under Chapter 7 the company's direction is taken over by court-appointed trustees, who may liquidate it by selling off the company or, as sometimes happens, try to run it themselves.

Chapter 7 is often a bloody experience in which a company's debtors, employees, vendors, and customers get royally screwed. The trustees or receivers appointed by the courts may have corrupt personal, political, or professional ties to the judge. Their legal fees may eat up whatever of value is left, thus keeping legitimate debtors from getting anything back. And political considerations, such as pressure to prevent employee layoffs, can keep terminally unprofitable companies running until all the assets are gone. Given the chances for shenanigans and everyday incompetence, Chapter 7 is a dark place whence few return.

Chapter 11 Voluntary bankruptcy filed by a company at its discretion. Under Chapter 11 the current management remains in control of the company, unless the judge says otherwise. Chapter 11 invites hanky-panky. It can be used for various nefarious purposes such as cheating a company's pensioners, breaking labor union contracts, and dodging potential damage judgments from suits by outraged customers. The purpose of a Chapter 11 bankruptcy is to give a troubled company a moment of peace from its pursuing creditors in order to come to new terms with them and reorganize itself so that it can come out of bankruptcy and resume its business on a profitable basis.

Chapter 13 Bankruptcy for individuals, not businesses, under the Bankruptcy Act, and thus of no interest to the devil.

chartism (technical analysis) Chartists use a form of stock market divination that combines elements of tarot card reading, Ouija, and table knocking. They have a language of their own, which includes terms such as *breakout, V formation, saucers, ascending tops,* and *rising bottoms.* The chartists' ability to forecast the price of a stock is as reliable as many another method but will not yield anywhere near the profit obtainable by simple, technologically backward cheating.

Christmas club They don't exist anymore, which is a shame because they were an occasion for moderate mirth among those who weren't members. Christmas club membership was obtained by opening a bank savings account, usually in early January, and for the next eleven and a half months putting in money to pay for next Christmas's presents. Christmas clubbers got no interest on their savings, unless it was a "Yo-ho-ho, did we fleece you!" from the management, but interest rate awareness among the fleeceable masses seems to be greater now than it was a half-century ago.

churn A broker's buying and selling a client's securities to generate fees for himself, not profits for his customer. Churning is illegal and unethical, words which are dumb oxen (oxymorons) on Wall Street or anywhere else stocks and bonds are regularly traded. One who has been churned has an understandable impulse to call a lawyer, but let that hand be stayed. It is nearly impossible to drag a broker in front of a judge. An easier way to get your money back is to bet your friends that you can climb up the north slope of K2, or spend three hours in a steel cage with two hungry sharks.

circuit breaker The rule that limits or halts trading securities when the market suddenly starts crashing downward. The circuit breaker is supposed to prevent a stock market from going into "free fall," a condition that the industry hates and fears more than any other. Why it does is hard to say, except that the people who run stock markets and the government officials who supervise the business hate sudden, big price moves, especially drops. It shouldn't make any difference if a stock loses a fourth or a third of its value in a day or month, but the people in the business crave what they call an "orderly" market—that is, one in which prices go up or down in tiny gradations. To that end, circuit breakers have been instituted, but what they accomplish and what good they may do is disputed.

Claiborne, William As far as we know, he was the first businessman in what would become the United States. Claiborne (circa 1587–circa 1677) had a not uneventful career, which included having Lord Baltimore order his arrest for inciting the Native Americans to gosh knows what. In 1629 he hooked up with a firm of London merchants, Claberry and Company, and got a license to trade corn, furs, and other commodities in New England, thus earning himself First Businessman title and a footnote in a few dry histories.

class warfare 1. Annual mud tussle between the freshmen and the sophomores. **2.** Much feared, often denounced though nonexistent strife between nonexistent classes in classless middle-class American society. **3.** Cry of alarm raised by the rich at the suggestion of a tax increase.

classified stock Nonvoting stock. Owners of classified stock get to share the profits and the risks but not the decision making. This kind of stock is issued by heads of companies who want you to invest but don't want to cede control. Two examples of well-known companies controlled with classified stock in the interest of two families are the *New York Times* and the *Washington Post.*

Clay, Henry (1777–1852) A three-time presidential candidate and huge figure in pre–Civil War American politics, his contribution to business was in unflinching and unflagging support of domestic manufacturing by excluding the importation of foreign, competitive goods. Just how important Clay was to the businessmen of his time can be seen in the sixty-six-foot-high, cast-iron memorial to him in Pottstown, Pennsylvania, once the heart of coal country. There the old boy stands to this day on top of a Doric column that can be seen for miles, a hero to the iron industry, and to the coal industry it depended on. So don't let anybody tell you that the modern United States was built on non–government-interference and free trade (see **protective tariff**).

clerk Permissible in terms such as "law clerk" or "Clerk of the House," but frowned on when used for sales personnel or bank clerks. The word is on its way to obsolescence thanks to title creep, a form of punky egalitarianism which demands that supermarket stock clerks be called associates.

closing costs What stands between you and your new house. Closing costs can include the fees for those lawyers you didn't hire and don't want from the lending institution, prepayment penalty, lender discount, real estate agent fee, and mortgage brokerage fee. Some of these costs will be paid by your giving points (for which, see **basis point**), which means these sums will be added into your mortgage and you'll be paying interest on them. As the person with the stubby pencil adds up the items, your temperature rises *pari passu* until you're ready to call the whole thing off, but you've sold the old house and, if you do call off the sale, you'll lose your earnest money and you'll have to pay most of the closing fees for not closing.

COLA Not a soft drink but an acronym for cost-of-living adjustment. Many government programs and private contracts contain COLA clauses, which call for changing payment schedules when the cost-of-living index takes a jump. The biggest COLA is the annual Social Security adjustment. It's also one that conservative politicians are forever trying to do away with, because then inflation would clip Social Security payments, without any elected official having to go on record as voting for a cut in Grandma's pension money. Inflation has been a constant in American life since Dwight Eisenhower, so business people hate COLAs and will do most anything to wiggle out of granting them to their employees or their vendors.

collar One of those Wall Street words, which, generally speaking, indicates a limit of some kind, such as an instruction to a broker not to buy a bond that yields less than a stated amount of interest.

collateralized debt obligations (CDOs) or **collateralized bond obligations (CBOs)** (See also **asset-backed security** and **securitization**.) Yet one more example of high finances selling the same thing over and over again, and with each transaction taking yet another cut, fee, or commission. CDOs are manufactured by taking a bunch of bonds or mortgages or anything else that seems to spit out a trickle or stream of money and putting them in the same vat, mixing them up until they're stiff, and then slicing the resulting mixture into cuts, or tranches, each of which is then sold off. If each slice or tranche is the same, the buyer will have more security against a loser-lose-all default than he would have if he had just bought one bond from one company. But CDOs are not necessarily tranched that way. The mass can be cut so that some slices are very safe and have a low interest pay-out and others are very risky and have a high interest pay-out (see **toxic waste**). Items like CDOs are invariably described as "sophisticated financial instruments," which you may take to mean that the institutions who buy them don't understand what they are doing.

company jet The company jet was probably first introduced as a management tool/perk by Edgar Ingram of White Castle hamburgers. He was up and flying around on inspection tours of his far-flung, fast-food outlets before there were jets, even before Lucky Lindbergh had touched down in Paris. There is a 1927 photograph of the fast-food king about to climb into a two-man, open-cockpit biplane with the company logo on the side. He survived several emergency landings in cornfields and lived long enough to see radar and cement runways.

company store Chiefly a store in what was called a "closed company town," where mill or mine workers had to make all their purchases. Since employees often fell into debt, the company store was one of the methods used to keep laborers in industrial peonage. But management soon learned it wasn't fooling anybody with this form of social control. By 1848 company stores were the cause of strikes in the Pennsylvania anthracite fields. Six years later Maryland outlawed them, but the company store remained a feature of the landscape for many decades. It was not, however, a feature in every company town. Many, possibly even most, company towns had independent retail outlets.

company town A place dominated in fact or imagination by a single industry, as for example Washington, D.C. (government and politics) or Las Vegas (gambling). The expression dates from the time when companies did, in fact, build towns to house their employees. (See **Pullman**.) One of the first, Lowell, Massachusetts, was built in the 1820s by the Merrimack Textile Company, to house mill hands, young women who were overjoyed to leave the family farm for the new factory jobs, which paid cash wages, provided clean and respectable housing, and offered a modicum of independence.

Save for a very few towns built by addleheaded, idealistic industrialists, most company towns were built to attract, hold, or discipline factory workers. The inhabitants of these unhappy places were required to live by rules laid down by the company or be fined. Some were god-awful, such as those in the Pennsylvania coal fields and the Carolina cotton mills, where the workers and their families lived like Arabs in the Gaza Strip. In some "closed towns," even the rail and road approaches were owned by the company, and outsiders were barred from entering.

compatibility Compatibility, or the lack thereof, has been the bane of business and customers alike for the better part of two centuries. The first telegraph companies were incompatible; the first railroads ran on different-width tracks, so that it was only after they all finally agreed on the same gauge that freight and passenger cars were able to move from one set of tracks to another. The electrical power industry warred over direct current versus alternating current. Nor is the compatibility issue settled. The clash between inches and the metric system can be seen in the incompatibility of nuts and bolts and thousands of other pieces of hardware.

The history of electronics has been one long war about compatibilities. (See **IBM**.) American cell phones won't work in Europe. Competing incompatible systems have plagued television, where the battle has been fought over which system of color broadcasting or high definition to use. There is a never-ending struggle between Betamax and VHS tape, and the computer industry has come close to destroying itself and bankrupting its customers because of its endemic compatibility problems.

Trade associations (see **Hoover, Herbert Clark**) are often the place where industry standards are hammered out, but participants in such meetings are wary that the Department of Justice's or the European Community's antitrust people will label an innocent meeting to set technical standards a conspiracy to restrain trade.

Sometimes customers set the standard. They chose the technically inferior VHS system over Betamax. And sometimes the government resolves compatibility questions, as has often been the case in electronics. But the outcome is not always happy, because the Federal Communications Commission's dillydallying not only keeps things bottled up for months and years, but on occasion the government gets it wrong—and once a government office makes a wrong decision, it takes a couple of millennia to get it right.

compensation committee A committee of the board of directors of a company charged with fixing how much the top executives are to be paid. In making the determination, the committee members are supposed to take into account how well the executives have performed and how much men and women in similar positions in the same industry are paid. Their responsibility includes protecting the rights of the stockholders by not overpaying. That compensation committees fulfill any of these duties adequately is subject to much skepticism. The failure of committee members to do their job is explained by their being the CEO's stooges, being overpaid for their own board services, and/or being halfwits—or by having company CEOs serve on their own boards of directors. Executive compensation in money, benies, and perks often runs into the tens or hundreds of millions and bears no relationship to the value of the services any executive can render to any organization. Whether the titanic discrepancies between the money paid to the people at the top of American corporations and the wages of all the other employees breed resentment or a sense of hopeless worthlessness or bitter cynicism is not known.

competition Much honored in the breach. Businessmen have been known to recommend it for others whilst pleading an acute cardiac condition precluding their taking part in the exercise themselves. Until recently, when free market dogma ended meaningful public discussion of the topic, businesspeople had been careful to distinguish healthy competition, which was good, from "cutthroat competition," which was bad. Alas, there has always been difficulty in getting businesspeople, government, and consumers to agree on what is healthy and what is cutthroat. (See **pools, trust, holding company**.)

competitive analysis and intelligence Licit spying on or gleaning information about a competitor by legal means. The appetite for skivvy on the other guy is such that getting it is a recognized service with its own trade association, the Society of Competitive Intelligence Professionals. Since 1996, limits have been placed on this kind of commercial peekaboo by the passage of the Economic Espionage Act, and it goes without saying that no reputable company would ever, even in the wildest moments of panic or avarice, stoop to illegally sucking proprietary information out of the other fella's computers.

If the United States government with all its police forces wasn't able to keep a seemingly endless stream of classified information to itself, the likelihood of even the most resourceful of corporations succeeding for any length of time is slight. From Colonial times forward, stealing information and violating patents have played a part in American business development. Probably the best defense against the competition filching your company's secrets is coming up with new secrets. While they're shoplifting the old stuff, you're stealing a march with the new.

conglomerate (noun and verb) One of the more destructive business fads and a godsend to the 1950s–1960s generation of Wall Street flannelmouths. The word should have been "congloberate" because the rationale for the conglomerate was that superb managers could successfully assemble and run dozens and even hundreds of companies in unrelated businesses; these vast corporate hodgepodges would be resistant to the business cycle and continue through thick and thin to report healthy growth numbers every quarter.

Motives for conglomerating were varied. Some company executives had a visceral resistance to paying out profits in the form of dividends to their stockholders. RCA (Radio Corporation of America), afraid to buy companies in its own field because of government antitrusters, went on an irrational shopping spree that netted it a sporting clothes company, Hertz rent-a-car, a carpet company, a frozen food company, and a publishing house. The only thing they had in common was that they had nothing to do with electronics and broadcasting, the only areas RCA people were competent in.

At one point a conglomerate called Ling-Temco-Vought owned, *inter alia,* a cable company, an airline, a meatpacking company, a car rental company, and a basic steel mill and couldn't run any of them satisfactorily. (See **Ling, James Joseph**.) Harold Geneen, the CEO of ITT, an absurdist conglomerate that included Scott's lawn products, the Sheraton Hotel chain, Wonder Bread, and countless more, said, "At the peak of our expansion we were buying an average of a company a week."

Such acquisitions were obtained by watering stock (see **watered stock**), borrowing money, and playing on the feeble brains of the cupiditously gullible. The healthy growth numbers were achieved with an accounting trick called pooling, by which it was declared that business had grown again, although in fact nothing had changed save a few figures moved around a ledger. In the fullness of time, which was ten years or less, the conglomerators crashed and burned, and the world of business said with one voice that it had learned its lesson and would never again let itself succumb to idiot enthusiasm, even as, a few calendar pages away, the 1980s and 1990s were waiting for them.

Consols Readers of eighteenth- and nineteenth-century British fiction will recognize these annuities, which supported endless numbers of upper-middle-class people in countless novels. Consols, a contraction of consolidated annuities, were sold by the British government starting in 1751 as a means of handling public debt. In time they came to be thought of as synonymous with financial security. They were supposed to go on paying forever, but the financial devastation wrought by the First World War on Britain destroyed the foundations on which consols sat. By the end of the Second World War, they were on their way to being a thing of the past.

consumer An American, a citizen, also any person old enough to have money and spend it. "Every man is a consumer, and ought to be a producer," wrote Ralph Waldo Emerson in 1860, when the word suggested waste and destruction, as in "all the furniture was consumed by the fire." Forty years later that connotation of the word had all but dropped out of ordinary speech. By 1897 the Sears, Roebuck catalog contained a "consumer's guide," evidence that a century ago the consumer was already on his way to enthronement as the central person in the American universe.

consumer protection   The way some businesspeople scream about it, you'd think the idea was a Marxist-Leninist device to destroy capitalism as we know it. In old Rome, government officials made sure honest weights and measures were used in the market. In Ye Merry Olde England, a King's officer saw to it that the ale sold to the public was properly brewed. In the United States, Congress passed a law in 1836 requiring the inspection of boilers on steamboats, which had an unpleasant tendency to blow up. The government being the government even then, the steamboats continued to blow up at a jolly rate, and, try as business may, it has not yet been able to kill off enough of its customers to materially affect P and L, counting house lingo for profit and loss, for you liberal arts majors.

Although you'd never guess it from reading some periodicals, business does not always oppose consumer protection. You may not think too much of the motives, but large businesses sometimes welcome consumer regulation, because of the costs it imposes on smaller competitors. Some businesses have welcomed inspection and certification laws since these enable them to enter foreign markets otherwise closed to them. Another plus of consumer protection is that companies can turn it into a form of government endorsement, with advertising slogans proclaiming things like "USDA Grade A beef" or "Meets All Government Standards." It must be good if the government says so, and the devil, at least not this one, never lies.

consumer price index (CPI) This is the famous cost-of-living number put out every month by the Bureau of Labor Statistics, which causes the hysterical personalities who give us the television news to announce "the cost of living remained tame last month," or "the cost of living jumped up, a sign it's getting out of control." In times of high inflation such as the 1970s, when most people's salaries bought less and less each week, the monthly announcement was a major news event.

The CPI purports to tell us if the dollar in our pocket bought more or less or the same as it did the month before. To get the CPI, Department of Labor employees, quaintly named economic assistants, fan out everywhere to record the prices on something like eighty thousand items that we commonly buy. Then the mathematics begins, and out comes what we look on as the inflation number.

It necessarily is imprecise because it is impossible to keep track of the prices of the millions of things offered for sale. Although thoughtfully done, the process is fraught with political controversy since so much is riding on it, including many contracts and government payments, which are changed according to the inflation rate.

consumerism **1.** The movement for the protection of buyers from shoddy goods or dishonest sales practices. **2.** The doctrine that consumer buying drives the economy and that a slump in consumption will bring on hard times. Shop till you drop, baby. That oinking noise you hear in the background is the sound of prosperity.

contingent liability A snake in the grass or a snake in the footnotes of a company's financial report, which is usually where you will find the little bugger. A contingent liability is possible future bad news for the company, such as losing a pending lawsuit, getting smacked with an adverse decision in a tax dispute, and various pieces of paper (endless in their variety) containing the promise to pay money if such and such an event occurs (see **exposure**).

contract   A worthless agreement enforceable at law, at enormous cost, great peril, and vast frustration.

contraction   Yet one more word for when business heads south. Whether it's a slump, a slowdown, a correction, a turndown, a pullback, a recession, or a depression, all the vogue words for "business sucks" have been invented to put the best possible face on things and cheer the troops up. Sis-boom-bahing may be taken to be the rankest hypocrisy or the minimum, indispensable rah-rah to stop businesspeople from climbing into bed, pulling the covers over their knitted brows, and turning to the wall. There comes a limit to cheerleading when those doing it begin to look like inane jerks, as happened to the Republicans in the early 1930s with their insistence that "prosperity is just around the corner." Sometimes talking it up ain't the same as getting it up.

contrarian   A Wall Street type who is down when the majority opinion is up, and vice versa, in giving advice and assessing the situation. A true contrarian is a rara avis and is confused with the Gloomy Gus or the Happy Heather. A Gloomy Gus is a man blessed or cursed with a bear market personality. In good times or bad, he's always predicting the worst, which makes him a genius about half the time and a pain in the ass the rest. A Happy Heather is the reverse. She's twittering gay little songs and finding silver linings in hurricane clouds when everyone else is heading for the storm cellar. A contrarian is not the same as a curmudgeon or a grouchy cynic, a description that fits the author of this dictionary.

cook the books Falsification of a company's or corporation's financial records with the intent to deceive. Sometimes books are cooked to hide defalcations and sometimes to make a company's position look better than it is. The whole system of distributing capital through the financial markets is based on buyers and sellers knowing what the hell it is they are trading. Such knowledge depends on two things: having a uniform set of rules for keeping the books and obeying them. As anyone who has studied an annual corporate report will tell you, there are a thousand ways to fool an unshrewd investor without cooking the books, but, if in addition to employing a thousand and one legal tricks of misdirection, the actual numbers in the ledger are false, the system falls. Book cooking was raised to cordon bleu quality in the first years of the twenty-first century when it was learned that the chefs and sous-chefs of the boardrooms had whipped up multibillion-dollar, fantabulous confections outdoing anything theretofore coming out of the kitchens of fraudulent corporate dishonesty.

core inflation rate A term of deception. Whenever the monthly consumer price index comes out showing a big jump from the month before, soothing voices are shortly to be heard saying not to worry, darlings, "the core inflation rate" hardly jumped at all. The core inflation rate is the cost of living minus fuel and food and whatever else may have taken a leap upward. The justification for subtracting some things from the cost of living index is that commodities such as food are "too volatile," meaning they bound around a lot, as if that made any difference. An inflation index has to reflect all prices; otherwise it's meaningless. Prices go up and down. That's what prices are supposed to do. To take them out of the index for behaving naturally is an intellectual absurdity, albeit an irresistible one for people with a political motivation to convince the public that inflation is being held in check.

cornering the market or **market corner** It is a devilish thing to do, but it's not as easy as you might think. Cornering a market means getting control of so much of a stock or a commodity that you can force the price up and up and up. There have been many examples in business history, the most famous of which was the 1869 attempt by Jim Fisk (1834–1872) and Jay Gould (1836–1892) to corner the gold market, something that could only be contemplated if the federal government did not offer any of its gold hoard up for sale. That required bribes to persons close to President Grant. These little emoluments having been paid, the plot went forward and the price of gold went up and up and up, but Grant himself, who was straight as a die, eventually broke the corner by putting government gold on the market. When the corner broke, there was something close to panic in the streets of lower Manhattan. Fisk apparently got caught in the collapse of the gold price, but the wily Gould appears to have gotten out in time with a profit commensurate with the standards of the Gilded Age.

In 1980, two Texas speculators, the brothers Bunker

and Herbert Hunt, in cahoots with some Saudi Arabians, made a bid to corner the market in silver. They were successful enough to drive up the price from around $1.30 an ounce to a point where it wobbled around at over $50 before the Government moved in and changed the trading rules, which sent the price down and the speculators down even further, to financial disaster, on Silver Thursday, March 27, 1980.

corporate America A spaceship covering the equivalent of half a continent, floating over the collective consciousness of the United States. Every so often, the spaceship moves and parks itself in a somewhat different place, but, more exciting and alarming to the inhabitants, it will sometimes change its shape and color. Every so often it emits a light ray and zooms certain select men and women up to the spaceship or zooms them back down to earth with many eye-popping tales, some wonderful, some horrible, but opinion is divided over what to believe.

corporate governance There are libraries full of books on this topic, but, whatever the theories, corporations are run by their chief executive officers (CEOs) without let or hindrance. The CEOs are appointed by boards of directors, who are elected by the stockholders, which tells you nothing.

In many, probably most, corporations, the outgoing or retiring CEO appoints his successor. He is able to do so since his board of directors, whose pay and perks are effectively controlled by him, are, if not his lap dogs then his collaborators, allies, or co-conspirators, as the case may be.

Technically, a corporation's owners, the stockholders,

could vote to throw the management and board out, but this rarely happens. (See **proxy fights**.) The system of corporate governance dates back to the early days of corporate organizations, when most companies' stockholders were few in number and lived in the same general vicinity as the company's home office. In this clubby atmosphere, the company's president—the grandiloquent title of chief executive officer is of twentieth-century coinage—worked under tight supervision. Nowadays corporations have thousands of stockholders living everywhere who don't know each other or much about the affairs of the company they collectively own, and, being unorganized, they are incapable of exercising any direction or control. Every year they are sent ballots to vote for members of the board of directors, but, since they don't know who they are, they either throw their ballots in the wastepaper basket or they vote for the company slate.

This system of self-perpetuating management has been the occasion of gross imposition on the shareholders of many companies and not infrequently resulted in damage to corporations of signal importance and value to the society at large. Nevertheless, though many clever fellows have tried, no one has come up with a workable scheme for the reform of the present system of corporate governance. (See **outside director**.)

corporate paternalism A corporate form of paternalism reemerged after World War II, particularly during the height of the Cold War when government and big business strove to show that American workers were better treated than workers in the then Soviet Union, which, of course, ended in Chapter 7 bankruptcy. (See **paternalism** and **Chapter 7**.) It was, in part, indirectly subsidized by the government through loosely audited, overly generous defense contracts.

IBM, a huge war contractor, was once famous for its benevolently paternal relationship with its employees. Even during the Depression, when IBM was supplying the growing New Deal bureaucracy with office machinery, it managed to hold to its no-layoff policy. In the 1950s it was among the first to offer major medical insurance, along with a generous retirement program. Nineteen fifty-eight saw the abolition of all hourly workers at IBM, as everyone went on salary and was cut in on an employee stock purchase plan.

The benies ensured that unions didn't have a prayer at IBM. In the easy money atmosphere of those years of little foreign competition and juicy government contracts, unionized businesses acceded to a series of lush contracts that amounted to a joint management/labor–sponsored paternalism. The living was easy and the costs were out of sight as large chunks of American industry became high-cost noncompetitors, first in world markets and then on their home ground.

Corporate paternalism all but died with the ending of the Cold War and the gigantic reorganization of big business that followed, as terms like *downsize, outsource,* and *outplace* became commonly used verbs.

corporate welfare An invidious term used in political discourse. Corporate welfare, or privilege, has been defined as including special tax breaks, access to cheap credit, subsidies, police power, and the right of eminent domain. Catching a private enterprise accepting corporate welfare is supposed to mean catching a corporation violating its own free market rule of separation of government and business. In their oratory, both pro- and antibusiness forces premise their arguments on the existence of a time when markets were free and pure, and the private sector got nothing from the public one. That's all bosh.

Government subsidies of business date from George Washington's time, when a third of the costs of the nation's stagecoach businesses was subsidized. The reason was the mail. The first telegraph line from Washington to Baltimore was paid for by a congressional appropriation. While much corporate welfare is boodle and corruption, much is not. Government and business have been thoroughly intertwined for two centuries. To separate them you would have to dismember the nation.

corporation (the) When Adam Smith, the first and best expositor of the free market, wrote in the eighteenth century, there were no corporations as we think of them. In his time and in the early years of the United States, corporations were monopolies granted by state legislatures, usually for the purpose of building a bridge or road. It has taken the better part of two hundred years for the corporate form to reach its present shape and nature, and it is still changing.

In the early nineteenth century, the dominant forms of business were single proprietorship or partnership. Incorporation began to be used as a way of raising money by selling stock. Purchasers of stock were liable to be called upon to put additional money into the corporation, and they were subject to paying their share of a judgment, if the corporation were successfully sued. In that era charters of incorporation were only obtainable by act of the state legislature. The incorporation documents held clauses specifying what line of business the corporation could enter, what kind of property it could own, and where it could conduct business. Corporations were not allowed to buy stock in other corporations. As the years went by, these restrictions were loosened or abolished, and corporations gained such special privileges as limited liability—that is, stockholders could not be held responsible for the crimes, or shall we say the torts, committed by corporations they owned.

Many decades before equal protection was conferred on African-Americans or women, corporations were entitled to a full palette of human rights. In the mid-1880s, the courts ruled that corporations were "persons" (*Santa Clara County v. Railroad,* 1886) and thus, under the 14th Amendment's due process clause, were entitled to the protection of the Bill of Rights and most of the other rights conferred on human beings by the Constitution. To be fair, corporations can't vote, although what's one vote compared to the clout gained by contributing millions of dollars to the campaign?

The power, size, and reach of the corporation is every bit as responsible as big government for making Americans feel like Lilliputians in their own country. The cruel, reckless, and stone-hearted bureaucratic corporation is a fixed element in the American imagination, as is the corporate record, laden as it is with incidents of brutality to its employees, violence to the environment, and dishonesty to its customers. However, without this social organization, we would have moved but a small distance from the unending manual labor and the short life spans which were the fate of Americans in the generation of the Founding Fathers.

coupon bond and **coupon clipper** Coupon bonds are a thing of the past, but you can still insult someone who's old enough to know what you're talking about, by calling him or her a "coupon clipper," meaning a person living on unearned income. Time was when some bonds came with coupons, which were detached by their owners every six months and presented to a bond agent, who paid the interest owing on them. (See **stock certificate**.)

credit agency These are the people who, in the opinion of many, snoop into your affairs, find out things about you that didn't happen, fail to find out things that did, and then ruin your reputation so you have trouble buying a car, a house, or a tank of gas. Once they done you wrong, nothing less than an act of God or Congress (is there a difference?) can get you unbesmirched. Nevertheless, absent this obnoxious business, the world would come to stop. We can't live without it, even if living with it is a constant aggravation.

credit card The first reported use of plastic or the third-party credit system (you, the merchant, and the card company) occurred in 1947. Charge-It, as it was called, was good only in the stores within a few blocks of the Flatbush National Bank of Brooklyn. Lining up tens of thousands of merchants to use a card is no small organizational feat, but eleven years later the Bank of America had a crack at it and started what would become VISA. Forty years later, half the country was in hock up to its ears, but there is nothing new about that. It's credit that made it possible for all those pianos to turn up in Victorian parlors. In 1867, Artemus Ward, a poor man's Mark Twain, told his countrymen, "Let us all be happy, and live within our means, even if we have to borrer money to do it with." And an 1882 edition of the *New York Volks-Zeitung*

quotes an immigrant housewife saying, "I buy everything on credit until I get no more, then I go to another
store and do the same thing there."

Though families in perpetual debt may not be new, the
credit card, of which a billion and a half have been
issued, may have legitimated the idea of debt as something you never pay off but only pay on.

By 1997 the Smithsonian Institution was selling a Ben
Franklin Discovery card, the use of which, the Smithsonian explained, would net their owners free U.S. Savings Bonds. Franklin, a businessman who knew the
difference between profit and loss, would have tossed
Poor Richard's Almanac into the fire at the thought of getting a bond paying 5 percent in return for borrowing
money at 20 percent.

credit reporting As commerce and manufacture
expanded in the early 1800s, businessmen for the first
time were having to trust people far away whom they had
never met and knew nothing about. Merchandise might be
shipped out to country stores and never get paid for. The
fate of many a business hung on the proprietors' hunches
as to the creditworthiness of their customers. Then came
Lewis Tappan (1788–1873) who, when he wasn't spending
every dollar and every joule of energy on the abolition of
slavery, was starting up the information industry. In 1841
he established the Mercantile Agency, which lined up
lawyers and others in a position to know in a thousand
communities across the country, to write reports on the
soundness, creditworthiness, and reliability of local businesses and their owners. (It is said that Abraham Lincoln was one of Tappan's paid informants.) Distant

manufacturers subscribed to Tappan's service to get a line on whom to extend credit to. In 1850 Robert Graham Dun (1826–1900) joined the firm, which would eventually take his name.

As the years rolled on and America became an industrial-commercial nation, the Mercantile Agency's service became even more indispensable. By the 1870s the company, which today bears the name of Dun & Bradstreet, would have ten thousand people sending in reports to satisfy five thousand requests a day for information. By the 1890s Dun's firm had gone multinational with offices in France, Germany, South Africa, and even Australia.

Snooping and nosing around has never made people popular. Back in the earliest days, Tappan was accused by the *New York Herald* of conducting "an office for looking after everybody's business but his own," which, as business became more specialized and larger by unquantifiable magnitudes, was exactly what was needed. The busybodyism to which the *Herald* had taken such exception revealed itself to be a cornerstone of a commercial age hourly more dependent on ever more specialized information. By 1899 the need for specialized business information had progressed to the point that Alfred M. Best (1876–1958) started a company, A. M. Best, that confined itself to scoping out insurance companies to rate them on solvency and their ability to pay off claims. Today, the finding, packaging, and selling of information is a major industry.

crook-honesty ratio (also called **the slimeball or dirtbag quotient**) The CH ratio, or the SB quotient, was set up to tell people if business is more or less honest than it used to be. Every year is assigned a number greater or less than one hundred. Years with numbers under one hundred are those during which crookedness productivity fell, years in which there was a dishonesty recession. The last time the quotient, sometimes referred to as the "gross domestic swindle number," fell below seventy five was 1829, when it was widely believed the end of the world was nigh. The quotient shot up to one hundred and fifty in 1830, the largest single, one-year gain until 1933, the year the American banking system collapsed—but some contest that number, saying that it had more to do with just plain bad news than entrepreneurial theft and white-collar robbery. Public opinion surveys show that a majority are convinced that whatever year the poll is taken is the most dishonest year in history, but ethicists and econometricians working together using sophisticated regression analysis of sigma-denominated data have proven that the year-to-year variation in thievery varies little when seasonally adjusted, which it seldom is.

Curb Exchange (New York) The name given in the early 1800s to the place of business of traders too poor, too dishonest, or too badly connected to be members of the New York Stock and Exchange Board (later simply the New York Stock Exchange). The Board, with fixed fees, more money, and social status, did its business inside, while the financial riffraff had no choice but to do their buying and selling on the street. Hence the name Curb Market. And there out on Broad Street, winter and summer, the traders stayed for a century, until, in 1921, they built themselves a suitable edifice at 86 Trinity Place.

The Curb Market handled lower-priced stocks and did well at it. In 1952 it changed its name to the American Stock Exchange and began to specialize in derivatives (see later entry) and other financial exotica. In 1998 the old Curb Market merged with the National Association of Securities Dealers, where it chugs on indoors and out of sight of the investing hoi aristoi.

customer In times past, a person who customarily bought from a particular retailer. The word is falling into disuse, possibly because it triggers an imaginary picture of a level of attention and service now available solely to the extremely rich. Thus "the customer is always right" is a maxim uttered by spats-wearing floorwalkers in black-and-white movies. The known-by-name customer, a concrete person to be kowtowed to by the staff, has been replaced in the modern, discount retail barn by the unknown consumer, an abstraction identifiable only by demographic group. High-volume, low-margin retail operations cannot recognize individuals, let alone cater to them, if they are to make a profit. This holds true whether the operation is a grocery store or a health maintenance organization (HMO). The economics for hand-holding aren't there, a fact that contributes to America feeling like a society of sharp elbows.

cyclical and **contracyclical stock** Contracyclical stock, such as food and drug companies, is supposed to hold its value in bad times. This is on the theory that people eat and take medicine even when in reduced circumstances. Of course, those in overly reduced circumstances are customarily called "the hungry" and they don't buy food. They steal it. A drag on profitability. Cyclical stocks, which are most stocks, do what their names suggests. (See **business cycle**.)

daisy chain Two out of three definitions are quite wicked. **1.** This is the nice definition—a chain of daisies made by children. **2.** Three or more decidedly naked persons linked to each other by simultaneous sexual activity of it-matters-not-what sort or gender. **3.** This is the really nasty —a small group of market manipulators bidding up the price of some obscure stock until they've got the suckers hoodwinked and buying in, whereupon the manipulators sell out and leave the gulls with baskets full of shares nobody will buy. (See **pump and dump**.)

davos See **sinister doings**.

dead cat bounce A rise in stock prices the day after they have smashed into the sidewalk. Since he has nine lives, hope remains that a cat, after being chucked out of a twentieth-story window, will, nonetheless, bounce. If there is bounce after life for cats, so also for stocks. Cat lovers are not to take umbrage. Misbehaving securities are also referred to as dogs.

dead-end job   A job most of us have but which we view as a violation of the 14th Amendment of the American Constitution. Jobs that don't lead up to the top are looked down on by the angry, greedy, envious many, who believe that, just as democracy guarantees them fifteen minutes of fame, it promises them a fifteen-minute residency atop the pyramid.

debt   The flip side of credit, and the center of perpetual moral, emotional, and financial turmoil. Companies may go into debt by outright borrowing or by selling bonds. The terms and conditions under which money is lent to companies are infinite in their variety and complexity and bear no similarity to personal debt except that, like you and me, one way or another, and at one time or another, the borrower has gotta pay the money back or come up with a helluva good excuse.

Although borrowing is indispensable for businesses, small and large, there are no hard and fast rules as to how much debt a company should take on. Generally, it makes sense to borrow if you can make more with the borrowed dollar than it costs to borrow it. There are even times when the failure to borrow is stupid. Montgomery Ward, the first and once the largest and most important retail mail-order house in the United States, mistakenly decided at the end of World War II to hoard cash in its vaults and failed to borrow for expansion. Its primary competitor did, and Montgomery Ward entered a decline that ultimately led to bankruptcy.

debt coverage ratio The relationship between how much money is coming in every month and how much must go out to pay on loans. Given the proclivity of some corporations to hide how much they really, really owe, it ain't always easy to determine debt coverage ratio.

debt service The money a company must have to pay next year's interest on money it has borrowed in the form of loans or bonds. Debt service also includes the money set aside to repay the principal on the same loans. The next question is "ability to pay"—that is, does the company in question have enough money coming in to meet its debt service? You'd be surprised how often that little question is brushed aside by stockbrokers and stock buyers when they're in their rutting season.

debt-to-equity ratio The relationship between what a company owes and what a company is worth. It's a way of calculating what would be left in stockholder value if all the company's debts were paid off. Needless to say, companies perfused with debt usually don't have the rosiest of futures, something it's nice to know before one decides to invest.

debt-for-equity swap Though stockholders in a busted company, which has gone into bankruptcy, get bupkes, bondholders are supposed to get first pick over the remains. And they do, if there is anything left after the masters-in-chancery, the lawyers, the accountants, and the consultants have slaked their appetites. What ordinarily happens is that the company, now shorn of debts, is "reorganized" and brought out of bankruptcy with the former bondholders now owning stock in the company in satisfaction of the loss of their bonds. The company is now supposed to go on to a new, long, and profitable life, and this has been known to happen, but companies have also been known to flap and cluck and fall back into bankruptcy again. This time the former bondholders are truly wiped out.

deep-in-the-money option (See also **options**.) A financial instrument that is supposed to give the buyer the right to buy a stock, a bond, or a bundle of currency at a certain price for a certain period of time. Although it doesn't look like it and doesn't appear as such on the borrowing company's books, this strangely named bird is really a disguised loan. Not exactly crooked but hardly straight, it's another gimmick that a nimble-brained schemer can put to use, and at the turn of the twenty-first century more than one corporate crook did so to a fare-thee-well.

default The worst word in business this side of defalcation, fraud, and running off to Rio with the company's funds. Default is the failure to pay interest or the principal on a loan, be it a bond or some other solemn promise. If you fail to pay your mortgage, it's a default, but the word is usually reserved for companies and nations that have welched on their obligations.

Owners of bonds in a defaulting company can entertain hopes of getting some of their money back someday somehow (see **debt-for-equity swap**), but when the bond issuer is a government entity, particularly a national government, its bondholders are subject to being told to blow it out the other end. There are notable and noble exceptions, such as the governments of the United States and the United Kingdom, whose promises have been as good as gold.

defined contribution pension plan   The notorious 401(k) and other similar plans allowed under the tax code. In the last quarter of the twentieth century these plans crowded out the older defined benefit pension plans in thousand of companies. The old plans guaranteed retirees a stated income and other benies for the rest of their lives. By the 2000s, in most corporations only the CEOs and other corporate officers had defined benefit plans; the peasants were stuck with one form or another of the 401(k), in which employees, and often employers, put money into private retirement accounts. Unlike the CEOs, who know exactly how much money they are going to get on retirement, the beneficiaries of the 401(k) accounts have no idea how much will be in their accounts on the day of their retirement. All depends upon how profitably the moneys in these accounts have been invested, and for hundreds of thousands, if not millions, things have not gone too terribly well. In many instances employers have manipulated the accounts to the disastrous disadvantage of their employees, but there is one consolation. The stockbrokers handling the transactions in these accounts have fared quite well, thank you. They get their fees and commissions regardless of how small a pile of shavings the investments have dwindled into.

deflation   Inside out inflation. During an inflation prices rise even as the purchasing power of people's dollars falls, thus causing them to buy today, since things will cost them more tomorrow. During a deflation the opposite occurs. The average price of everything for sale drops. The purchasing power of the dollar increases month by month, thus causing people to postpone shopping today, since the price will be lower tomorrow.

During an inflation the smart thing is to go into debt because the dollar you borrow today, you can repay with a ninety-cent dollar tomorrow. During deflation, debt is to be avoided since the dollar you borrow today you will be obliged to repay with a dollar that buys $1.10 worth of merchandise tomorrow. During inflations, interest rates go up; during deflations, interest rates go down.

delist (a verb, not a noun) The action of throwing a company and its stock out of a stock exchange. This is done when the price of a company's shares drops below a dollar and stays at this pitiful level for some time; it is also done when there is a scandal, or the company has failed to live up to some set of financial conditions. Delisting is the equivalent of a court-martialed officer having his insignia of rank cut off in front of his former command.

Dell Computer Corporation   Computers caught the imaginations of young American males as nothing had since the advent of cars and radios. The fascination with these things, the low startup costs to get into the business, and the fractured nature of electronics—an industry with an infinity of parts—combined to afford opportunities for gifted business fanatics such as young Michael Dell (1965–), who had his own business up and running before his twentieth birthday.

Dell resembles a nineteenth-century combined manufacturing and service company like Singer Sewing Machine, but Dell sells, via telephone and Internet, a custom-configured product that will not be manufactured until an order is placed. The product is designed by Dell and is assembled by Dell, but its parts are made by other companies hundreds and even thousands of miles away.

Deming, W. Edwards (1900–1993) Until the 1980s, nobody had heard of this guy. Then the Japanese began cleaning the American clock with higher-quality, lower-cost cars and electronics, and the world was told that this heretofore unknown person was the management consultant who had taught the Japanese how. Suddenly Deming was elevated to super-guru level, as American managers of every stripe learned his fourteen points in an attempt to jack up quality and productivity. In large measure American business did perk up, and how much of the credit you want to give to Deming depends upon which expert you talk to.

demographic (noun, singular) As in "the female nine to twelve demographic." The word often denotes a population chunk that business intends to outfit with a collective identity and its own behaviors and consumer tastes. From hip-hop and goth to soccer mom, creating a group consciousness moves merchandise and sells services. It also gives the impression of a society composed of morons and faddists, excepting only those too poor to bother with or too near death to be scooped up into a demographic. The power of business to create social groups or groupings, be they permanent, à la teenagers, or transient, is one more marker of how business shapes culture.

department store Although the local merchant and the general store have a death grip on the American past as depicted by Courier and Ives, the people who lived on those prints actually began shopping in department stores in the 1870s. That's when Roland H. Macy perfected this form of retailing. Compared to the often dingy, jumbled local store, the department store was a treat, even without the music and the displays. Lower prices and panoramic variety brought in the customers. High volume enabled pioneer department store owners such as Marshall Field, John Wanamaker, and Jordan Marsh to bypass wholesalers and extract lower prices from manufacturers, while the departmental organization of the stores made it possible for management to track what sold and what didn't, who was efficient and who wasn't. Management by numbers had arrived in retailing, and the results were inexpensive—some might say cheap—merchandise for the masses. (See **catalogue merchandising** and **chain store**.)

depreciation (See also **amortization**.) It's amazing that a dry accountant's word can cause the fuss, trouble, and catfights depreciation has sparked. Depreciation is applied to expensive, long-lived, physical items such as factory, office buildings, and heavy machinery and equipment, but not land. On a company's books, depreciation represents the steady loss of value of such things on account of aging, use, and obsolescence. How depreciation is calculated, and on what, is the subject of much arm wrestling, since there are tax consequences and bottom-line consequences depending on which of various methods is chosen. The methods with names, such as straight-line, double-declining-balance, and so forth are too tedious for devils with attention deficit disorder to dwell on.

Short-lived items such as books, software, and small pieces of office equipment are "expensed," as they say, meaning that the entire cost is deducted from the revenue in the year the item is bought. This lowers a company's taxes, and, therefore, precipitates battles with the tax people over what should be depreciated and what should be expensed. Needless to say, going the other way—depreciating what should be expensed—is very wicked even unto fraud. Depreciating ordinary costs of doing business such as maintaining the company's trucks is done to make it look as though the company is making more money than it is. Ah, the temptations are so many and the virtuous road so narrow.

In the nineteenth century, when many businesspeople had little experience with companies that had invested vast amounts of money in machinery, depreciation wasn't to be found on their books. They sometimes woke up to the unhappy realization that they had been losing money, when they thought they had been booking a nice profit. Although it is very, very wicked to do it, contemporary CEOs of enfeebled corporations, and their confederate CFOs, have been known to hide depreciation, thereby giving investors, creditors, and vendors the impression that their financial health is more robust than it is.

deregulation Putting a company and/or an industry on the honor system. Deregulation is based on the belief that, if companies are allowed to do business without let or hindrance, life expectancy will jump to 114 years. After the fall of Communism, Russia, tutored by the best minds from the best American universities, deregulated itself, but, unhappily for the locals, life expectancy dropped to 50, after which the American consultants left. In the United States the electrical utility industry was deregulated and, while life expectancy in California did not shoot up, electric bills did. Deregulation of electricity does have its pluses. Without it Enron couldn't have begun to buy the publicity it received. In a matter of months, Enron's cockeyed E corporate symbol achieved a fame that took corporations such as GM and Coca-Cola a century to attain. (See **natural monopolies**.)

derivative A security (or often enough an insecurity) whose value is derived from another security. If that makes no sense, the people who write—i.e., think up and sell—derivatives often appear to have an uncertain grasp of what their derivatives are. In 1998 Long-Term Capital Management, an exclusive trading house for the trillion-aire class, with a Nobel Prize winner in economics in the management, fouled out selling its own derivatives and was only saved a trillion-dollar loss—literally a trillion—by a private-public rescue expedition mounted by central bankers scared out of their striped pants (which they haven't worn for generations). They feared that the entire financial world would crumble as a result of the games played by the fools, mad persons, or crooks at Long-Term Capital, who came within a hair's breadth of accidentally starting a financial chain reaction that might have consumed the world.

However, there are some derivatives that are simple. If, for a trifling sum, you buy the right to sell a certain stock for a certain amount of money within a certain length of time, you have bought yourself a derivative, not a big fancy derivative, but a derivative whose value depends on the price performance of the stock you don't own. If the stock drops, you'll make yourself a bunch of money thanks to your derivative. If the stock goes up, you'll lose whatever you paid for the right to buy the stock. (For the mechanics, see **put,** as in puts and calls.)

There are myriad derivatives, many with beguiling acronyms such as BEARS (Bonds Enabling Annual Retirement Savings) and CUBS (Calls Underwritten By Swanbrook, whoever or whatever that may be) and DIAMONDS and SPIDERS, and on and on. Some of these are derivatives themselves, so we sometimes have derivative piled on derivative, and then when you get to the custom-made, one of a kind derivatives, even the people who think them up don't understand them. They are of such complexity, entailing gallimaufries of contingent buy, sell, resell, pledge, loan, and borrow instructions around the globe, and depending upon layers of "if-then" orders written into complicated trading programs, that only computers can execute them. People and institutions who you'd presume would understand the derivatives they were buying and the financial risks entailed, have been known to be just as confused as everybody else. At one point, such mighty firms as Procter & Gamble and Bankers Trusts sued their derivatives dealers, claiming that they had been hornswoggled into huge losses after buying derivatives that they didn't understand and their brokers didn't explain. On the question of whether or not this stuff is pure chemin de fer or baccarat, see **futures**.

dignity of labor A quality found among immigrants and the late Jesus Christ, carpenter, and much admired by the leisured classes.

diluted shares or sometimes **fully diluted earnings per share** Profits or earnings can be divided by the number of shares of common stock in the possession of investors, but potentially there are others besides the owners of common stock who can get cut in, such as owners of preferred stock, stock options, or company bonds that may be converted into stock. If you count up all these possibilities and divide them into the profits, the result is earnings per diluted shares, a lower figure than just plain old earnings per share, but a helpful one because it's good to know how many people might come to the luau and get their fingers sticky on the roast suckling pig.

discount retailing The present dedication to competition is a conviction only fitfully shared by earlier Americans. There were no price wars at the rural general store, and up to the mid-twentieth century most manufacturers offered their merchandise at list prices, a one-price-for-all policy that was sanctioned by New Deal–era fair trade law. Retailers who cut prices could be brought into court, and were. To get around the policy, the big chains made arrangements with manufacturers to provide them with house brands: a stove bearing the manufacturer's name would carry the list price; the same stove, bearing the house name of the chain, could be sold at a discount.

Polk Brothers in Chicago beat manufacturers' list prices by offering a huge trade-in to customers who brought in any piece of inoperative junk. Though it took prolonged court fights to bring about price competition, the ingenuity of the discount merchants did in list prices. Once the buying public got the idea that they were being made to pay eye-popping markups, the system collapsed.

Nevertheless, we are not quite in consumer price competition nirvana. See **price signaling**.

disinflation   Said to occur when the rate of inflation, the rate prices have been going up, slows down (unlike deflation, when prices actually drop).

dividend   Your share of the profits. After all of a company's expenses are paid, what's left over is the profit, part of which is divided, hence *dividend,* among the stockholders, should the CEO and the board of directors so decide. And a lot of times they don't. Many companies pay no dividends, and people buying their stock can only expect to profit on their investment by selling the stock after it has risen in price. No guarantees here. It might not rise; it might just stay at the price at which it was bought, in which case the purchaser might just as well have kept the money in a china sugar bowl. The shriveling, if not the disappearance, of the dividend contributes to pressure on management to do whatever needs doing to drive up the price of its shares.

Some companies, which do pay dividends, make the amount so small that the postage on the envelopes they send the dividend checks in costs more than the amount of the dividend.

The failure to pay a dividend may or may not be a sign a company is in trouble. A firm that doesn't pay dividends because it has no profit to pay them with may be a corporate knacker on its way to the boneyard, but a young company, husbanding its cash, may become a profitable dividend payer later on. Some companies have been enormously profitable but prefer to keep plowing the money back into the business instead of rewarding the stockholders. In the nineteenth century Andrew Carnegie's steel company was a famous example of this; in the twentieth IBM followed this policy, and in the twenty-first, there is Microsoft.

dogs of the Dow The name of a system for winning in the stock market by buying the ten cheapest stocks in the Dow Industrial Average. There are more systems for winning in the stock market than there are in Las Vegas. Needless to say, they all work and you may rely on any of them to get very rich.

don't fight the tape Wall Streetese for *qué será sera*. The tape in question is the ticker tape, which once upon a time slithered out from under a glass dome during trading hours, showing the moment-to-moment flutterings of the prices of stocks. Tape fighters are people who think the price of a security is too high or too low, or say things like, "the market is oversold (or undersold)," meaning that the price isn't what it ought to be. But truth to tell, the price is what it is, and woe betide all who gamble their money not recognizing that.

dot-com **1.** In less than ten years, business took a complicated, difficult to use scientific and military system of communication and turned it into a commercial service that hundreds of millions of people cannot do without. Nothing, not even flu epidemics, has spread so far, so fast, and so pervasively. Dot-com stands for one of business's greatest accomplishments. **2.** The word has also come to stand for the drunken speculative orgy of the latter part of the 1990s. (See **bubble**.) The commercial prospects for the dot-commery in general and the

Internet in particular were grossly exaggerated, but it was the Internet that made the personal computer a next to indispensable appliance in every home. As with television, radio, the automobile, and the railroads, people were swept up by deliriously silly hopes for profits, but the new industries and their utility were real enough. So were the profits for businesspeople who kept their heads on their shoulders.

double-entry bookkeeping Bookkeeping itself is at least as old as the Egyptians, whose clerks can be seen hard at it, scribbling their entries into papyrus journals in ancient pictures on pyramid walls. The systems used, the cash journals and records of that kind, were OK as far as they went, which for enterprises of any complexity and volume is not far enough.

In 1494 a Renaissance monk, Luca Pacioli, published an instruction manual for double-entry bookkeeping, a maddeningly tricky but indispensable method of record-keeping that gives a full and accurate picture of the state of a business. The expression "balance the books" comes from Fra Pacioli's double-entry system with its two columns, one for all outflows and one for all inflows. The devil simplifies here but, please, remember that he is in the details. Once mastered, the good friar's methods afford executives, even now in more complex forms, the tools of analysis, management, and control without which gigantic, world-straddling commercial organizations could not exist.

Dow Jones Industrial Average (DJIA) There was a Mr. Dow, and his first name was Charles, and it was he in 1896 who thought up the index, which then was the sum of the prices of twelve important stocks divided by twelve. He printed it every day in the *Wall Street Journal,* started and owned by him and a Mr. Jones (first name Edward). Of the original companies in the index, only General Electric remains; many another has come and gone as the total number of companies represented has been increased to thirty.

The way the average is calculated has changed. Nowadays, the prices of the thirty are put in a statistical Waring blender, and they flip the switch and pour out the number.

Personally, I like the sound of the names of companies that used to be in the Dow and that are now less than an echo from the steam whistle of the Midnight Flyer: U.S. Cordage, Victor Talking Machine, Pacific Mail Steamship, and Hudson Motor Car. They sit better on the ear than McDonald's, Hewlett-Packard, and Walt Disney, which have taken their places.

The Dow Jones seems to have been invented as a marketing device to get people interested in buying stocks at a time when—if you can believe such a thing!— respectable people viewed buying the shares of industrial companies as only a step and a half away from betting on the ponies. In the 1890s men with their bowlers squarely on their skulls bought bonds or, if they felt rather daring, shares in railroad companies.

Purists, cranks, crackpots, financial analysts, and grinds insist that the DJIA is an inadequate tool, but the fact remains that when anybody asks anywhere in the world, "How'd the market do today?" they want to know if the Dow went up or down. The Dow Jones company offers a hamper full of other indices, which is the Latin plural of index and why Wall Streeters use it is beyond me. There are dozens and dozens of other indexes

(English plural), all of which have their advocates. If it isn't information but action you want, you can buy shares in funds that mirror the indexes.

DRIP (dividend-reinvestment plan) A number of large corporations will sell their stock to small stockholders without going through brokers, whose services can be quite expensive. The dividends from stocks in these plans are often automatically reinvested in more stock without commissions being charged. There are a number of variations in these plans, all of which, by their nature, encourage holding a company's securities long term. In an era when the top officers of companies are in and out short term (three to five years) carrying away bags of loot and leaving a bad smell and sickly company, long term can have its disadvantages.

Drucker, Peter F. (1909–) Although he hates the word, which he correctly equates with charlatanism, the Austrian-born Drucker is considered the guru of all gurus of management theory. No writer-lecturer in recent decades has commanded the respect of business executives as Drucker has, but his work is without the brainless neologisms and formulaic rubbish that characterize the clucking squawks of most bestselling business writers. In simple but not simple-minded prose, for more than sixty years he has given the business world a stream of imaginative and yet practical advice and observation. Whether you buy it or not, at least you can take it seriously.

dry promotion The award of a grandiloquent title, unaccompanied by a pay raise or any increase in responsibility. It fools the suckers every time.

due diligence A term of art usually meaning that you must look before you egg somebody else into leaping. Before Company A buys Company B, the officers of Company A must investigate Company B with due diligence or, if they end up taking a bath, risk getting sued by their stockholders. Bank officers are supposed to, and sometimes actually do, exercise due diligence in examining the credit qualifications of someone or some company applying for a loan. Due diligence sometimes means you can't just go through the motions of doing something you have agreed to do, but must shake a leg, get out there, and give it the old college try.

dumb New Coke.

dumber Most very large corporate mergers and acquisitions, the kind that are announced with brass fanfares. The greatest leveraged buyout acquisition of the 1980s about which books were written and movies made, the RJR Reynolds-Nabisco takeover, was a painful flop, with the winners losing billions. Most recently the glamoroso purchase of Time Warner by AOL has been written off as a wet firecracker. The ink was scarcely dry and the celebratory champagne hardly drunk when the new company's stock began its long swoon. In both instances, the deals made macho sense, pride sense, and glory sense, but not business sense. A mere desire for millions cannot account for the stupidity of the principal players. Their greed should have saved them, but it wasn't powerful enough to overcome other brain-paralyzing emotions.

dumbest Trying to defuse a widening public-relations crisis, a top executive at Philip Morris USA apologized for a company-funded report calling cost savings from smokers' early deaths one of the "positive effects" of cigarette consumption (*Wall Street Journal,* July 26, 2001).

dump Predatory pricing engaged in by foreigners. Evil companies from abroad, foully subsidized by their foreign governments, dump goods in the American market for under the cost of making them. The strategy is to bankrupt American competitors, then jack up the prices, thereby recouping earlier losses and reaping monopoly profits.

The American government can and often does retaliate against dumping, but this is a murky topic. Any manager will tell you that knowing the costs of production when there is no politics involved takes some doing, but in dumping controversies there is politics aplenty and plenty of sneaky ways of slipping subsidies to producers —and it's not just wicked foreigners who do it.

Dutch auction A bass-ackwards auction in which the price is gradually lowered until somebody in the audience raises a hand. Persons of Dutch descent do not seem to take umbrage at this term, although a prickly Hollander might say it reenforces the stereotype of the stingy Dutchman.

earnings   The payoff, what's left after meeting all of a company's expenses of every kind and sort. That sum, and sometimes it's a surprisingly shriveled one, is divided among the stockholders, except when it isn't, and then it's called retained earnings, but not retained by you. Earnings would be a number subject to reprehensible manipulation by unscrupulous CEOs if there were such people. Announcements of earnings that are not calculated on the basis of GAAP are not only suspect but may grossly overstate the real condition of a company (see **profit**). There may be a difference between earnings and profit, but it's a devil of a definitional problem, and this imp hasn't solved it.

earnings management   Fidoodling with the books to make the quarterly per-share profits a penny or so higher than anticipated by stock market analysts. For a year or two, there are an infinite number of ways of making things look better (or worse) than they are. One of the cutest is taking out an insurance policy that pays off if earnings do not reach a certain figure. The insurance money goes on the books as earnings, and the investing public is hoodwinked into thinking the company is more profitable than it is. For CEOs and their corporate co-conspirators, who live and die and profit by the price of the company's stock, ways of throwing up misleading or meaningless or—dare one say it?—dishonest numbers abound. If they can kick up the price of the stock long enough to cash in their options, they do not worry about the long run because they will be long gone when that time comes. For the modest investor holding the stock for a retirement account, well. . . . (See **whisper number**.)

easing Lowering interest rates, especially if it's done by the Federal Reserve Board Open Market Committee. Contrast "easing" with "stringency," a word used for a tight-money, high-interest condition. Beware: if you use the word "easing" you may be taken for a professional and be expected to know all the other argot of high finance.

Eastman, George (1854–1932) Shortly before he took a gun and fired a bullet into his heart, George Eastman wrote a note in which he said, "To my Friends My work is done Why wait? GE." His work, judged by its effect on business and culture, was prodigious. From the time of Eastman's birth to his suicide, America—indeed the world—thanks in no small measure to him, changed from a place where graven images were rare and expensive to a place where images, still and in motion, were on their way to becoming ubiquitous artifacts that everyone made, cherished, studied, and surrounded themselves with. To Eastman, a self-taught, Sunday afternoon experimenter in photographic technology, goes the credit for making cheap, easy picture-taking available to the millions with his inventions of film and the inexpensive Brownie camera, with its slogan of "You press the button, we do the rest." It was Eastman, also, who provided Thomas Edison (see **Edison, Thomas Alva**) with the film he needed to complete his motion picture system.

By hiring the chemist Henry M. Reichenbach to perfect transparent film, Eastman pioneered the assignment of technical personnel to do specific pieces of industrial research. A globalist long before the term had been coined, Eastman spread Eastman Kodak across the globe a century ago. His near monopoly of the American photographic market got him an average profit of more than 170 percent, even as he lowered his prices to capture more customers.

Though Eastman seems a candidate for robber baronhood, the honor doesn't really fit a man who monopolized an industry that wouldn't have existed had it not been for him. Moreover, though a classic profit maximizer, Eastman parted company with many of his fellow industrialists during World War I by not charging what the traffic would bear. He hated the labor unions, but instead of using goons and thugs, Eastman fended them off by paying high wages and providing medical services, lunchrooms, industrial safety programs, bonuses, and opportunities to buy company stock. To a large extent, Eastman only amassed money to give it away, quietly and sometimes anonymously. Long decades before it was fashionable, Eastman was giving sizable amounts of money for African-American education. (For more on that, see **Rosenwald, Julius**.)

EBITA   When you see this term, run like hell. It is used to paint pretty and often misleading pictures of a company's condition for would-be investors. It stands for what a company has left after it's paid immediate expenses such as salaries, rent, and the like, but *before* it's paid the interest on the money it owes, its taxes, or amortization—that is, the money set aside to replace old equipment, be it machines or software. Thus the financial health of a company viewed through EBITA, or earnings before interest, taxes, and amortization, looks a lot brighter than it would through EAITA, or earnings after interest, taxes, and so forth.

Edison, Thomas Alva (1847–1931)   In the old photographs, Edison looks like the pluperfect boring, irrelevant, dead white man, but by the time Edison died he had been granted more than a thousand patents for the inventions that he and his associates brought forth over the decades. Though he was most famous for such minor advances as the incandescent light bulb, the electric storage battery, recorded sound, motion pictures, and quadraplexing (sending four messages on the same telegraph wire at the same time), Edison was a businessman. He invented things for which he believed there was a market. The business bearing his name became General Electric. As with many of the largest figures in business, the Wizard of Menlo Park (NJ), as the papers and a once-adoring public called him, was a system builder. Thus, when he had perfected the incandescent light bulb, he put together an entire electrical system—central power station, distribution, and transmission lines, etc.—to make it work. For several years in the 1880s, he left workshop and lab to spend his time selling and installing the systems in a number of cities. Business to Edison was not an afterthought.

The Wizard started out as your prototypic lone inventor in the shed, but one of his inventions was a social organization —the bringing together of technicians, engineers, and scientists to work under one roof in an invention factory. Although it took them awhile to learn how to do it, the lesson of what Edison did was not lost on some business executives (see **research and development**).

emerging As in "emerging market" or "emerging nation." Emerging from what is not stated, but whatever the emergers are emerging from, the implication is that you don't want to be there. The term is the latest in an ever lengthening line of euphemisms, which include *developing, undeveloped, third-world* or, going farther back in time, *primitive, simple,* or even *savage.* Each new euphemism is a light coat of paint applied over an older, darker one. For a while, the older color may not seep through, but sooner or later it does, and it's necessary to apply yet another coat, or euphemism, lest the feelings of the undeveloped or the not-yet-developed or whoever get bruised. If you are a businessperson, however, or an investor, the word *emerging* should be a red flag signaling the possibility, nay the probability, of problems, such as inflation, currency restrictions, strange bookkeeping practices, devaluations, nationalizations, terrorists, rioting, and a general want of the stability business needs to flourish.

England The land whence American business sprang, a fact that may come as news to Americans, who believe that everything good and worthwhile has its origins in the United States. The foundations of English business practices go back to late-medieval Italy and sixteenth-century Holland, but they had taken on distinctive forms of their own by the time the London stock market opened in 1690. Thenceforth, if not earlier, North American business copied the English, particularly as English businessmen put steam technology to work to foment the Industrial Revolution. Not only did England lead the world with the invention of such trifles as the railroad, but the great early nineteenth-century American advances in canal and railroad building were paid for by English investors.

equity The value of a property or a company after deducting every claim on it, such as the unpaid balance of a mortgage, other loans, outstanding bonds, taxes, and the like. For instance, some people "own" a house without having any equity in it, meaning that if the house were sold and the mortgage, taxes, and other bills paid off with the money from the sale, none would be left for the "owner." Hence an unknown number of millions of people who think that they are homeowners are actually renters, but they don't know it. The stockholders in companies that go bust often learn that when the company's bills and bondholders are paid off, they have no equity and their stock no value whatsoever.

Erie Canal The first of innumerable joint undertakings between government and private investors, the canal linking Lake Erie with Albany, and therefore to New York

City via the Hudson River, was too costly an undertaking for business to do alone. The money to build it was supplied by the state of New York and private investors. Completed in 1825, on time and on budget, the Canal paid off for all concerned. New York State got rich, and the tolls paid the investors back with a profit.

Some things demand too much capital or pay off too slowly or are too risky for private money alone. Canals, railroads, highways, and air transportation are the biggest and most obvious examples. Countless others, some more and some a lot less successful, are there for the finding.

ETF (exchange-traded fund) One more attempt by man and woman to obtain safety, security, and guaranteed profit. Since the odds of making money by selecting individual stocks to buy are putrid, somebody came up with the idea of selling shares of bundles of them, picked to represent the price behavior of all the stocks on an exchange together. Thus, if the market as a whole goes up, shares of your ETF should go up by the same percentage. No more of the disheartening experience of seeing the prices on all stocks except the ones you own go up, while yours go down. Unhappily, sometimes the reverse happens and the average price of shares on a stock market goes down, even as four or five stocks are shooting up into the stratosphere.

ETFs are another form of diversification, the conviction that the safest way to make money is by investing in a variety of securities, on the assumption (which sometimes is born out and sometimes is not) that when one kind of investment goes kerplop, another kind goes kerzoom. Mutual funds are also attempts at diversification, though they are run by people who select individual stocks for the fund, such people being by turns brilliant, stupid, lucky, cursed, honest, crazy, or crooked.

ethicist A person in the employ of a large corporation whose job it is to tell the CEO right from wrong. And how does an ethicist know right from wrong? The person has a PhD from a name-brand institution, ears sensitive enough to hear when God whispers, or a stout paycheck.

Everleigh, née Lester, Ada (1876–1960) and Minna (1878–1948) The Victorian sisters who first applied modern merchandising, i.e., advertising, to the sex industry. From the turn of the last century until 1911, the sisters were the proprietors of the nationally known Everleigh Club, America's most luxurious whorehouse, located in Chicago at 2131 South Dearborn Avenue, wherein the establishment's high-society patrons enjoyed such appurtenances as its famous $15,000 gold-leaf piano and its $650, 24-carat cuspidors; its champagne, caviar, lobster, and fried oyster suppers; and its library of handsomely bound volumes, which, one suspects, may not have been overly used. Other services were supplied in chambers with names like the Japanese Throne Room and the Louis Quatorze Room, by wholesome young women who were paid $50 a pop in an era when the girls on the street were known to perform for as little as a quarter. It cost $10 just to walk into the Everleigh Club, and by the time a spoilsport mayor closed the place down, the sisters walked out millionaires.

excess Until recently the excesses of top-ranked businesspeople were taken to be company jets, perks and perky young people on staff, preposterous emoluments, a bully's temperament, and the pride which goeth before a fall—about half the time. Latterly, the world has learned that executive excess is a standard of living that would leave Peter the Great or a Renaissance pope jumping up and down and moaning with envy. Even Pope Alexander VI, the Borgia pope, who lived like an American CEO, didn't have an $11,000 shower curtain. He didn't have a shower.

A second kind of excess is the unstoppable propensity of the business mentality to go too far, usually by a failure to control inventory. Car companies build too many cars, hotel companies build too many rooms, steel companies build too much production capacity, and, most recently, electronics, which was supposed to be immune from the mistakes of the past, demonstrated that it not only could overproduce, but could bring forth excesses that rivaled any and all of the inventory gluts of yore.

exposure   Only distantly related to the indecent kind. The word used for any threatening financial blow to the corporate belly. Its application is vaguer and looser than that of a liability and sometimes harder to recognize, since the company has no legal responsibility to pull back the raincoat and publicize the danger it may be exposed to.

401(k) 401(k) stands for disillusionment, worry, and finding out that the golden years will be paid for with lead bars spray-painted gold. (See **defined contribution pension**.)

Fair Disclosure Rule This is the talk-to-everybody or talk-to-nobody rule promulgated by the Securities and Exchange Commission. The purpose is to ensure that big fishes and little fishes get information about a publicly traded company at the same time, so that nobody can decide to buy or sell a company's stock based on information not available to everybody else. The rule was put forward because CEOs were meeting with stock analysts and other representatives of the big-fish brokerages and giving them the lowdown on what was coming up with their companies. The rule is yet one more move in the long chess game between the inside information sharpies and government cops who are charged with the job of making sure it's an even-steven market for everybody. How successful this law enforcement activity may be is a matter of conjecture.

fair trade Trade without "predatory" pricing. Predatory pricing is one of those terms that scares the hell out of you, but means different things, depending what your interests are. At the turn of the twentieth century, with the rise of the American Fair Trade League, fair trade meant preventing mail-order houses and chain and department stores from underselling local merchants.

By 1937, forty-two of the then existing forty-eight states had passed fair trade laws of one kind or another. In August of that year, President Franklin Roosevelt reluctantly signed a national fair trade bill, thus bringing into existence a fifteen-year era of non–price competition in the United States. Consumer groups howled, but manufacturers liked the arrangement almost as much as local merchants, and who is to say how much it's worth to shop in a place where they know you?

The battle to stifle retail price competition has long since been won by the big national and supranational merchandisers, but the term is still with us and much invoked by American manufacturers threatened by lower prices from abroad. None of this is new.

In the 2000s the fair trade slogan is used by nations variously defined as underdeveloped, developing, laggard, poor, oppressed, or retarded. Whatever they are called, many of them cannot sell their agricultural products in the United States, thanks to tariffs, quotas, and the like. If they could, it is believed that they would stop being underdeveloped, stupid, poor, etc., and become self-supporting and would therefore stop whining and fussing.

fallen angels   Not excessively nubile, teenage runaways down at the bus depot. Nor are fallen angels the splendid spirits cast out of Heaven in *Paradise Lost.* Fallen angels are once gilt-edged bonds issued by companies with long histories of steady profits and prudent management, which subsequently go bad. AT&T stock, which for a century paid dividends with the regularity of a bond, is a prime example of a four-star security bought for certain income, which dropped out of financial heaven and went into free market free fall.

false bottom   Not a cosmetically assisted derriere but the foolish belief that a stock or the market has fallen as far as it can, when worse is yet to come.

family business   Although politicians spout off about them a lot, family businesses do indeed exist. Those that are richly successful do not usually stay family businesses after a couple of generations, because the heirs want to spend money, not spend time making it. Nevertheless there are businesses that remain family-run for long periods. One charming example is C. F. Martin & Co. of Nazareth, Pennsylvania, founded in 1833 by Christian Frederick Martin (1796–1873), who brought the craft of guitar making over from the old country. For almost two centuries the Martin family has run its business with as much harmony as that made by its highly regarded string instruments.

family farm A term used for a now extinct socioeconomic unit. For all practical purposes the family farm has gone the way of the family-owned everything else. There are about as many family farms left in the United States as there are drugstore soda fountains. The phrase "family farm" is customarily bandied about by politicians whose pockets have been filled with bribes—that is, campaign contributions—by agribusiness giants looking for subsidies, tax breaks, and protection against foreign competition.

Farmers, whether members of families or not, are growing old and dying out. Sentimental blubbering about a way of life that disappeared generations ago aside, their vanishing numbers are nothing to cheer about. A nation that can't feed itself is at the mercy of those who do feed it, but farming is a highly skilled, high-risk, lonely occupation, requiring knowledge of mechanics, agronomy, hydrology, ecology, law, chemistry, accounting, and God knows what else. And God knows what happens when the last of them retires and the whole country is officially declared a suburb. *Postscriptum:* The family farm ought not to be conflated with the large-scale industrial farm, sometimes owned by a family, sometimes not. These enterprises could not stay in business without large subventions from Washington, D.C. The classic family farm gets almost no dough from the government.

Fannie Mae and **Freddie Mac** (Nicknames for Federal National Mortgage Association and Federal Home Loan Mortgage Corporation.) Despite the cuddly names, these are huge, stockholder-owned outfits. Their names betray their governmental origins in the 1930s, when, as now, Washington's policy was to increase home ownership and back the construction industry. Fannie and Freddie do this by buying home mortgages from banks and savings and loan associations and reselling them, hence making sure the banks always have money to lend for new mortgages. The two are now private sector entities, but special ones. They don't have to pay state and local taxes, and the business world is convinced that, though the Federal Government is not legally bound to do so, it would step in as a last resort to make good on any bad debts. Let it also be said that even though Fannie and Freddie have made a small group of insiders a lot richer than they ought to be, the organizations have helped make America a nation of homeowners, which, as any television commercial will tell you, is the pithy heart of the American dream. On the other hand, government backing has made Freddie and Fannie low-risk, low-cost, rock-solid, high-profit, privileged corporations with one foot in the private sector and one foot in the Treasury, and that drives competing, true private-sector companies wild.

After generations of staying quietly in the background and making indescribably large amounts of money, in recent years Fannie and Freddie have gotten themselves a lot of unwelcome publicity as it has come to light that this brother-sister combination has been fiddlefaddling with the books to hide just how much do-re-me they've been raking in.

Let us also give a quick nod to the existence of Farmer Mac (Federal Agricultural Mortgage Corporation), a seldom heard from outfit with a reputation, doubtless undeserved, of performing no known service other than enriching the scalawags who have crawled in and taken it over. In Washington, you need only yell "Farmer down and in trouble!" and it rains thousand-dollar bills.

fast food As good an example of business shaping culture as you'll get—in this case, by inventing the centerpiece of American ethnic food, the hamburger. In the course of changing hamburger meat from something made of scraps, puppy dog entrails, and mouse droppings, which middle-class people would not dream of touching, into food they can't stop eating, business not only reconfigured what Americans put in their mouths but also the how, the when, and the where of what they eat.

The hamburger, loosely defined, goes well back into the nineteenth century; however, it was Edgar Ingram (1880–1966) who made it what it is, when he opened the first White Castle, the first-ever fast-food outlet, in 1921, in Wichita, Kansas. The American gut and the American derrière haven't stopped growing since. By the early 1950s the term *fast food* was coming into general use.

The essential fast-food formula hasn't changed since Ingram thought it up, although the execution varies considerably: consistent quality, the same (ahem) good taste every time, speed, cleanliness, take-out-ability, every store a look-alike, moderate price, and uniformity in all things. Ingram was a perfectionist whose perfectionism made White Castle a success. His insistence on the best ingredients led him to slaughtering his own beef and baking his own rolls (see **vertical integration**). His fanaticism for spotless stores and spotless personnel led him to pioneer the use of paper napkins, aprons, and other products, and create a profitable manufacturing company selling them to other businesses. To make sure that every White Castle was identical, he commenced prefabbing them in his own factory and shipping them to the store sites. These steel structures with their enameled surfaces, redesigned for gas stations—another exploding industry in the 1920s—put Ingram in yet a third profitable business.

So how come the country is littered with golden arches and not White Castle crenelations? Ingram would not borrow money or sell stock to raise money to expand fast enough to keep out the swarm of competitors who moved in on him. White Castle grew, debt-free, only as fast as his profits enabled him to grow. After World War II, Ingram left the field of franchising to McDonald's Ray Kroc, who made cardiology such a popular medical specialty.

fast track　A parliamentary rule in the U.S. Congress designed to get foreign trade agreements approved. (Fast track sometimes goes under the sweetened name of "trade promotion authority.") A fast-track rule requires that the vote on the agreement take place within a fixed period of time, and the vote must be straight up or down with no amendments. The reason for fast track is that foreign trade bills are good for everybody, every industry, and every region of the country in a general sort of way, and bad in a particular sort of way for many individuals, industries, and areas, since trade bills always open up more competition from abroad. Without the fast-track rule, congresspersons and senators, being the frail people they are, would buckle under to pressure by injured businesses and unions from home and would kill any trade bill by delays and/or nullifying amendments. A fast-track rule is no foregone conclusion. On at least one occasion, it has been voted down, and even when it is voted through, blood splatters can be seen on the Capitol's marble walls.

Father's Day   Once there was a Mother's Day, Daddy's Day was inevitable but quite slow getting off the ground, even with the backing of the Associated Men's Wear Retailers and the much repeated fact that the word *father* occurs in the Bible 1,650 times, as compared to a measly 311 for *mother.* Nevertheless, Mother's Day has always been bigger, since it was started circa 1906 by a tireless, mother-loving Methodist laywoman named Anna Jarvis (1864–1948). By 1908, twenty thousand people tried to crowd their way into the Wanamaker (department) Store Auditorium in Philadelphia, where the merchant prince John Wanamaker presided over the Mother's Day cere-monies. Well he might have, for Mother's Day is topped in retail sales only by Christmas, Valentine's Day, and the Easter bunny.

FICO or **FICO score**   An acronym derived from the name Fair, Isaac & Co, a company that produces algorithms for calculating creditworthiness. Although other ways of scoring are used, the score is still called a FICO. Since mortgages are mixed together, chopped up, and resold in pieces as bonds, it's important to have reliable formulae to predict what percentage of the mortgages underlying the newly created bonds will go south. The science of sto-chastics is applied to everything in business from assessing credit risk to quality assurance on the produc-tion line. It doesn't eliminate human judgment, but it lessens its influence in all kinds of decision making, an area where it has been found that, much of the time, a mathematical statement is preferable to human whim.

fiduciary   This is one of those words the very utterance of which is intended to make the suckers feel safe. It is verbal tapioca, financial comfort food. Meaning "someone who holds something in trust," it is applied to trust officers, executors of wills, bankruptcy receivers, and administrators of the property of minors and the mentally infirm. By and large, no group bears more close watching than fiduciaries. It would be an exaggeration to assume that every one of them will betray his trust, but it is hard to think of an area of business life where there is more unpunished larceny and fraud.

flip **1.** To sell a piece of real estate, stocks, bonds, or any property immediately after buying it. To turn it over quickly or flip it. Traders do this every day in the stock market and nobody thinks ill of them, but in real estate, flipping, which is nothing more than rapidly selling a property for more than you paid for it, can be regarded as sleazy, since, in certain social situations, profit too quickly realized is considered ill-got gains. **2.** Real estate fraud. The con works this way. The first sleazy operator buys a building for half a million dollars and sells it to the second sleazy operator for a million. The two of them bribe an appraiser and/or a loan officer in a bank to give them a mortgage of $900,000. Half a million from the mortgage goes to the original seller, and the remaining $400,000 is divided up by the crooks who do not pay the monthly installments on the mortgage but walk away from it and let the bank take the beating. **3.** Selling shares of stock immediately after buying them in an initial public offering. When a new stock is first put on the market (the **initial public offering** or **IPO**) a price is set for it per share, and a certain number of people and/or institutions are invited by the underwriters, the company handling the deal, to buy shares at the beginning price, with the proviso that they do not sell these new shares for some stated period of time. The company launching the new issue wants the price to go up, and that's less likely to happen if the first purchasers turn around and sell. Flipping is deemed such a breach of manners that flippers are not invited back to future offerings.

Ford, Henry I (1863–1947) An uneducated man, God only knows where he got some of his ideas, the good ones and the bad. The bad ones, especially his raging anti-Semitism, were so bad that they have all but blotted out the place he holds in the history of the modern world. Insofar as it can be said that a single person invented mass production, it was he. In the first third of the twentieth century, Fordism (as the modern factory and the moving assembly line were called before he himself coined the term *mass production*) had an impact on daily life deeper than that of the Internet on the last third.

Those first famous Model Ts rolled off the line into a nation with almost no paved roads, no gas stations, few mechanics, and no settled way of selling autos. Selling directly to the public was tried and discarded in favor of the type of dealerships Cyrus McCormick (see **McCormick, Cyrus Hall**) had already pioneered in the farm equipment industry.

In 1914 Ford flabbergasted the nation by announcing he was doubling the wages of his factory workers to an unheard-of five dollars a day and instituting a shorter forty-hour work week. This sometimes benevolent, sometimes malevolent talent had figured out that if people didn't have money in their pokes they could not afford to buy his cars. By the time of his death, his hateful eccentricities, his anti-Semitism, and his antiunion goon squads had destroyed his once enormous popularity and sent his company careening toward bankruptcy.

Ford, Henry II (1917–1987) Henry Ford's grandson lacked the engineering and inventive genius, not to mention the imagination, of the old man. He also lacked the old man's misanthropy, but he had business talent in exactly the areas where the grandfather had none and used it to save the Ford Motor Company from extinction. Prey to alcoholism and womanizing, Henry II nevertheless reorganized the company along the lines invented by Alfred Sloan at General Motors and demonstrated a remarkable ability to find and recruit a series of gifted executives who restored Ford Motor Company to health, no small accomplishment given that second acts in business are as rare as they are everywhere else.

form 10-K, form 8-K, and **form 10-Q** Sexy names thought up by the Securities and Exchange Commission for reports that virtually every company selling any kind of security to the public must file, under penalty of being frowned at or, occasionally, seriously punished. The 10-Ks are yearly statements of a company's financial condition; the 10-Qs are less thoroughgoing, unaudited quarterly statements; the 8-Ks are only issued when something of moment has transpired, such as a merger offer or the R&D laboratories' discovering a cancer cure. In other words, big good or big bad news that might affect the price of a company's stock or its credit rating may not be kept secret while insiders load up on the company's stock or dump it, depending on the news—something, of course, that no insider would ever think of doing. (See **insider trading**.)

franchises Nationally branded retail outlets owned and operated by small business people. Franchises are one of the reasons every part of America looks like every other part. Identical looks, identical modi operandi, and identical products are the center of the franchise system, which, however else you may want to criticize it, has taken much of the risk out of the small, retail business enterprise. Franchises combine some of the independence small business people love with big-corporation advantages, such as national brand advertising, lower-cost supplies owing to high-volume purchasing by the mother corporation, consistent quality, modern cost accounting, careful training of personnel, and various kinds of staff backup that would otherwise be out of the price range of small businesses.

The major legal, organizational, and procedural elements of the not-so-simple franchising system were worked out in the 1920s and 1930s by the big oil companies, which, under pressure of the ever growing number of cars, had to devise a better way of selling gasoline than delivering it to hardware stores in barrels. The oil companies got into franchising as a means of distributing a mass-produced industrial product—gasoline; food franchising, begun in 1935 when Howard Johnson opened his first store, was a different kettle of fish. The product was made and usually consumed in a restaurant of distinctive design and color, a signal to the automobile-driving public that the quality of the food and the menu were familiar—and reliable—commodities.

The franchise explosion dates from the 1950s with the arrival of operations like McDonald's, which benefited from the tens of thousands of miles of new highways and the exponential growth of suburbs engineered for autos and inhabited by the first generation of Americans who had the money and desire to eat out. Whether fast foodery is a net plus or minus aesthetically and nutritionally is a topic for argument. There's no arguing, however, about the drab, mass-produced predictability with which franchises have disfigured the land.

Franklin, Benjamin (1706–1790) He ought to be the patron saint of American business, except that he wasn't a Christian, had a common-law marriage, and fathered an illegitimate child. Perhaps the most gifted human being ever to draw breath in North America, he was an enormously successful businessman, making his money in printing, book publishing, and newspapering. His legacies to his nation and the world are too numerous to be listed here, but none was more important than that which he left to the businesspeople who have come after him: the achievement of an overarching success without backstabbing, bullying, cheating, overweening pride, arrogance, dishonesty, or an unseemly love of luxury. Franklin taught that you can succeed in business while treating others with kindness, honor, and charity. It is a great shame that he was too immoral to be considered a role model in our times, when standards are higher, but, what the hell, George Washington used to invite him over for dinner.

free enterprise system A metaphysical ejaculation out of the mouths of politicians, Chamber of Commerce orators, and editorialists, used to beat people over the head whose advocacy is contrary to the speaker's interest. Although, other than two uses in the **Epic of Gilgamesh,** the term is not to be found in any sacred writings, in the

United States it is deemed to be a gift of God, and to disparage it is to blaspheme against the honored dead.

free trade Said to exist when goods and services flow from nation to nation without impediments such as tariffs, or deceptive barriers such as phony health regulations and environmental rules. A synonym for free trade is "pie in the sky," but down on the ground no nation, not even the United States, which is famous for demanding it, is close to razing the fences of protection. Realists will tell you that they are happy to settle for freer trade.

front-running One of those tricky things brokers do behind your back. A client phones in an order to buy a large block of stock, and the broker, realizing from the order that those shares are about to spurt upward, puts in his own order first. He thus gets the stock cheaper than the customer and makes a larger profit. Sometimes the broker's purchase may cause the price of the stock to jump up, costing his customer even more dough. That's front-running, and brokers who do it may have to wait a few minutes longer to get on the squash courts.

Fuller, Alfred Carl (1885–1973) At one time, the Fuller Brush Man was as familiar as the cop on the beat, a trusted figure whom the nation's chronic labor shortage has chased off the streets and into nostalgia-land. At the apex of the company's fame, residents of every middle-class community in the United States knew their Fuller Brush Man and awaited his visit and the free sample he brought. His reputation put him in a different league from door-to-door magazine, aluminum siding, or presentation peddlers. In common with those of other highly successful sales organizations in American business history, such as

IBM, Fuller dealers—they were not called salesmen—were imbued with a Messianic fervor for self-improvement and community uplift. Fuller's brushes, like Mary Kay's skin care products, were decidedly superior to the competition. It is not true that a mad-dog, enthusiastic sales organization necessarily sells crap. You've gotta get out there and hustle to sell the good stuff, too.

Futurama Exhibit In preparation for the 1939 New York World's Fair, General Motors hired Norman Bel Geddes (1893–1958) to design a huge, three-dimensional, panoramic model depicting what city and suburban life in America would look like twenty years hence. Needless to say, the automobile had free run of the Futurama, which turned out to be not too far off the mark. Did General Motors and Bel Geddes reflect the tastes and desires of people or shape them? Or was it a little of both? Business has been determining the size and shape of physical objects since the dawn of consumerism. So strongly recognizable is the corporate style that many people jump back from it and seek to own objects that seem to come from another time. Hence, the love of retro, but, of course, retro is but the business styles of thirty or forty years ago. Objects from the premanufacturing age do exist. They are expensive and of limited use.

futures, futures market, futures contract A futures contract is a contract to buy or sell something at a certain price on a specific date. That something can be the much giggled-at pork belly, or gold, or British pounds, or Euros, or wheat, or other securities. You don't have to own the thing when you contract to sell it, but there's no wiggling out of it. If you have not sold the contract to someone else, on its due date you must come up with the wheat or the gold, or pay over its cash equivalent. If you have a futures contract to buy and you haven't sold the contract by the due date, you must accept delivery on the fifty carloads of grain or the ten thousand dozen grade A eggs, or the suddenly depreciated bonds stipulated in the contract. The important part of a futures contract is that it is a contract, not an option, so that on the due date you must perform.

Futures contracts, and the futures markets where they are bought and sold, made their appearance around the time of the Civil War and were immediately a source of controversy. On June 17th, 1864, in an attempt to suppress erratic price jumping, trading in gold futures was prohibited by the federal government. Henceforth, the precious metal might not be contracted for sale except by its owner. The regulation had no discernible effect, and, with an astonishing alacrity for a government agency, it was abandoned several weeks later.

To this day, a sizable body of opinion holds that futures trading is a useless speculative bog whose denizens are animals with long noses and sharp claws. Nevertheless, for many people the futures market is a protection from the vicissitudes visited on honest toilers by speculation and the ordinary unpredictability of prices. Farmers looking to lock in a price for the grain they've sown, manufacturers doing the same for raw materials they will need in the future, and companies doing business overseas and seeking to prevent their profits from being wiped out by currency fluctuations, all have recourse to the futures market, which couldn't function without speculators.

Gates, William Henry (Bill) III (1955–) Businessman and technologist, tediously and endlessly encomiated for being the richest man in the world. When you get into the realms of who's richest, the counting can get a trifle imprecise. As the cofounder of Microsoft, Gates isn't in the league of a Thomas Edison, a John D. Rockefeller I, or a Sam Walton, men who created or reshaped industries that touch on the daily lives of tens of millions. Although Gates is an adept technologist and a gifted businessman, in his case, pure, blind luck played a larger part than it usually does. Microsoft's first and main product, the operating system of the personal computer, was spectacularly profitable more because of a business misjudgment at IBM than its own modest virtues. Had IBM elected to buy this operating program, rather than lease it from Gate's company, it is unlikely that Gates would have mounted to such heights. Despite his popularity with the adoring masses who mistakenly credit him with the introduction of the PC, he has earned a secondary fame as the despised monopolist of the electronics industry. A substantial subset of his customers are also known to present the symptoms of Tourette's syndrome—ticks, howls, and obscene ululations—at the mention of the man's name. This has nothing to do with the monopoly accusations, but rather results from the famously shabby unreliability of his principal product. You can't be sure how the nondead are going to wind up, but, as of this writing, Gates may die with as much money as Henry Ford or Andrew Carnegie, though with a slighter imprint on business or world history.

Generally Accepted Accounting Principles (GAAP)
GAAP is a fluid, ever changing body of precedents, traditional practice, and rules, as published by such professional bodies as the Financial Accounting Standards Board. Don't try to understand this stuff unless you are ready to make a study of it, which may or may not avail you, since GAAP is frequently honored in the breach, as the ENRON scandal taught an investing public brought up on the fairy tale that auditors were people you messed around with at your peril. Legend has it that a company that wants to pass muster is expected to keep its books according to GAAP. A company whose books are adjudged to be not in accordance with GAAP is supposed to land in deepest, darkest doo-doo, but a CEO is more likely to be eaten by a shark than to suffer the embarrassment of getting caught and punished in any meaningful way for GAAP violations. As a consequence of certain regrettable revelations in the first years of this

century, CEOs of large firms are now required to swear by their mamas' memory that their financial statements are accurate. For those who cheat there is the threat of the perp walk but, except for one or two offered up as a public example, the big boys seldom get jugged.

Generally Accepted Auditing Standards (GAAS) The rules as to how an audit is conducted, as laid down by professional accounting organizations. The standards include the responsibility of the auditors to include an honest, or at least somewhat revealing, statement as to the financial condition of the company, but there is a built-in conflict of interest that makes frank auditors' reports something of a rarity: the auditors are paid by the people whom they audit. Modern business history is cluttered with accusations by stockholders and lenders of *soi-disant* outside accountants who, after the scandal broke, looked more like co-conspirators than take-no-prisoners bean counters intent on telling a corporation's true situation. Of late, some courts have begun to hold accountants liable for misrepresentations in prospectuses (see **prospectus**) and corporate reports. Calls for reform anent auditing and reporting are recurrent. After the investing public has gotten a new, particularly thorough hosing, laws of questionable efficacy are sometimes passed, as happened in 2002. (See **Securities and Exchange Commission**.) But after a certain point, regulation may assist people who practice trompe l'oeil accounting by creating gooey, opaque complexities behind which the awful truth can be concealed. Regulation may also give the guppies and other small fish the erroneous impression that claims for the stock they are buying have been vetted by the government.

geezerism Getting old before your chronological time. In business you can't be too young to start trying to look younger and damn the cost of the plastic surgery, the hair plugs, or the personal trainers. In some places looking older will get you fired but in others it's not the image but the numbers that will cost you your job.

Although it will never be admitted, even if proven in a court of law, many businesses make it a point to get rid of employees before they get too old purely for bottom line reasons. Too old means when their salaries get too high or their potential retirement benefits grow too large. Persons in their Viagra years, or even in their forties or younger, may be too old for some organizations unless they're in the upper-management ranks. (It may take a dynamite charge to blow an octogenarian CEO out of his leather boardroom chair on to the deck of his yacht.) In some companies a geezer is anyone with a family, because family men and women are harder and more expensive to move around. Hide the photos of the kiddies in a drawer while you reflect on yet one more example of business effecting the shape and content of family life.

Giannini, Amadeo Peter (1870–1949) Born in San José, the son of one of the thousands who came to California in the 1849 Gold Rush and didn't strike it rich, A. P., as he was called, started out making a success as a fruit and vegetable wholesaler, but when he switched over to work in the tiny Bank of Italy, he found his true calling. At his death, his Bank of Italy, renamed Bank of America, was the largest financial institution in the world, even exceeding in size the great New York banks, whose owners despised him for his Italian extraction and feared him as the ferocious, endlessly ingenious, indomitable competitor he was.

While immigrant ethnic groups in a few cities had started banks to serve their own people, Giannini went out to win the business of every group. His customers could transact their business in a half-dozen different languages, even as he was changing banking from a carriage-trade business into one that served the working masses. Breaking the mold of upper-class exclusivity, A. P. shocked the banking world not only by advertising but by going out onto the streets and canvassing for business. The single greatest innovation he brought to the industry was the introduction of branch banking, which was fought both by local bankers and rival money center banks, who were threatened by Giannini's ability to corral new accounts by the hundreds of thousands.

Wall Street's fear of Giannini was echoed by the American left. The inhuman "Bank of the West" in John Steinbeck's *Grapes of Wrath* was clearly meant to be Giannini's Bank of America. But there were two sides to this argument. The local banks with whom Giannini competed offered fewer services and charged much higher interest rates on loans, which they were less likely to make. Without the credit Giannini supplied to farmers, California could not have become an agricultural wonder. It was Giannini's bank that financed the construction of the Golden Gate Bridge and provided the wherewithal for money-starved Hollywood during the Great Depression. Among many other films, Bank of America money paid for the making of *Gone with the Wind, Snow White,* and *Mr. Smith Goes to Washington.*

Mr. Giannini had to go to Washington himself when Wall Street and the Hoover administration conspired to take the bank and its sister, the Transamerica Corporation, away from him. As a pioneer in democratic capitalism, Giannini had campaigned to sell his stock to ordinary people, and several hundred thousand came to support him in the most extraordinary proxy fights in business history. In the 1932 presidential election, Giannini threw his support to Franklin Roosevelt, but unlike other business figures in politics, he had more than money to offer. He had people, his stockholders and his depositors, who came out to help Roosevelt carry the state by record numbers.

Today A. P.'s ambition to see national branch banking has become a reality, but not as he would have hoped. Instead of legions of loyal customers, there are millions complaining about the high costs and poor service.

"I've always vowed I'd never become a millionaire," Giannini said, and he never did. He left an estate of less than half a million. His coin, some said, was power, but his will to power carried with it the idea of the equal consumer republic that has come into existence.

global economy (the) When international trade grew to a magnitude that jolted the seers who make their livings discovering new epochs, they proclaimed the epiphany of a global economy. New, different, unique, extraordinary!

Well, maybe, but 4500 years ago Sumerian businessmen were operating on an international scale, with agents in offices abroad selling goods from the homeland to buyers who paid in strange coin. If the Sumerians, the Greeks, the Romans, the Arabs, and merchants of China and medieval Europe were not part of a global economy, it's only because they thought the world was flat.

There never was a time when an entirely self-sufficient, economically isolated United States got along without having extensive commerce with others in distant places. (See **protective tariff**.) As early as the Jefferson administration (1801–1809), an American foreign trade embargo caused such hardship that New England almost seceded from the Union. By the second half of the nineteenth century, American business, joining American agriculture in peddling abroad, was swarming overseas (see also **multinational corporation**).

Although the term *global economy* was not used a century ago, big business already had a global mentality. The slogan "Sherwin-Williams Paints Cover the World" appeared in 1894, and it was in that time that Chauncey Depew (1834–1928), political fixer and bagman for the Vanderbilt interests and president of the then-mighty New York Central Railroad, trumpeted, "Let production go on . . . let the factories do their best, let labor be employed at the highest wages because the world is ours."

What is new is the speed and the scale with which business in the twenty-first century has penetrated so many foreign cultures.

globalism The belief that the world should be open to free trade, with nations sacrificing a degree of their autonomy to a superceding international law. Every place and country would make its living by specializing in what it does best and most efficiently. One place would grow the wheat, another would make all the automobile tires, and yet another would make the machine tools. Globalism strives for total interdependence and with it, of course, comes total dependence on others, a disturbing prospect for jingoes, cynics, and close readers of human history.

globaloney The doctrine that unfettered world trade cures warts.

gnomes of Zurich   "The gnomes of Zurich and their related goblins" were first introduced to the world in 1964 on the pages of the *New Statesman*. It may have originally been a coinage of British prime minister Harold Wilson. Regardless, various good and evil acts have been attributed to the gnomes ever since, and, although still vaguely associated with the banking capital of the Republic of Switzerland, they now are invoked as the intermittently good and intermittently wicked magic imps who live under the Alps and control the world.

gold   A mineral, whose symbol is Au and atomic number is 79, possessing a power equal to sex to agitate the imagination and cause people to do silly, dangerous, and even fairly illegal things, such as robbing Spanish treasure galleons and cheating at cards.

Gold is also a commodity like wheat and wool, so that its price is subject to change as supply and demand ebb and flow. In the last one hundred years, people who have held gold either in ingots, in coin, or as stock in gold-mining companies have made a financial killing with it or have themselves been killed by it. As a medium of exchange, it has progressively gone out of favor in what we are pleased to call the advanced nations because the stuff weighs a ton.

gold bug   Despite its drawbacks, gold's advocates have never died out, and you will find people today who will tell you the gold standard is the only reliable protection for keeping the value of money. During the administrations of Presidents William McKinley and Jimmy Carter, gold sentiment abounded, but by the turn of the twenty-first century such opinions had become fringy.

gold standard   In the good old days, you could take a ten-dollar bill to the nearest bank and exchange it for a ten-dollar gold coin. That was the gold standard.

After the Great Crash of 1929, the United States switched to a modified gold standard, keeping vast amounts of gold in government vaults at Fort Knox, Kentucky, to "back up" paper money. This involved huge shipments of gold going back and forth across the Atlantic Ocean, cumbersome money manipulations, and quirky restrictions, such as making ownership of gold by American citizens illegal.

The gold standard played a part in the financial crises and "panics" of yesteryear. A shortage of gold, or a "stringency," as they used to say, could bring on hard times. A big gold strike could result in so much money flying around that prices would rise and inflation would set in.

Gompers, Samuel (1850–1924)   Born in London's East End of poor working-class, Jewish parents, Samuel Gompers immigrated to New York with his family in 1863. He went to school, and, simultaneously, worked at a cigar factory. The cigar makers, in the Jewish tradition of respect for learning, hired a man to read to them every day while they worked. Thus, the young Gompers was introduced to the ideas of Karl Marx, Ferdinand Lassalle, and trade unionism. His idealism and the introduction of cigar-making machines pushed Gompers into a career of union work. Gompers was one of the key figures who, in 1886, established the American Federation of Labor, which elected him its president, a post he held until his death. As much as any single person, it was Gompers who steered American unionism away from socialism or communism. He had a repugnance for a governmental role in union work, but the Republican Party was so hostile to unionism that during the Woodrow Wilson administration (1913–21), Gompers effected the marriage of organized labor with the Democratic Party.

Samuel Gompers bequeathed to American trade unionism its often fierce patriotism, its tradition of resistance and suspicion of government in the workplace, and its preference for private collective bargaining with employers. But American business executives, unlike Europeans, have never really accepted unions and waged such constant war against them that by 2000 union representation in private-sector companies had shriveled into something approaching impotence. The irony of the defeat of unionism is federal government regulation of the workplace, which has caused more than one corporate executive to die of indigestion after eating a plate of nails in fury at the intrusive and entangling bureaucracy that confronts every employer, but you can't have it both ways, fellas.

goodwill This kind of goodwill has little to do with peace on earth and altruistic urges. A slippery word, it is the difference between what a company is worth and the price somebody pays or overpays for it. The worth of the company is all its buildings, cash, machines, patents, money owed, etc., minus what it owes. Say that's a million dollars—but another company buys the joint for two million bucks. The second million is called goodwill. So how come goodwill is worth so much? If we're talking about a company like McDonald's, the goodwill is, among other things, the Golden Arches and Ronald McDonald—intangibles that are so famous and so well thought of by a broad stripe of the public that they're worth a lot. A company's reputation is valuable goodwill. A good rep will get you customers, so it's worth something. But when, as sometimes happens, a company is sold and the goodwill portion of the deal is ridiculously high, it usually means the hanky-pankies are out. This can involve such things as hiding the true cost of the purchase, making it look as if the purchasing company is more profitable than it is, and opening up various delicious opportunities for the principals in the deal and their lawyers and brokers to come by gains, which if not exactly ill gotten, aren't exactly honestly gotten, either.

Government National Mortgage Association (Ginnie Mae) A federal government agency that guarantees the full payment of securities created by putting home mortgages of various kinds together. The banks that originally make the mortgages collect the monthly payments and send the money to Ginnie Mae, which speeds it on to institutions or individuals who buy the securities. If a homeowner skips a payment or defaults, Ginnie Mae makes it up; thus Ginnie Mae securities are considered as good as gold. The inspiration for such agency-like, government-sponsored enterprises can be traced back to the efforts of the New Deal under President Franklin Roosevelt to blow life back into the moribund housing industry and put a roof over people's heads during the disaster years of the 1930s.

government-sponsored enterprises (GSEs) These are incongruous, private, shareholder-owned corporations that enjoy federal government backing and special privileges. Their origins date back to the desperate improvisations of the Great Depression. Two of the best known

GSEs are Fannie Mae (Federal National Mortgage Association) and Freddie Mac (Federal Home Loan Mortgage Corporation).

greater fool theory A belief espoused by people buying a stock that is laughably overpriced because they are sure someone else will buy it from them for more. However, contrary to reason as it may be, there comes a time when the supply of fools has been exhausted.

greed Moralists call it the greatest vice; economists call it the profit motive. The line between a decent return on one's capital and labor and antisocial piggery skips around from point to point. The admixture of pandemic greed and optimism that infects all businesspeople is the occasion for business's highest ascents and widest, smoking holes.

greenmail Money paid to an obnoxious stockholder to get him to sell his shares and clear out. Obnoxious behavior may include demands to pick board members, sell off parts of the company, or do any number of things the management doesn't like. To rid itself of a greenmailer, a company is usually forced to pay more than the shares are selling for in the open market. (See **premium**.) Greenmail is a pejorative term coined by greenmailees to suggest that the greenmailer is some kind of extortion artist. Managements succumb to greenmail when they are afraid the greenmailer might sell his shares to a third party hungering to pull off a hostile takeover, or because the greenmailer is acting out in front of the press, threatening lawsuits or finding other ways to make life miserable in the boardroom.

Greenmail is not illegal and, while considered a tasteless way of making money, it may have a tonic effect on stodgy companies run by people who are too dumb or too complacent to maximize profit. Or it may just be privateering, which is allowed but tut-tutted. Greenmailers prosper in periods when money is plentiful for mergers, acquisitions, and takeovers, thus making it easier to terrify jittery CEOs.

Gross, Samuel Eberly (1843–1913) If not the inventor of the housing development industry, Gross was certainly a founder. His Chicago-based operation was prototypical of large-scale real estate promotion, even as it is carried on to this day. Not only did he sell tens of thousands of lots in his many developments but also thousands of homes to working-class families, starting at a hundred dollars down and ten dollars a month. Gross's advertisements, replete with an angel floating around brandishing the sword of "justice," announced the coming of "The Working Man's Reward," that is the single-family, detached house with a little land around it for a garden and a bit of lawn.

Gross was anything but the stereotype raper-pillager real estate developer. Among the first in his line of business to appreciate the setting as well as the house, his projects came with paved streets, gas lighting, and other public utilities.

The American Dream of a nation of middle-class homeowners begins with Gross, whose contemporaries looked on what he was doing as an antidote to the violent and dangerous radicalism roiling the country in the 1870s and 1880s. "A city of such houses is safe from anarchy," a local writer declared. Besides making no small contribution toward the eventual ending of class warfare, Gross was a good businessman, although, like so many real estate visionaries, he apparently died broke or the next thing to it.

Group of Five (G-5), Group of Seven (G-7), Group of Ten a.k.a the Paris Club (G-10), Group of Fifteen (G-15), Group of Twenty-Four (G-24), and, lastly, **Group of Seventy-Seven (G-77)** The members of these groups are governments; the smaller the group, the richer the country represented. The G-77, which actually has over a hundred members, is made up of the lame, the halt, and the blind and doesn't do much more than lobby the smaller groups and beg for handouts, the polite word for which is aid. G-10, the Club of Paris, has indirect control over lending to financially distressed governments. These groups, in some form or other and whatever their drawbacks, are necessary adjuncts to the economic governance of a world whose parts are ever more intertwined.

growth The *summum bonum* of business. Every year, every quarter, every month, every week must be bigger and therefore better than the previous one. Companies, or their CEOs, brag about how many consecutive periods have seen increased earnings. It is widely held that a company or person who doesn't grow is dead. But, of course, like cancer, growth can kill you as companies arrange spurious transactions in which they sell their merchandise and immediately buy it back, just so they can show their volume of sales is up.

Although it may or may not get a CEO black looks from the shrewder stock analysts, presuming they haven't been bribed, corporations do sometimes borrow money, hide the existence of the loan, and use the money to buy another company, thereby making it look as though the corporation is brimming over in profits and growth.

Hamilton, Alexander (1757–1804) Revolutionary War hero, political propagandist, secretary of the treasury under George Washington, and advocate for government support of industry, most notably the protective tariff.

In 1792 Hamilton, through the instrumentality of the Society for Useful Manufactures, hired Pierre L'Enfant, who had drawn up the District of Columbia's land use plan, to design an integrated industrial-residential development on the banks of the Passaic River, where a steep falls would provide power for textile mills and other factories. With pledges of capital from wealthy Americans and Europeans, the state of New Jersey chartered the corporation and promised a ten-thousand-dollar investment and a ten-year tax exemption for the city-to-be, which was named Paterson in gratitude to the governor. Only the name survives, for before things were fairly up and running the workers walked out in what has come to be regarded as the first industrial strike in American history. Shortly thereafter, they were locked out by management in what is regarded as the first industrial lockout. Hamilton and L'Enfant fell out, the investors, hit by hard times, failed to come through with needed capital, and in the end the Paterson development never happened, but the idea that the perennially labor-strapped United States would find its true future in machines and industry certainly endured.

happy talk, spinning, blowing smoke, or **just plain bullshit** Some of the terms used to describe CEOs talking up their company's prospects when they know perfectly well the outlook for near term is less than promising, or possibly even bleak. The purpose of such CEO oratory is to keep the price of their stock up. Until 1995, such misleading speech might result in a class-action lawsuit, but that avenue was barricaded with passage of the delightfully named Private Securities Litigation Reform Act of 1995. In general, small investors, without the power to retaliate financially against the management of a company or a stockbroker who has run a con on them, can expect no easy time getting satisfaction from the law courts, which, more often than not, are closed to them. They must hope for redress via a mandatory arbitration procedure, where, candor compels one to say, the aggrieved customer does have a better chance of prevailing than of winning the lottery, but how much better a chance it is difficult to say.

Harper, Martha Matilda (1857–1950)   At the age of seven, Martha was sold away from her family by her none-too-sentimental papa to be a serving girl in a Canadian village. By Lord knows what energy, perseverance, business intelligence, and guts, she took her place in the history of commerce in 1888, when she opened the Harper Hair Dressing Parlor, in Rochester, New York. In due course hundreds more Harper Method parlors were established in North America and then in Europe.

They are noteworthy because they represent a development in sales and distribution different from the dealership systems invented and advanced by Singer, McCormick, and Ford. Harper Parlors were owned by their operators, who were trained by Martha. Mindful of her own growing up, she recruited poor "girls" of her own social background as franchisees (see **franchises**).

The Harper Method establishments, while not uniform in looks and design (see **fast food**), were furnished with equipment sold by Harper, and the materials used in them were bought from Harper-owned factories. Thus, sixty years before the franchise explosion hit the country, Martha Harper invented an effective form of it.

The male franchisers who came later do not seem to have been influenced by her, probably because the Harper Method was isolated from men, existing in a female ghetto and sharing the high ethical standards of what was then the women's culture. Martha herself was a serious Christian Scientist, and thus her Method was based on healthy practices and a healthy frame of mind. Though it put her at a competitive disadvantage, she opposed dying hair, permanent waves, marcel heating irons, electric hair dryers, and anything injurious to the health of hair and scalp.

Martha Harper is a doubly important business figure because of her efforts to make women's values a standard in commerce. She failed and is forgotten, and thousands of women executives, oblivious to such questions, have chosen to put aside their heritage and drop down to the ethical level of the men. Martha was doomed in a commercial society in which people pay to have the fat cut off their fannies and their tits enlarged with silicon sacks.

halawa A system for transferring funds without leaving a paper trail. The word *halawa* is supposed to be the Hindi word for trust, but this devil has more hind than Hindi. Regardless of what it means in Sanskrit or Arabic, to work the system depends upon a network of people who trust each other. It is supposed to be used by terrorists for financing their activities around the world but, for all we know, it may be used by business to escape currency regulations or taxes.

hedge fund A souped-up mutual fund on crystal meth, which takes risks ordinary mutual funds will not go near, a hedge fund is restricted to rich people and institutional buyers, such as Harvard University and various pension funds. Under the law, hedge funds do not have to make public what they are up to, which contributes to a sense that they have their ways of getting to the head of the line and scooping up opportunities the serfs and penny-ante investors never get to sniff. Recently the serfs have been clamoring for hedge funds of their own because they have heard stories of doubling, tripling, and quadrupling investments faster than it takes a croupier to deal the cards. The big, exclusive hedge funds, with their inside track on grabbing the tastiest financial lamb chops, have delivered souped-up profits—but in business, where there is an upsy-daisy there is always the possibility of a downsy-daisy, too. (For the mother of all downsy-daisies, see **Long-Term Capital Management**.)

Hello Kitty This small, white, cloyingly cute animal without a mouth was born in Japan in 1974. Though the kitten in question, said to be female, starred in no movie and has no known history or back story—unlike Mickey Mouse or Barney—nevertheless, for thirty years she has appeared on every conceivable kind of merchandise from tiny little purses to radios, toasters, and, it is written, vibrators, but that may be a foul canard. What is gospel truth is that Hello Kitty's company, Sanrio Ltd., is worth half a billion dollars and stands as living proof that it is possible to make, if not a silk purse out of a sow's ear, a hell of a lot of money out of licensing a pussy cat.

hemline theory The theory holds that the price of stocks follows the hemlines of women's skirts. A variant has hemlines dropping during peacetime or recessions, when manufacturers want to sell more cloth, and rising during war and prosperity, when material is scarce. Since women began wearing pants and fashions in hemlines began to be both up and down at the same time, depending on which woman you happen upon, the hemline theory has gone back to the shop for a makeover.

HMO (health maintenance organization) A private-sector system of payment for medical care that has astonished the other high-tech nations by providing all people residing in the United States with advanced and lavish care. That the health figures in many other rich nations are significantly better than those for the U.S. is on account of a statistical aberration that will sooner or later be corrected, and then the American model of private-sector early death and laissez-faire, painful life will be adopted by all right-thinking societies, except the French, who hate us.

Hoffa, James Riddle (Jimmy) (1913–1975) President of the International Brotherhood of Teamsters (1957–1971), probably the victim of a political persecution by Robert F. Kennedy, attorney general under his brother, President John F. Kennedy. Vilification at the hands of the Kennedys has made Hoffa the personification of corrupt union bossism, an honor that rightly belongs to others. In actuality Hoffa, though only sprouting bumps where others might have full-fledged angel wings, was loved by rank-and-file union members for bringing home the bacon to the ordinary truckdriver.

Under Hoffa, the Teamsters Union acted as a legal means for the trucking industry to wiggle its way around the Sherman Antitrust Act (see **antitrust**), making it possible to dampen competition through quiet price rigging and market division. This is a largely unremarked role long played by unions in industries where there are many little companies and no big, dominant corporations. The garment industry is another example where unions not only regulated competition but lent entrepreneurs capital and thus became, if not partners, then at least business allies.

holding company One of the clunkier forms of industrial organization, a holding company is, in one version, a company that owns controlling interest in a number of companies all in the same industry. In another version, a holding company may be a company that holds controlling stock in another company, which owns a controlling interest in another company, and on and on in daisy-chain fashion, but always in the same industry. This form of business organization was devised in the latter part of the 1880s to dampen profit-destroying competition and to placate the growing public furor over the trusts, which also were invented to rein in competition. (See **trust,** third definition.) A holding company that controlled most of the companies in a given industry could allocate markets, divide up profits, and prevent competition, but they were hard to run because of their byzantine internal communications, and they could be expensive because so many of the holding company's units were unnecessary duplications. When, in 1903, the federal courts ruled that Northern Securities, a holding company that controlled two formerly competing railroads in the Pacific Northwest, was illegal under the Sherman Antitrust Act, big business lost its enthusiasm for holding companies—always with certain exceptions, of course—and decided to go the merger route (see **merger**) instead.

home equity loan Before it was called a home equity loan, it was simply a second mortgage, a form of borrowing that conservative, middle-class people of the past shunned as expensive, dangerous, and profligate. Such borrowing was unthinkable for the honest bourgeois of yore, who invited the neighborhood in for a mortgage-burning party after the last payment had been sent to the savings and loan association. Putting a second mortgage on your house used to be an act performed only out of dire necessity, but in our time people think nothing of getting a home equity loan to buy trinkets after they have maxed out their credit cards.

Hoover, Herbert Clark (1874–1964) The only president (1929–1933) to distinguish himself as a businessman, and he did it big time. (Presidents such as Jimmy Carter, James A. Garfield, and Rutherford B. Hayes might be classed as businessmen, but their business was small-scale farming, and the devil doesn't accept that. The two George Bushes' activities seem to have been so intertwined with their political connections as to rule them out of consideration. Lyndon Johnson died with enormous holdings, particularly in broadcasting, but these had been extorted, if not stolen, by political finagling.) Hoover, who had nothing to do with door-to-door vacuum cleaner sales nor any connection with home appliances, was a mining engineer and company executive in Australia and in China, where in defense of the business interests he organized the fire brigades in Tientsin during the Boxer Rebellion in 1900. In 1907 Hoover started his own company, opening offices in New York, London, San Francisco, and Russia; by 1913, it had some 175,000 employees and was running mining operations around the world.

Generations before the term "global economy" was coined, Hoover was practicing it, and as secretary of commerce (1921–1928), he reorganized his department to assist American firms to do business abroad. Thousands of parts in the automotive, plumbing, hardware, and building materials industries were standardized under Hoover, who made it a specialty to get businesspeople to cooperate on such vital if pedestrian necessities as uniform sizing. (See **compatibility**.) As secretary of commerce, he was the key figure in organizing the nascent airline and broadcasting industries into forms that would govern them for the next half-century of growth and development.

Although subsequent to leaving the White House Hoover was considered an opponent of governmental presence in business, in his heyday he inserted the Feds into areas they had never gone before, such as financing private enterprises and mobilizing public opinion to pressure the steel industry to adopt the eight-hour working day.

Hooverville Hoovervilles were the domiciles of choice for persons in straightened circumstances during the Great Depression. A Depression-era cluster of private-sector, affordable housing named after the thirty-first president, Herbert Hoover, it consisted of structures built by their occupants out of bits of found lumber, tin cans, and tarpaper, situated on squatter land down by the railroad tracks.

hope The sine qua non of all business undertakings and, when capitalized, the Arkansas birthplace of William Jefferson Clinton.

horizontal integration The organizational antithesis of the vertically integrated corporation of the past, which strove to own and control its operations from extracting raw material from the earth to the finished product. Modern companies are protean in form. You never know what they're going to look like. What you thought was a division or an owned-and-operated subsidiary may actually be part of a multilayered pyramid of legally independent entities, controlled by one or more holding companies. The arrangement facilitates borrowing money, selling stock, and quickly adjusting to changed circumstances. It also makes it difficult to sue. Even if you win, you can't get at the honey pot. (See **vertical integration**.)

horizontal merger   Mergers are usually classified as horizontal or vertical. A horizontal merger is one in which two companies, say two computer manufacturers or two airline companies, exchange wedding vows. If two large companies are involved, the resultant corporate big boy with some ungodly huge market share may find itself athwart the antitrust laws. On the occasion of every big merger, there is a debate over whether the government should stop it, a decision that revolves around such questions as: When is big too big? If it is a monopoly, is it a bad one? Will competition be stifled? Since no objective answers to questions of this character are remotely possible, the decision is ordinarily settled by deadly political knife fighting.

human resources   Formerly known as personnel. The switch over to human resources betokens the same efficient use of people as the organization's use of inhuman resources. And, before deplaning, please check to make sure you have all your personal and impersonal belongings.

Iacocca, A. Lee (Lido) (1924–) To his boss, Henry Ford II (see **Ford, Henry II**), when Iacocca was president of the Ford Motor Company, he was "that goddamn wop," but to the American public during the 1970s and 1980s he was the hero-executive of his period, the pitchman who personified the corporate good guy. As chairman of the Chrysler Corporation, Iacocca made himself famous telling the millions via television ads, "If you can find a better car, buy it."

Iacocca was a rare bird, a major success at two different companies, first at Ford and then at Chrysler, which he led from the edge of bankruptcy to a resurgent prosperity, with the help of a $1.5 billion government loan. The loan was paid back in a gloriously well publicized moment, which did nothing to mollify critics of government "bailouts." In the end it was all for naught, thanks to the chronic, excess production capacity of the worldwide auto industry. An ever-weakening Chrysler was finally wiped off the New York Stock Exchange after being bought by German-owned Daimler-Benz. Nevertheless, there was that moment when, as with an earlier automobile giant, Henry Ford I, serious, sane, and stable people were nursing an Iacocca for President boomlet.

IBM (International Business Machines, Big Blue) You can have your Microsofts and your Intels, but the single most important corporation in the computer universe has been IBM. It began life in 1911 as the Computing-Tabulating-Recording Company, manufacturing everything in the way of small machines from meat slicers to punchcard tabulators. In 1914 C-T-R hired an out-of-work businessman named Thomas J. Watson (1874–1956) who, after graduating from the Miller School of Commerce in Elmira, New York, had worked as a door-to-door peddler selling organs and sewing machines.

Sloughing off meat slicers, Watson, the new head of the renamed IBM, concentrated on office equipment by expanding the product line, thanks to his engineering lab, but primarily through purchase of other companies. Nevertheless, by the end of the 1940s, IBM had 90 percent of the punchcard market, the most advanced information-processing technology available.

Business genius seldom goes from parent to child, but it did in the Watson family. (For an example of a family where it didn't, see **Radio Corporation of America**.) Tom, Jr. (1914–1993) returned from the Air Force in 1946, pushed his reluctant father into computers, and the rest is history. (See **System/360**.) Within twenty years, IBM had computerized virtually every large organization in the

United States. The Watsons understood you can have the best gizmo in the world, but it doesn't mean jack if you can't sell it. (See **McCormick, Cyrus Hall**.)

As Young Tom wrote, ". . . technology turned out to be less important than sales and distribution methods. We consistently outsold people who had better technology because we knew how to put the story before the customer, how to install the machines successfully, and how to hang on to customers once we had them." (See **antitrust**.) They held on to 'em by virtue of a stunning sales and service organization. Any time, day or night, that an IBM product went on the fritz, a telephone call would summon a serviceman literally within the hour.

The company's reach was worldwide. By 1955 it had offices in eighty-two countries, and its practice of manufacturing where it was doing business and of staffing from top to bottom with locals enabled IBM to wiggle around trade barriers. It also made IBM seem, if not native, then less American and more globally neutral.

In a commercial and cultural sense, what we call the information age was, until well into the 1980s, the IBM age. It was the only computer company anybody had heard of, and the corporate motto, THINK, given it by the monomaniacal elder Watson and almost as well known as the pledge of allegiance, was the material for countless cartoons and jokes. The IBM employee, male, white, and Protestant (the company hired no people of color, no Jews, no Roman Catholics), clad in a blue suit and white, buttoned-down shirt, was the personification in the public imagination of the Cold War–era organization man.

idols and **images** The landmarks of the American soul are mostly business creations, be it the Empire State

Building, the Million Dollar Mile, Rodeo Drive, or the stuff that gets in between the brain cells, the commercial plaque that coats our consciousness: The pause that refreshes, Just do it, We try harder, The breakfast of champions. And the jingles: Momma didn't sing you no lullabies, It's the real thing, You deserve a break today, A little dab'll do ya, I wish I was an Oscar Meyer Wiener. The Energizer Bunny has been running around since 1989; the Marlboro cowboy climbed on his horse in 1955, and you can't get the damn fool off it; and Elsie, the Borden bovine, dates from the 1930s. The companies change, the words and pictures linger. Aunt Jemima has been making breakfast for over one hundred years.

immigrants For a country that is perpetually strapped for workers, there would be no modern business without immigrants. In the past, immigrant ethnic groups have played dominant roles in countless industries. Railroads, department stores, and steelmaking were developed and led by Scotsmen; from the turn of the last century, Arabs played a major role in small-town retailing across America; Italians did the same in construction; Croats in California built up a world market by introducing new methods of cultivating, packing, and shipping fruit. In our era, business is dependent on importing technical personnel from south Asia, the Philippines, China, and Russia. If engineers, biomedical researchers, software designers, and dozens of other specialists weren't brought in from abroad, thousands of American enterprises would face daunting problems.

Industrial Revolution Unlike other famous revolutions —American, Chinese, French or Russian—the dates of the Industrial Revolution can't be fixed. And unlike Washington, Mao Tse-tung, Lenin, or Danton, the principal figures in this upheaval had no idea they were leading a revolution. No mob of industrialists and technicians stormed the palace, but instead a vast number of interconnected events took place over at least a century. For all we know, the Industrial Revolution is still going on, since it brings with it changes in family life, morals, government, and culture as it continuously throws up new practices and institutions, while overthrowing and forcing the abandonment of ancient ones.

inflation Inflation occurs when the value of money deteriorates and it buys less. Example: If your great-granny and great-grandpa had put $100 in a mattress in 1913, and you discovered it in 2000, you'd need $1743.82 to buy what the 1913 C-note could, though back then you couldn't buy a color TV, antibiotics, and much more at any price, so these comparisons are somewhat labored.

There is nothing new about inflation. When the Roman Empire was young, people devalued money by shaving bits of silver off coins, thus making them worth less. The government did the same thing by secretly lessening the silver and/or gold content of the coins. Debasing the currency was made easier with the coming of paper money: governments simply printed more of it. It became easier still when money came to exist in the form of electronic postings in a computer. A few keystrokes and there are ten billion dollars more than there were a second ago.

Although some people are misguided enough to think that inflation is conducive to prosperity, it plays hob with business. Lenders, fearful the dollar borrowed today will be worth only fifty cents when it's repaid tomorrow, jack up interest rates. Executives are forced to compute what something really cost or what a payment was really worth against the upward change in the numbers, leading to terms such as *nominal prices, real prices, deflators, inflators,* and *the money illusion.* The train of consequences from inflation is endless and endlessly adverse.

initial public offering (IPO) Putting stock in a company up for sale for the first time to everyday investors. That initial offering is seldom sold on a first-come, first-served basis. Many games are played by the brokerage firm or firms handling the deal, so that some people get to pay the original asking price for the stock, and some have to pay more, maybe a lot more, depending upon the degree of buyer hysteria surrounding any given IPO. Some customers may get the ground-floor price by promising not to sell their new stock for a given period of time, lest they depress its value.

When it comes to IPOs, some of the prestigious names in the securities business have been impinging on the Devil's own work by selling IPOs to their ovine customers when they know the company issuing the stock hasn't got a snowball's chance in the nether regions of avoiding bankruptcy.

The above does not begin to describe all the hanky-panky surrounding some IPOs, and from time to time the cry for reform can be heard, however faintly, wafting its way down Wall Street's fabled canyons. Where it goes and what it does after it's finished wafting is not known. There is naught to do but to put up with the crookedness, since new companies reach a point in their development when the original backers want to back out or cash in their chips, or they run out of money and new funds are needed. So a baby company has to go to a wider public, even though it means a small group of strategically placed, sanguinivorous lawyers and brokers raking in money out of all proportion to their labors. It also must be grudgingly conceded that some brokers do run a financial risk of the IPO failing, meaning the stock sells for less than the initial asking price, and for those monkeys to hazard their money, large profits must be dangling from the banana trees.

insider information Company secrets. Whether insider information of any value stays inside is a matter of conjecture. If the United States government couldn't keep the atomic bomb a secret, what are the odds that a company's new product line will not stray into outside hands?

insider trading Use of a company's secrets by an employee or privileged insiders, i.e., lawyers, accountants, brokers, or consultants, to make money trading the company's stock. You can get fined or jailed if caught at it, but either people in positions to know are wonderfully honest or—as in dope smuggling, where many are called and few are arrested—for one reason or another, transgressors are seldom pinched.

Insiders trade on insider information because even the pros can't make fast money in the stock market without cheating. Long-term investors can make slow money without cheating by using their noggins, but for making fast money—that is, betting on the day-to-day fluctuations of the price of a share of stock—luck and brains won't help you with the Goddess of Chance, so some of the boys and girls in the business have ways of making their luck a little luckier. Betting on sure things is more profitable, and if you can't do that, the way to make money in the securities business is by charging fees and commissions.

Insider trading is a topic with its murkier aspects. There are, for example, outsider-insiders. A friend who works for Global Glory Pharmaceuticals gets drunk and tells you that his company has a cure for breast cancer, and you, having remained sober, borrow every dollar you can get your hands on to buy glorious Global stock. That is insider-outsider trading. You may or you may not get jugged for doing it, depending on whether or not the Securities and Exchange Commission (SEC) gets up on the wrong side of the bed. The confusions are endless. To take the above hypothetical example a step further: What if you don't buy Global Glory stock but innocently tell your paramour about it, and he/she does buy the stock and makes a bundle? Is that an SEC no-no or a yes-yes? The Devil only knows and he's not telling.

installment buying The universal instant gratification and the path to drunkenness, child abuse, and debt. Installment buying's legions of editorial detractors never fail to include in their remonstrances against financial self-indulgence that our prudent and frugal ancestors would be shocked by a generation that thinks nothing of taking on mountains of debt to enjoy transient fripperies. All of which is eyewash.

insurance As Saudi Arabia is to oil, the insurance industry is to money. The one sits on top of ocean-sized pools of the black stuff, and the other sits on top of the same sized pools of the green stuff. Almost no enterprise of any size exists that doesn't have at least a little insurance-company money invested in it. Insurance is a vast and vital source of capital for other businesses and a vast and vital source of endless controversies.

The modern insurance giants grew up in the decades immediately after the Civil War, using what was termed "industrial insurance," a system of selling coverage to the masses, imported from England by John Fairfield Dryden (1839–1911) at the Prudential Insurance Company. This was back in the days before they had the Rock. Instead they had skillions of untutored agents canvassing working-class areas to sign up people for $150 life insurance policies, with agents coming around every week to collect ten cents, making this very costly coverage. Many families couldn't keep the policies in force and, since they got back none of the money they paid in on their lapsed polices, the companies made out like bandits.

The banditry did not go unnoticed. The industry was repeatedly investigated, castigated, and exposed. In 1907 John Rogers Hageman (1844–1919), president of Prudential's foremost rival, Metropolitan Life, was indicted on ten counts of forgery and perjury. One of the accusations laid against him was that he prepared false annual company reports, a fact that ought to bring comfort to people lamenting that operative ethical standards used to be much, much higher. If we're going to hell in a hack, it's the same old hack.

Even though the cost of industrial policies was high and the agents selling them were on the same ethical level as the presidents of the insurance companies they worked for, there is, as always, another side to it. These policies paid enough to cover the funeral costs and leave some money for the family members to get on with their lives. This was an age when there were no safety nets and little reliable private charity. For tens of thousands of working-class white and African-American families, these insurance policies were what saw them through. Even now, in a business society that claims that uncertainty— unforeseen ups and downs and sudden winners and losers—is necessary for growth and prosperity, that insurance is often about all millions have to cling to.

insurance broker A person paid to find the best deal for someone or some company seeking to buy insurance. Alas and alack, some of the largest and most respectable insurance brokers have discovered that it is to their advantage to find the best deal for themselves. Instead of placing insurance contracts with the company offering the most advantageous terms, they place them with the insurance company offering them the most money under the table. As President Ronald Reagan was wont to say, "Trust, but verify." He was talking international politics, but the rule holds true in business, too. The skunky part is knowing how to verify. (See also **reputable firm**.)

intangible assets Young ladies and gentlemen cursed with buck teeth, acned skin, and shriveled derrieres but blessed with a smiley-faced, peppy optimism are said to have intangible assets, meaning, of course, that others rarely have an urge to pat their buns. In business, intangible assets are not quite so nugatory. They include things you can and can't touch, such as leases, copyrights, permits, licenses, computer programs, patents, and that will o' the wisp of business termi- nology, goodwill.

intellectual property Any patent or copyright with enough value to be sold and/or stolen. Intellectual property includes movies, songs, genetically engineered seeds, designs of every kind for everything and what is loosely called trade secrets which include manufacturing processes, organizational arrangements, and how information is handled inside a company.

In recent years American business has gone nuts over foreigners, especially Chinese foreigners, stealing intellectual property. The claimed losses are enormous; the real losses may be very large but excessive whining about having one's secrets ripped off is a chump's game (see **Slater, Samuel**). Sooner or later some clever devil (but not this one) will find a way around the patent or just steal it, which is costly to the losing stockholders but often beneficial to the world at large, which profits from having secrets unlocked and put to use by larcenous competitors. Instead of reliance on lawyers the best defense of intellectual property is inventing something new and better, thereby staying ahead of the game.

interest The cost of using somebody else's money. Basically, interest comes in two flavors, simple and compound. Simple: the interest on a hundred dollars lent at 10 percent for two years will be twenty dollars—or ten dollars for the first year and ten dollars for the second year; the same loan with compound interest will be twenty-one dollars. The extra buck was earned on the first year's interest of ten dollars. Compound interest is great stuff if you are the lender, but if you are the borrower, as anybody in debt to a credit card company knows, that compounding can kill you.

Many business loans and the interest thereon are of

such labyrinthian complexity that knowing the difference between simple and compound will not rescue the traveler who has chanced on those foggy shores.

interest rates in general Whatever the prevailing interest rates may be, they are always too high. It is fixed dogma that low interest rates bring prosperity and boom times, high interest rates recession and Hoovervilles. But no interest rate is too high if a businessperson can borrow at the high rate and use it to pay the interest and still harvest a profit. No interest rate is low enough, even if it's zero, at those times when you can't make a profit no matter how you invest it. In the trough of the Great Depression, interest rates did actually hover around zero, and much good it did anybody. Conversely, in the 1980s many a business borrowed money at very high interest rates through junk bonds and was able to turn tidy if not exorbitant profits. Which is not to say that a drop in the interest rates at certain moments doesn't give business just the goose it needs. What's high and what's low is subjective. (See **loan shark** and **usury**.) The movement of interest rates up or down is even harder to predict than the movement of stock prices.

International Monetary Fund Started in 1945 as a mechanism for carrying out the Bretton Woods agreement, the Fund has achieved the distinction of being the single most hated international institution. Supplied with vast amounts of that which makes the world go 'round, the handful of rich nations that make up the IMF sweep in wherever economies are ailing and in return for lending them money to get them out of their pinch, extracts promises from the governments in question to amend their ways. Then the economic life of the self-same countries collapses, with the lower classes reduced to beggary and the middle classes forced to drive taxi cabs and sell soft pretzels on the street corners. It has been proposed that Fund officials wear bells around their necks like lepers of old to warn the population that poverty and want have just deplaned at the airport.

in the long run In the long run, dearie, it'll all work out. In the long run the market always goes up, in the long run everybody gets rich and retires to Florida. The phrase is a favorite bromide used by economists, stockbrokers, and politicians to soothe frightened people. Clairvoyants, such as security salesmen and elected officials, pooh-pooh short-run thinking, but, instead of allowing oneself to be lulled by vapid cooings, one might remember British economist John Maynard Keynes's (1883–1946) sardonic remark on the subject, to wit, that in the long run we'll all be dead.

invest, investment, and so forth This word has a straightforward definition of putting money or work into something to get a profit, or as those with machine brains say, it's input for output. But beware of "investments" in which no specifically named individuals can expect to profit, such as investments in jails, airports, juvenile delinquency, or baseball stadiums. These are not investments. They are expenditures.

investment banker The top of the line (see **merchant banker**) in the finance industry, investment bankers do nothing so grubby as solicit accounts, peddle car loans, or hook the innocent on the credit card habit. Investment bankers arrange for new issues of stock, either by buying some or all of the issue themselves and then reselling the shares at a profit, or by arranging for others to buy while getting a fee and "other considerations," as they say when they don't want outsiders to know the details. Big stock deals are done by small wolf packs of investment bankers, or—as they like to style them—syndicates.

Though the profits of investment bankers are incommensurately and indefensibly large compared with the real costs of their services, investment banking is an important channel for getting money to start up a new business or expand an old one. Investment bankers compete furiously in every way, except, it seems, in price. The industry's reckless indifference to the consequences of what it raises money for makes it at least partially responsible for frightful episodes of waste such as the dot-com bubble.

When times are booming, this is a much more profitable line of business than selling shoes, oil well drilling, gold mining, or drug peddling, and the opportunity for yet greater gain by financial treachery has made the name "investment banker" something less than a synonym for probity or rectitude. There is a reason that men like Rockefeller and Carnegie found ways to finance their enterprises without recourse to the local investment banker.

investment trust The name used in the 1920s for a mutual fund. The idea of selling shares in a company whose business was owning shares arrived from England in 1889, only becoming an important factor in the American stock market in the 1920s, when investment trusts became the rage. By the end of the decade, they'd gone bonkers and were doing such intelligent things as lending money to speculators who lent money to investors who used the money to buy shares in the investment trust. The metaphor that comes to mind is of a salamander eating its own tail. Needless to say, by the decade's end, disaster overtook the investment trusts, of which there were hundreds with enormous amounts of people's money. The ensuing stench was so putrid that when investment trusts were resurrected many years later, they had to be renamed and repackaged. Hence, the mutual fund.

janitors insurance, or **broad-based insurance,** or **corporate-owned life insurance, COLI** for short
Insurance taken out by a company on the lives of its employees, janitors included, with the beneficiary being the company, not the employee, who is oblivious to his being worth more dead than alive to his boss—or to his ex-boss, for the insurance may continue after the employee has gone on to better things. Profits from the life insurance payments are not taxable, thus people stand to get rich if they are lucky enough to see all their employees carried off by a return of the 1918 flu pandemic.

Japan An island nation due west of Silicon Valley which was once so rich that Americans feared that Nipponese businessmen (women don't go in for that sort of thing there) would buy all the golf courses and skyscrapers in the United States, put them on boats, and ship them back to Tokyo. It was believed that the Japanese were harder-working and smarter-working than Americans. (For more on this, see **Deming, W. Edwards**.) The Japanese were also supposed to have achieved a coordination between business enterprises and the government, which made it inevitable that they would become the Number One economic power of the world. Books about how the Japanese did it were bestsellers and the fly-by-night, flea-bitten lecturer/teachers who infest the world of business were everywhere preaching Nipponism. The vogue peaked in the early 1980s, and since then, by a physiological process not yet understood, the Japanese started to lose IQ points and get dumber. By the early 2000s they came to be looked down upon as an obtuse and dense people with little talent for business. Since they are declining in population, and will, according to the best projections, have become extinct by the end of the twenty-first century, no one pays attention to them anymore, except to remind them occasionally how wrong they are.

job creation, as in "It'll create new jobs." Whenever these words are spoken, you may be certain that somebody has a hand out for public money to pay for one of those lalapalooza money losers. You invest for profits, not jobs. If the thing makes money, the new jobs will be there. Investing for jobs is leaf raking, as they used to call the jobs a desperate government created during the Great Depression because nobody knew what else to do.

Johnson, John Harold (1918–) The business careers of successful African-Americans born before a certain date are invariably stories of achievement against the worst odds; Johnson is no exception. Born in Arkansas, the son of a sawmill worker and a mother who worked in the white folks' houses, he found a way to attend the University of Chicago, and then the big idea hit him. He borrowed five hundred dollars, using his mother's furniture as collateral, to start *Negro Digest,* more or less a black version of the *Reader's Digest.* The publication's success was ensured after Johnson got Eleanor Roosevelt to write a piece for it. Johnson went on to start *Ebony* and *Jet* and branch out into broadcasting.

junk bond Rubbish and trash are worthless, but with junk you never know. Junk bonds are issued with high interest rates by companies deemed to have such dubious prospects that they may not be around long enough to pay that interest, let alone repay the principal. High-yield bonds, as those who sell junkers prefer that they be called, are ranked below "investment grade" and are therefore not purchased by pension funds, endowments, or others whose first responsibility is not to lose the kiddies' money. But anybody with an eye for nosing around secondhand stores will tell you there are great bargains to be had in junk shops, if you are willing to blow the dust off the merchandise and take a close squint, and if you're smart enough to recognize what it is that you're holding in your hands. Those who are smart enough are often quite rich.

Kay, Mary, née Mary Kathlyn Wagner (1915 or 1918–2001) Perhaps the last of the major business-women to be confined to the woman's ghetto. (See **Walker, Madame C. J.**) As she would later say, "In 1963 [the year she started her hugely successful cosmetics company], the social forces that now support the financial and legal equality of women had not gained public favor. And yet here was a company that would give women all the opportunities I had never had. I don't think God wanted a world in which a woman would have to work fourteen hours a day to support her family, as my mother had done. I believe he used this company as a vehicle to give women a chance."

Mary Kay, as she liked to be called, started her company with five thousand dollars and her twenty-year-old son to take care of administration, while she did her evangelistic recruiting of "consultants," that is, door-knocking sales-women, of whom there were tens of thousands. Her yearly pep rallies cum sales meetings were famous for the splashy, expensive prizes, such as pink Cadillac convertibles, awarded top producers. In the last year of her life, Mary Kay sales were well over a billion dollars.

Colorful and articulate as she was, Mary Kay has to be seen as one of a procession of entrepreneurs figuring out ever better ways to get a salesperson's foot in the door of the American home. (See **Fuller, Alfred Carl.**) In 1886, when he began what became Avon Products, David Hall McConnell (1858–1937) flashed on the thought that a female foot could get in that door easier than a male foot, and thus a certain Ms. P. F. E. Albee became the first Avon Lady. Thousands of others soon followed, thereby opening a new path into the business world for women of the Victorian period.

In the 1920s, Wearever Aluminum, using a male sales force, came up with a new wrinkle: get one woman to host a party for her neighbors, to sell the cooking products line. In the 1930s, Stanley Home Products began using women to organize the sales parties, but a high point of sort was reached in the early 1950s, when Tupperware parties became something akin to a national fad. Although the hundreds of thousands of women engaged in these sales organizations seldom made good money, distribution systems that rely on large sales forces are cruelly expensive. Thus, as with many another activity, business has sought to move sales from man to machine, that is, from labor-intensive to capital-intensive methods. Enter such maddening practices as telemarketing and spam, but electronics has also brought dozens of other less obnoxious means of making a sale.

People who don't do it for a living look down on sales and are irritated by sellers, but, however it's done, selling is an indispensable part of every distribution system.

Keogh Plan Named after its author, a long-forgotten New York City congressman, Eugene J. Keogh (1907–1989). His plan was the first (1961) of a stream of tax-sheltered savings programs. The Keogh was designed to help self-employed people save for their retirement, but they are now available for every purpose and in a variety of forms (see **pension**). The hitch is that the plans' owners must decide how the money is to be invested, and a lot of us aren't very good at that.

Kondratieff wave or **cycle** Named after Nikolai Dmitrijewitsch Kondratieff (1892–1938), who may be the discoverer of the Halley's comet of world economics. Kondratieff waves of good times and bad have been circling us every fifty years or so for several centuries, or so it is held by those who buy the theory, and that includes some major names in the study of economics. Whether this kind of thinking is theology or science is in dispute, but until the 1980s the woods were full of big theories about economics and business. Big theories have lost popularity and are no longer discussed by earnest young persons in bierstubes. That does not mean that theology, magic, voodoo, witchcraft, and superstition have fled the world of business. (See **Chartism.**)

labor organizations Unlike its counterparts in Europe and Japan, American business management has never made its peace with unionism. The history of violent strife between unions and management in America has no parallel elsewhere. Until the end of the Cold War, business had to stomach unions, if only because in the propaganda contest with the communists, public displays of union busting simply would not do. With the coming of President Ronald Reagan and the winding down of the Cold War, American business was able to resume its own private war against trade unionism with devastating effect. Aided by the dramatic shrinkage of the most heavily unionized industries, business has enfeebled union power. If present trends continue, the only unionized workers around will be government employees, but even here the governmental entities are resisting by outsourcing work to nonunion private firms.

Business has been helped in its struggle to eliminate unions by unions themselves. For decades many a union official robbed the dues-paying membership with the same gusto as CEOs stole from their stockholders. As more workers shed overalls for white collars, they were increasingly dismayed at the image of the "labor boss" as a fat-assed, self-satisfied jerk in a Hawaiian sports shirt, chomping on a cigar, passing his time and spending his membership's money at a swimming pool in Balmoral, Florida. More than a generation has passed since the American labor movement—if you can call an aggregation of such sludgy organizations a movement—has had a national leader of stature.

The emasculation of organized labor has not been an unmitigated blessing for business. Managers may not realize it, but they have traded sitting across the negotiating table from the old-time union business agent for spending their days in court with their thousand-dollar-an-hour lawyers. Unorganized workers sue. They sue about everything, as the courts have become their grievance procedure.

The newer kind of worker, through professional associations and other nonunion organizations, has looked to the government to protect his or her interests, with the result that legislatures, regulatory agencies, law courts, and politicians now intermediate between employee and employer. This state of affairs has called forth an infinity of yowling by businesspeople, who are learning that government agencies can be more inflexibly difficult to contend with then labor unions, who, with the right pecuniary incentives, will make a deal.

leader Previously, a person either on foot or on horse, sword drawn, at the head of a column of soldiers running toward other soldiers who were shooting in their direction; in modern usage, a man or woman seated at a large desk screaming at subordinates.

leadership An undefined quality attributed to bosses on public occasions.

legacy (adjective) Pertaining to any business, practice, or product having attained an age of fifteen or more minutes.

Leidesdorff, William Alexander (1810–1848) An early California hotelier, land speculator, and real estate developer, Leidesdorff is considered the first African-American millionaire.

Leslie, Frank (1821–1880), male, and **Frank Leslie, a.k.a Mrs. Frank Leslie, née Miriam Florence Foline (1836–1914), female** This is a tad complicated but mildly amusing. It begins with Frank Leslie, the male, getting himself properly born in Ipswich, England, the land where he learned the craft of woodcut engraving, a skill he took to the United States and employed on behalf of P. T. Barnum to make glorious circus posters. In 1854 he changed what was ultimately to be called pop culture with *Frank Leslie's Illustrated Newspaper,* pioneering the use of pictures instead of words in American journalism. He also invented what we now call investigative journalism, beginning with an exposé of the "milk swill scandal."

By the time of Leslie's death, the business was bankrupt, but his wife, Miriam, a person to conjure with, changed her name to Frank Leslie, no doubt thinking that a famous male moniker would help her in a male-only business. The female Frank borrowed money, refloated the business and was so successful that she was accorded the soubriquet of the "Empress of Journalism." She went on to marry Oscar Wilde's half-brother and, when she passed to the editorial room in the sky, left what was a gigantic fortune at the time, two million dollars, to the woman's suffrage leader Mrs. Carrie Chapman Catt.

letter of credit   Good as gold. Used in international trade since the Italians thought it up in the Middle Ages, the letter guarantees that the bank issuing it is good for the beneficiary's purchases up to a stated amount.

letter stock or **letter security** See **private placement**.

level playing field **1.** My rules. **2.** A theological construct, a happy hunting ground where the young knights of the business Round Table contend with each other and, when the joust is done, refresh themselves in waters drawn from the clear rills and crystalline runnels whence the cash doth flow; a condition not unlike Heaven, where all is fair and no one loses.

leveraged buyout (LBO)   Buying a company with money borrowed from somebody else. It was the preferred form of brigandage in the 1980s.

Levitt, William Jaird (1907–1994)   Mass-producer of cookie-cutter housing for the lower-middle masses. Levitt's first and most famous development was the seventeen-thousand-plus single-family homes built in Nassau County, Long Island, New York, between 1947 and 1951, renting for $65 a month, or for sale for $7,990. Ultimately his Levittown would be the home of 82,000 persons, every one of whom was white. Thus began the exodus of the white millions from the older and now out-of-date housing of the nation's central cities. By having many of the parts of his houses made off-site in factories, Levitt reduced the skilled-labor component of his houses by 80 percent. His refusal to use union labor brought his costs down even further and, whatever you may think of his methods, they made it possible for a family with a very modest income to own a house with a couple of trees and a bush in the suburbs.

Financing for the various Levittowns was provided by the federal government by such happy devices as 115 percent mortgages for the entrepreneur, but even so, in his era Levitt was looked on by many as the man who made the home-ownership dream real—real, that is, for white people. "We can solve a housing problem," he declared, "or we can try to solve a racial problem. But we cannot combine the two." (For someone who believed he might combine the two, see **Rouse, James W.**)

Lewis, John L. (1880–1969) In the America of the 1930s and 1940s, this man was as well known and as controversial as Dr. Martin Luther King, Jr., in the 1960s. The son of Welsh immigrants, Lewis followed his father into coal mining and then went on to become a union leader. Lewis ascended to the presidency of the United Mine Workers of America when coal was king. A political conservative, indeed a Republican, Lewis in

1935, often using Communist Party operatives, led a gigantic union organizing drive that changed American history. Before Lewis, most unions solicited only skilled workers, such as pipe fitters and machinists, for membership. That changed when Lewis founded the Congress of Industrial Organizations (CIO), which went after all the workers in a given industry. In a matter of hardly more than months, Lewis's people organized upward of a million workers in the steel, electrical, rubber, and automobile industries and ushered in the era of big unionism, which was to last until the disintegration of the smokestack industries forty years later.

During the 1930s it was a tossup as to whom businessmen hated more, Franklin Roosevelt or John L. Lewis. There was much to dislike about Lewis, a tyrannical labor leader whose goon squad was equally good at clubbing his own membership, Communists who got out of line, or company finks. Within the mine workers unions, he tolerated rampant theft by lesser union officials, though he doesn't seem to have personally benefited from it. Nevertheless, Lewis was a national hero who was responsible for significant health and retirement programs and, unlike most union leaders, welcomed the introduction of high-productivity, labor-saving equipment.

Lewis, Reginald F. (1942–1993) Probably the first African-American billionaire, but calculating how much big money people actually have is always a little iffy. Born in modest circumstances, by all accounts a man as determined as he was gifted, he graduated from Harvard Law School and went into a high-level New York corporate practice, where he could press his nose against the fishtank and watch the barracudas at play. In no time at all, he joined the fun, and before he died in 1993 he borrowed to buy a declining sewing pattern company, rejuvenated it, and sold it for nineteen times what he'd paid for it. Next he took over Beatrice International Foods, which had sixty-four subsidiaries with twenty thousand employees doing business in thirty-one countries. No other African-American owned or operated a business remotely that size. His success marks African-Americans' leaving the ethnic business world to take their place on the larger stage of world business, as others followed him to become CEOs of such corporations as American Express and AOL Time Warner.

liability Any condition, situation, or act that carries with it the responsibility to pay. This is a no-wiggle-room proposition.

line of credit or **bank line** A promise by a bank to make available a certain amount of money for a firm to draw on for a stated period, usually a year. Lines of credit usually come with strings attached, requiring the borrowing company to do or not to do certain things.

Ling, James Joseph (Jimmy) (1922–) While it isn't possible to say for sure that this electrician from Ardmore, Oklahoma, invented the conglomerate, in the immediate post–World War II period he popularized this form of business organization, in which dozens if not hundreds of companies in unrelated fields are brought together through a bewildering crisscross of loans, stock swaps, divestitures, and buying and selling companies, or parts of companies, by the use of devices that boggle the ordinary mind. Ling's great corporate creation was LTV, a vast hodgepodge of companies in electronics, car rental, space, pharmaceuticals, sporting goods, steel, and so on. And on. By 1963 LTV was the twenty-fifth largest nonfinancial company in America. At its peak in 1967 its stock was selling for $169 a share; three years later it was going for seven bucks, and a few years after that LTV was bankrupt and Ling himself a part of business lore. His spirit lives on in companies such as Tyco, a recent example of a distressed and suffering conglomerate. But as long as there are executives with Alexander the Great complexes, conglomerates, wasteful and unmanageable as they are, will be with us. Presently General Electric is the world's largest conglomerate, and on Wall Street they swear that it is the one conglomerate that defies the history of these corporate megalosauruses.

liquid Anything of value that can quickly and easily be sold or otherwise converted into cash money is liquid. Anything that cannot is illiquid. (See **thinly traded**.)

list (verb), **listed** A company's stock is listed when, having attained a stated financial condition, it is assigned a symbol by a major stock exchange and posted for regular trading. For a young company this is the same as a bar mitzvah, a coming of age, and an occasion for champagne at the office and, in times past by men who ought to have known better, pinching the secretaries' bottoms. Now, according to recent studies, there is no pinching at all, or everybody, regardless of gender or preference, gets to pinch everybody else with impunity.

Little, Arthur D. (1863–1935) While Little may not have created business consultation as an occupation, he helped get it off to a good start. After graduating from MIT with a degree in chemistry, Little got a job in the paper industry, where he became an expert in technology, and then went out on his own as a consulting chemist, eventually founding Arthur D. Little, Incorporated, the first organization offering government and industry laboratory research and expert help in manufacturing, energy, marketing, and environmental questions. The inventor and perfecter of a number of industrial devices and processes, Little was a scientist-businessman whose career made a difference in many ways and many places. His work in showing how paper could be made from southern pine trees changed the economy of an entire region.

Probably his greatest contribution was selling Americans on using scientific research. Little, a multitalented man, propagandized for research by lecturing, writing, and devising publicity stunts, the most astonishing of which was turning a sow's ear into a silk purse in 1921. In truth he had to use one hundred pounds of sows' ears, plus various chemicals, to make not one but two purses, thereby demonstrating what research and development can accomplish—as well as showing that some people will stop at nothing to get their point across. The Arthur D. Little organization, which he willed to MIT, goes on to this day.

little guy or **little man** The little man took root in the American imagination as business structures got bigger and more impersonal. This Lilliputian figure, who must live by rules and tempos not of his own choosing, is famously depicted by Charlie Chaplin as the frantic fellow on the assembly line in *Modern Times*. (See **Taylorism**.) At first this construct of modern man was applied to the blue-collar classes, attendant on the coming of the age of big factories. But, eventually, middle-class people, even members of the professional classes, came to see themselves as little guys, ants on the toenails of corporate elephants. Bureaucracy, once a word whose use was restricted to political economists, invoked the near universal sense of individual helplessness felt by all confronted with private- and public-sector giganticism.

From mass production and mass advertising sprang mass man and his neanderthal egalitarianism, the faceless human being whose identity is his demographic group, whose political will has evaporated to reemerge as product preference. Once a citizen, he is now a consumer who can return the purchase if not satisfied but cannot shake his feelings of insecurity, displacement, and powerlessness. By way of compensation, he lives longer than human beings ever have before, his standard of living is exponentially higher, and he enjoys a leisure life his ancestors of the prebusiness age could not have dreamt of.

Although the little guy is the consequence of the big business era, from the 1930s on the sense of unimportant weakness in the face of bureaucratic enormity, which is at the heart of little-guy-ismo, came increasingly to be blamed on modern government—often with good reason. Big Brother, created by George Orwell in the 1940s to describe the nightmare Communist state, lives on as a shorthand word for all national governments of big business societies.

living wage A metaphysical concept, not without certain diabolic implications, propounded by emotionally unstable persons. It is not a business term and should not be employed in the presence of businesspeople. They break out in hives.

Llewellyn, James Bruce (1927–) Perhaps the first African-American to get into or at least near the highest levels of business. The son of Jamaican immigrants who inculcated the primacy of work in their child, Llewellyn worked his way through college and law school and in 1969 bought a small grocery store chain by using a lever-aged buyout, many years before it briefly became the financing tool of choice in the 1980s. He subsequently sold it at a great profit. Thanks in part to Jesse Jackson, the famous or infamous civil rights reverend, and his boycott against Coca-Cola, Llewellyn and his business associates were able to buy a major bottling dealership, which he soon built up into the eighth largest in the nation. Regardless of whatever means it took Llewellyn to get hold of a business, he didn't run it as a black busi-ness, as he explained to a magazine interviewer: "Black businesses have to [realize] that we are no longer a black business in the sense that we serve the black commu-nity, but we are a black-owned business selling to everyone. If you don't do that, you're walking away from ninety percent of the population."

In 1985 he and his partners became the first black businessmen to own a major network-affiliated TV sta-tion (Channel 7-Buffalo). Their bid of $65 million was accepted over a $90 million offer from a white group because of a provision in the tax law allowing the sellers a $30 million tax credit if they sold to an African-American syndicate. One more, distinctly modern, instance of the private and public intertwining.

load management This is the science and/or art of making sure that something you've invested pots of money in earns its keep. The trick to load management is to keep the equipment going all the time. When the electric utilities' generators are humming from customer demand, when the airliners are flying full up with passengers, load management is working and the company's making money. Airliners sitting empty on the tarmac are losing money; so are unused highways designed for peak travel time. Effective load management is what rescues profit from loss.

load mismanagement The games played by clever corporate types to conjure up an ersatz power shortage, which is then manipulated to extract exorbitant charges from bewildered, confused, and panicked public authorities, as in the great California power scandal of 2001.

loaded 1. Having lots of do-re-me, which is good. **2.** Intoxicated, which may not be good. **3.** With a fee attached. Whenever the word *load* appears, brace yourself.

loan shark A despicable sort of chap who lends money at rates of 20 percent per week or even more, which is against the law. People who borrow from loan sharks are terrible credit risks, and it is universal in lending, whether it is a hotsy-totsy corporation or an unshaven rummy working on the docks, that the riskier the borrower, the higher the interest on the loan. The loan shark's customers have no steady cash flow and no collateral. The high interest compensates for the trickly cash flow and, for collateral, the loan shark has in his employ a gentleman with a baseball bat. Among the coarse classes, loan sharks have been known to be called Shylocks, probably without knowledge of *The Merchant of Venice* or the fact that the use of the name is considered anti-Semitic.

A notch or two up the social scale of the high-risk, high-interest loan industry is the payday loan business. For hourly workers and other low- to moderately low-income workers who patronize them, payday loan offices offer advances on the next paycheck. In return for giving the lender a predated personal check, the borrower is given money minus the fee, which works out on a yearly basis to something around 400 percent interest. The next payday, the borrower deposits the paycheck, thereby covering the advance. While this is a valuable service for people who live on the financial margin, it is an expensive one. But the people who use payday loans have little choice when the car breaks down or some other nonroutine emergency expense falls on them. Reformers have been demanding some kind of price control cap be put on the business, but if they get their way, nobody can say what may happen. Will these payday check cashers, some of which are subsidiaries of our largest and most respectable financial institutions, get out of the business? Since the need for such loans will be just as great as before the reform, will the desperate borrowers resort to loan sharks and yet higher interest?

lobbyists Insinuating men and women from Gucci Gulch or K Street NW in Washington, where this nefarious class is said to have its offices. Though lobbyists were descried in Washington and various state capitals in the 1860s, the occupation's antiquity has not spared these genial persons, many of whom are defeated politicians, from the contempt in which they are held by the civilian population.

From time to time the urge to reform, purify, rectify, banish, control, police, and otherwise supervise lobbyists seizes the public, but the work is like going after the cockroaches in a New York City apartment. When the clouds of insecticide dissipate, there are dead critters aplenty, their antennas drooping, feet up in the air, and x's in their eyes, but twenty minutes later the damn things are running over the top of the stove again.

They exist because the government has been a unique and necessary source of money for business since the earliest years of the Republic. Without the information provided by business trade associations and individual companies, biased though it may be, legislatures and government agencies would be blindfolded and lawmaking in a complicated, technical, and business-dominated society would not be possible.

Lohman, Ann Trow (1812–1878) Born to poverty in England, Lohman immigrated to the United States to become rich and famous or, if you will, infamous, by selling contraceptive materials and abortifacients. Based in New York, she advertised her products in newspapers across the country and established branch offices in Boston and Philadelphia.

Long-Term Capital Management The name of a hedge fund that either did or did not do one of the biggest flop-polas in the history of finance. In retrospect it seems that the two Nobel Prize winners in economics who ran Long-Term Capital Management did so many deals of such complexity that neither they nor their computers under-stood what they had gotten themselves and their fancy-pants investors into. By September of 1998 it seemed that the fund was about to go kaput, taking with it a mere $3.6 billion and raising fears that, in consequence, the financial dominoes across the globe would fall, bringing down the world. In panicky reaction to this highly unwelcome prospect, the Federal Reserve Board organized the big banks and investment houses into an emergency rescue operation, and the worst did not occur. A body of expert opinion exists that insists that, had the Fed done nothing, nothing bad would have happened to the world. However that may be, the Long-Term Capital Management story reveals that the people running high finance have, thanks to a pathological mixture of greed, heedless pride, and quickness with numbers, built financial structures like those of the electrical grid. Most of the time they work OK, but every so often they go flooie, the world comes to a crashing halt, and nobody quite knows why or quite knows how to fix them.

macaroni defense Only from Wall Street do you get corkers like this one. The macaroni defense is used by a company fighting off a hostile takeover and consists of issuing bonds that must be redeemed, i.e., bought back, for more than their purchase price, if the company is taken over. The bonds, you see, expand like macaroni when dropped in hot water.

Made in the USA Prove it.

magic numbers If you step back, which they don't, and take a cool look at what businesspeople do, you see that it is a parlous life they lead. There are no sureties. Bankruptcy lurks. Litigation threatens. Amid such nerve-racking uncertainty, human beings look for signs and portents. In the past they have looked for clues to the future in the shapes of clouds and the contents of chicken guts. In business they look to magic numbers, numbers that flash on the electronic boards, daily, weekly, or monthly, and provide a key to the future. The magic number changes, but there is always one or even two or three for which people hold their breaths. For a while in the 1970s, it was the price of gold. That was superceded by the prime interest rate, the Nasdaq, the consumer price index, the Federal Funds rate, M1, the Dow Jones, and the price per gallon of sweet Texas crude oil. Nothing human beings have ever built rivals the universe of business in complexity, so the likelihood that one or two numbers in a series can tell much is rather small, but when it's dark and you don't have a flashlight, any handrail will do.

mainstream (noun and adjective) Noun: A place the speaker, writer, or advertiser stands in the middle of; majority opinion. Adjective: Respectable, timid, stodgy, scaredy-cat, brain-dead. A mainstream church: a church with high prestige and few members; mainstream political opinion: sludgy, standpat, conventional sentiment.

mall "Seen one, seen 'em all." — C. Hitchens

manager One without whose specialized skills business bureaucracies could not exist. This kind of manager, as contrasted to a mere boss or top man or director, emerges as a distinct occupation in the last quarter of the nineteenth century, when executives came to believe in a science of management. In the first quarter of the twentieth century, the manager, with his briefcase full of administrative techniques, would burst the bounds of business to become a popular hero of sorts. The scientific management idea was exported to the Progressive political movement, resulting in such things as the push for nonpartisan and city manager government. While often overpraised, overpromised, and abusively applied, modern management is not all hokum preached by jive-ass, circuit-riding business charlatans. A body of specialized knowledge, indispensable to running enterprises, does exist, and the whitened bones of companies that failed to apply it litter the back issues of our major business journals.

manual labor An un-American activity.

margin The portion of the price of a stock you put down when buying it on credit. The broker lends you the rest of the money, for which he charges you interest that may be as high as that on your credit card, so the stock has to do some fancy upward zooming for you to make a profit. Do not try it at home.

marginal The multiple meanings of this word revolve around additional payments in or payments out when another number changes, as, for example, the "marginal" increase above what you owe when you are jumped into a higher tax bracket. If production is increased, the profit per widget will rise or fall, and that difference is the marginal increase or decrease. From this tool of analysis come marginal cost, marginal efficiency of capital, marginal revenue, marginal tax rate, and marginal who knows what else. The idea of marginality is dear to the hearts of businesspeople and economists, who use it in scores of ways to figure costs and profits and make decisions.

margin call   Two of the saddest words in personal finance, customarily uttered by a boy broker twisting the tips of his moustache or a girl broker doing something else of an unmentionably threatening character. The call is a demand for more money after the price of the stock bought with a loan secured by the selfsame stock has dropped. If the stock continues to gallop south, more calls will follow. A failure to pay results in the stock being sold out from under one's fanny.

marketing   Newfangled word for old-fangled selling.

market maker   The same as a specialist, except that market makers do it for cheap stocks not listed on high-status stock exchanges.

market share   The percentage of overall sales of a product or service controlled by one company. It is an article of faith in business that unless your company has the largest or at least a very large market share, you are in for trouble. It is believed that only the number one and two companies in the same industry will survive and prosper. Although you would think that a large market share is best obtained by offering the highest quality possible at the lowest possible price, it does not always work that way. In the automobile industry, for instance, car companies have sometimes chosen to sell at a loss rather than lose market share.

McCormick, Cyrus Hall (1809–1884)   McCormick is often given credit for inventing the reaper, the machine that cuts grain, but, in fact, he was *an* inventor of the reaper. Often, when the time is ripe, more than one person comes up with a variation of the same idea; McCormick's career is an illustration of how inventing something of great utility is only half the job. Unless the invention gets into the hands of the people who can use it, it's just a contraption gathering dust on the workshop floor.

McCormick broke new ground by mass-producing quality machines and getting them into the farmers' hands through a series of signal business innovations. He pioneered the dealer-franchise system, later copied by other industries that needed to both demonstrate and service complicated products. He put together a superior sales and distribution system and provided the customer with spare parts and timely service by factory-trained mechanics. By advertising and offering installment credit sales, the company got the reaper into the fields, where it was the cause of events, social and economic, that changed American and world history.

As the ever more efficient equipment demanded larger and larger acreage, it made agriculture a big business, which threatened the existence of the family farm.

mentor Originally the Goddess Athene in drag, advising the young Telemachus in the *Iliad.* Now a senior person or patron who guides, protects, and advances a junior in the organization, hence someone who mentors a protegé, and, hence again, "mentee." We await the coming of *mentic, menticizing, mentitation,* and *menticated* with ineffable anticipation.

merchant banker **1.** In the early nineteenth century, a merchant in the import-export business, who also performed banking functions such as issuing letters of credit. **2.** Modern merchant bankers do little of a mercantile nature, nor do they open accounts for walk-in customers. A merchant banker is one who, for an extortionate fee, gives financial advice, negotiates mergers and acquisitions, and underwrites new issues of stocks and bonds or other kinds of securities. For practical purposes, the term is interchangeable with *investment banker.* "Merchant banker" may sound more old-line and classy, but that kind of classy, if it ever existed, went the way of the Native American back around the time that J. P. Morgan, the elder, passed from the scene (for more about him, see **Morgan, John Pierpont**).

merger   Two or more companies coming together and losing their separate identities to become a single, integrated organization, but the word is loosely used to include one company buying another (acquisition). The financial aspects of merger deals are done in an infinity of clever ways, concocted by the legal and accounting professionals when at their worst. Financial razzmatazz aside, mergers basically get done via one of two routes: **1.** The stocks of the merging companies are thrown into one pot and a new stock is issued by the new, merged corporate entity. The amount of stock that owners of the old securities get back depends on the value assigned by the negotiators to each company's shares. So an owner of a share in one of the old companies might get back half a share or two shares. **2.** One company simply swaps its stock, on an agreed-upon ratio, for the stock in the other company.

The first merger wave splashed through the corporate world in the 1890s, and others of greater or lesser intensity have periodically been crashing on the shores of high finance ever since, especially in moments of giddy prosperity. The reasons for mergers are many and disputed. One oft-heard motive is suppression of competition by joining forces. Other reasons alleged and adduced for corporate copulation: Companies, unable to grow by themselves, can at least get bigger via mergers and acquisitions; mergers with no discernible business advantages except to lawyers and accountants are brought off by wily Wall Street operators whose noses can smell out a hundred-million-dollar fee with nary a snort nor a sneeze. Such unions are only possible because the CEO's concerned are flamboozable nebbishes; mergers are also a means of capturing the rights to new technologies; mergers have been pulled off by piratical personalities whose motive is to get hold of a company, loot it, and leave it without a thought that a valuable and useful organization has been destroyed; other mergers and acquisitions have been concluded by businesspeople who see large, unrealized value in parts of the acquired business, which the present management lacks the gumption to exploit for the stockholders; some mergers come about because of a CEO's Napoleon complex, which drives him to make his company grow by gobbling up everything in sight, and some mergers are conceived because the companies involved are a good fit, resulting in increased efficiency and better goods and services.

Mergers between companies in the same business, as when two banks become one, are often fraught with trouble, since the merged company, heavy with people in duplicate positions, is frequently riven by men and women scheming and backstabbing over who gets to stay and who must walk the plank. Clashes in "corporate cultures" are also common, with results that do not always augur well for the stockholders or long-suffering customers. The histories of companies subsequent to mergers is sufficiently spotty to cause the flag of caution to be raised on Wall Street when one is announced. There is a reason that the shares of the dominant merger partner, or acquiring company, almost always drop on the announcement of corporate nuptials.

Merrill, Charles (1885–1956) Although a doctor's son with a private-school upbringing, Charlie Merrill was a self-made businessman who, in 1914, started what ultimately became Merrill Lynch with a few bucks he'd saved from his last job and a lot of ideas. In the succeeding sixteen years, Charlie made a specialty in finding money for new businesses with no social status and therefore no allure for the aristocrats of finance such as J. P. Morgan and Kuhn Loeb. The aristos found money for railroads, steamship lines, steel mills, and a very few other select industrial corporations. Charlie hustled around and found the money for movie companies and, his specialty, chain stores, the new form of retail organization, which was delivering better, more varied, and cheaper merchandise to that new person on the socioeconomic scene, the nascent American consumer.

But by 1928 Charlie, who seemed to have a capacity for dispassionate analysis rare in any calling, had concluded that an enormous stock market crash was preparing itself. The conviction that a disaster was drawing near impelled him to take the train to Washington and visit retiring President Calvin Coolidge, whom he offered to make a partner in the firm. When Coolidge replied that he knew nothing about the securities industry, Merrill said he wanted him to spend his time using press and radio to warn people about the massive and mounting indebtedness and the tornado of speculation the market was caught up in. Seventy years later, the company that bears Charlie's name was far less forthcoming with its customers as the dot-com crash of 2000–2001 approached.

Coolidge said no thank you, so Charlie took the burden on himself as best he could, warning his firm's customers and his partners that doomsday was coming up fast. His partners couldn't see it, or greed didn't let them, but as the boss, Merrill ordered everything sold. It wasn't long before many had reason to thank Charlie, but the lesson is that Charlie and the others who saw the crash coming were like Cassandra, fated to know the future and be disbelieved. Much the same happened with the dot-com disaster seventy years later. The people who were wiped out were repeatedly warned that they had put their money and their hopes into dangerous nonsense.

After 1930 Charlie betook himself and his millions out of Wall Street and spent the Depression decade overseeing the Safeway grocery chain, of which he was the majority stockholder. At the end of the Depression, he reconstituted Merrill Lynch, which he had put in mothballs, and with his experience in chain stores and mass merchandising, pioneered making stock ownership mass ownership.

The United States government had been the first to sell securities to the whole population, beginning with the Liberty Bonds of World War I and the War Bonds of World War II, but Charlie Merrill was among the first to bring about the popular capitalism that is one of the most salient features of twenty-first-century American society. Merrill was not working out a theory. His only preachment was:

Take care of the customer first, and the customer will take care of you.

metrics A noun, the plural form of which cannot yet be found in the *Oxford English Dictionary*. A recent, unnecessary neologism, if it has meaning, it is anything having to do with a company, expressed in numbers or statistics. The use of the word is intended by the speaker to give the impression of technical competence and an all-knowing expertise.

middle class A subsection of the population that includes everybody, oddly enough. Modern social theology has it that there is no upper class and that "lower class" means talking with your mouth full. The possible existence of some kind of superclass is seen in the custom of addressing billionaires in television interviews by the title of mister or ms. Middle-class people are always called by their first names.

Milken, Michael R. (1946–) The Napoleon of American high finance, who made corporate continents rise out of the vast, black, primal sea and then fall back in. He is now roosting on his Elba, banished forever from anything to do with investments, after having served three years of a ten-year sentence and paid fines of about a billion dollars. He could afford the money. At his peak, Milken was raking in more than half a billion dollars a year, while being Exhibit A for the contention that security traders are compensated out of all proportion to their importance to the society.

Milken, as an employee of Drexel Burnham Lambert, seized upon the idea of using junk bonds to finance a group of wild-ass business hustlers in taking over a number of underproducing, slumbering corporations that were sliding down into extinction. Raising billions to finance the takeovers and mergers, Milken and the others who emulated him played a major enabling part in the reinvigoration of American big business in the 1980s, so perhaps he was worth what he was paid. In the decade or so of his greatest power, beginning in the mid 1970s, Milken provided the financing for such companies as MCI Communications, Duracell, and Viacom but also the wherewithal for piratical looters to get their grappling hooks onto the decks of poorly defended corporate treasure ships, which they left to founder.

The means Milken chose, as he found out on his sentencing day, when he all but had to be carried weeping and shrieking from the courthouse, were intensely illegal. The heart of his crimes was a conspiracy to control the prices of the junk bonds he was peddling by a variety of unlawful means. Had he pulled his tricks seventy-five or one hundred years earlier, he would not have been prosecuted, and not a few economic theorists believe he should not have been prosecuted now. However you want to judge him, it is well to remember that this briefly gigantic figure was not a swindler. Many of his junk bonds turned out to be gilt-edged investments; some went south, and some were used to finance businessmen who might at a distance of more than five feet be mistaken for gangsters. Milken is one of those men about whom you say that we should await the judgment of history, but a century from now history may still be arguing about this man.

minimum wage **1.** The least a business has to pay a worker. **2.** A law specifying the least a business must pay a worker. This law apparently is only obeyed when the amount of the minimum wage is allowed to sink over time thanks to inflation. Otherwise, if labor can be had for less than the legal minimum wage, labor is paid less. For the past half-century, politicians and academics have been at each other's throats over the utility or desirability of having a legal minimum wage. The jury is still out on this one, which may mean it is permanently hung.

monopoly A fighting word, or at least a much fought-over word. Its dictionary definition is a market in which something can only be had from one seller. The legal and political definitions, which are the ones that count, zigzag through the business world in confusion and controversy. The meaning of the word in law is different in the United States and Europe; it also changes depending upon which group of politicians is in office.

A monopoly may be a government creation, as with granting somebody a patent, which is the exclusive right to sell something and therefore the power to set the price without fear of being undercut by competition. From time to time the government has chosen to permit monopolies and supervise them. Communications, transportation, agriculture, and power industries are examples. A monopoly gushes so much cash that the cost of bribing the public officials sent to oversee it is negligible, and, while the devil is sure such dishonesty has never occurred, disgruntled persons persistently talk about the possibility.

For customers to feel the pain from them, monopolies need not control 100 percent of the market or be national in scope. An airline with less than all of the flights can, nevertheless, extract monopoly prices in a region of the country where it has its hub or hubs. Daily newspapers, almost all of which have declining circulations but are regional monopolies, have been able to keep hiking their prices.

monopsony An upside-down monopoly, that is, a market where there is only one buyer. Monopsony is as likely to give rise to naughtiness as monopoly, as can be seen in the perpetual scandals surrounding government arms procurement, a textbook example of a single-customer market. Quasi-monopsonical conditions may exist in the private sector if a manufacturer becomes dependent on a single, gigantic customer, such as a Wal-Mart or a Sears.

Moore, Gordon E. (1929–) A leading member of the group of white, Protestant boys of entrenched middle-class, professional origins, mostly from west of the Mississippi, who grew up to be the scientist-businessmen to whom the world owes the electronic-digital age. Although first-class scientific ability and business talent often do not go together (see **Silicon Valley**), they did in Moore's case, when first he brought together the team that started Fairchild Semiconductor, and then did it again, founding Intel. (See also **Noyce, Robert N.**)

mordida International trade term meaning baksheesh with a bite. Money exacted by an official for permission to do something illegal or something legal. Although the term is Spanish and said to be from Central America, the practice is universal. Building, fire, health, electrical, and plumbing inspectors in New York City, for instance, are famous for demanding money from legitimate persons for permits to conduct legal businesses. Functionally, there might not be much difference, but a distinction exists between having money extorted from one by an official and bribing an otherwise honest official so that you can get to the head of the line in a sludgy, motionless bureaucracy. Without baksheesh, grease, mordida, many a business operation would have a painfully slow go of it.

Morgan, Junius Spencer (1813–1890); John Pierpont (J. P.) (1837–1913); and **John Pierpont (Jack), Jr. (1867–1943)** These three were the principal figures in America's greatest finance dynasty. Through the banking institutions, they played the leading role first in guiding investment capital from Europe to America, and second in sending it back to Europe. The Morgan bank handled the financing and purchasing of military supplies for England and France during the First World War.

Other than Rockefeller, no name in American history has been more closely yoked to rapacious capitalism than that of Morgan. J. P., with his glaring eye and swollen, gleaming red nose—the man suffered from a disfiguring condition called rhinophyma—was the epitome of the robber baron in the popular political imagination of generations of Americans. In his top hat and swallowtail coat, he personified Mr. Moneybags. The Morgans, it was widely held, were the evil center of the "money trust," which was squeezing the life out of farmers and factory workers.

But if you compare the Morgans with modern "malefactors of wealth," as President Theodore Roosevelt denominated wicked businessmen, the Morgans come out looking pretty good. They put their money and their business organizations at the service of the nation during several horrendous financial crises, undoubtedly saving the United States from business panic and recession. In the twenty-five years before the creation of the Federal Reserve Board, the Morgans were the Federal Reserve. Snooty, cosmopolitan, arrogant, they used their financial power with responsibility. For all their distance from ordinary people, they were a class act, stacking up well against the greasy, shifty, contemporary barons of Wall Street.

J. P. Sr., was among the first to attempt to do something about the chronic problem of overproduction, overcapacity, and the attendant lethal competition, which followed the invention of mass production. After 100,000 years of scarcity, business had invented a new and unlooked-for source of pain—abundance, and with it, ruinous competition. To prevent companies from competing themselves into bankruptcy, Morgan wanted them to cooperate with each other, either through agreements to collude on prices, once legal, or by forming monopolies or amalgamating in some other fashion, through trusts or mergers and acquisitions. The United States Steel Corporation was one of Morgan's attempts at preventing suicidal competition. A century later the same devices are still being used, often with indifferent success.

Like investors of today, the Morgans also had to decide whom to trust and whom to stay away from when investing or loaning money. When all was said and done, J. P. Morgan relied on the character of the men running the firms he was putting capital into, but unlike today's world, Morgan's was small enough to enable him to know whom he was doing business with. In the twenty-first century you're always giving your money to strangers.

mortgage broker A person who gathers a home buyer's pertinent financial information and shops around among banks to get the best deal. This is a fairly new occupation whose numbers have grown rapidly in the past few years. It is said that there are about 25,000 of them. Mortgage brokers have begun to cut banks out of the process and place mortgages with institutions that buy the mortgages from banks. It has been a long time since banks kept mortgages in their vaults. The modern way has been to make the mortgage, sell it, and make more mortgages with the proceeds, which include profits to be sure. But now the brokers are coming along and eliminating the middleman. This change in the system has been made possible because of new computer software that enables a mortgage broker to qualify a borrower literally in a very few minutes. The downside is that the software grants or doesn't grant mortgages according to a given set of statistical parameters. If you don't fit, you don't get. It's not the way it was a long time ago, when a banker could say, "I don't care what her balance sheet shows. I know she is the kind of person who will pay back this loan." The lenders don't know whom they're lending to and couldn't care less, as long as the applicant fits certain specifications. The new way is quicker and cheaper, but it is the abnormal, the deviant, the person who doesn't fit, who, business history shows, is the one who does great things.

motel In 1951, Kemmons Wilson (1913–), a Memphis, Tennessee, real estate man, piled the wife and kiddies into the family jalopy for a trip to Washington, D.C. Along the way, they were forced to stay in what were then called motor or tourist courts, catering to travelers negotiating the two-lane highways of the period. Not unlike Saul of Tarsus, somewhere along the road, Wilson was struck with the conviction that what America needed was dependable, clean, convenient, modestly-priced road accommodations. Back home in Memphis, he built just such a place and called it Holiday Inn, after the movie of the same name, which starred Bing Crosby, a chap who strode the theater marquees of his time like the entertainment colossus he was. Just as Mr. Wilson was building his first Holiday Inn, Dwight Eisenhower was ensuring their success by starting construction on the interstate highway system. Less than thirty years later, there were 1,700 Holiday Inns, all clean, all comfortable, all the same with their swimming pools and their color TVs.

multinational corporation A company with factories or other fully developed divisions or subsidiaries in two or more countries. A firm that simply exports its goods or services but has no real organizational presence in another nation is not a multinational.

Singer Sewing Machine (see **build a better mousetrap**) was the first full-blown multinational corporation, but by the 1880s, thanks to transcontinental rail service, the oceangoing steamship, and the transatlantic telegraph cable, American multinationals were well established all over the world. In Europe, famous firms such as Baldwin Locomotive, Hoe (printing presses), Eastman Kodak, Otis Elevator, Standard Oil, Babcock and Wilcox (boilers), and Metropolitan Life were familiar, going concerns. U.S. business activity overseas stimulated London publishers to bring out a spate of books with titles like *The American Invasion* and *The Americanization of the World.*

Although the power and influence of multinationals entered a period of phenomenal growth and complexity following World War I, it is a mistake to think that *multinational* is the same as *supranational.* A few companies were entangled with the Nazis during World War II, but most American multinationals have remained American in outlook and loyalty. Though there are examples aplenty of these organizations plowing up the virgin rain forests and inculpating themselves in dirty deals of every kind, imaginable and unimaginable, the predictions of a planetwide government of multinational corporations, running the world on their terms, have not come to pass. With all their faults and acts of exploitation of man and nature, multinationals have played their part in raising the living standards of many societies.

mutual fund Originally shares in mutual funds or investment trusts were offered as a means by which people of modest means could buy a security representing stocks in a wide variety of companies, which they otherwise couldn't afford. This is the "don't put all your eggs in one basket" theory, although Andrew Carnegie, who was no slouch as an investor, is supposed to have said, "No, do put all your eggs in one basket, and watch the basket." It worked for him, but so did everything else he attempted.

Although there are funds that reflect the overall price of the stock market, thereby relieving investors of the burden of picking winners, most mutual funds are more selective, so that the buyer must choose between thousands of specialized mutual funds. Picking one is not unlike making a buying decision in the dentifrice section at Wal-Mart—endless varieties backed up by an infinity of claims and misleading statistics.

The more successful managers of the bigger, more famous mutuals are accorded star status, which they get to keep until the next major market slump. It is a rare manager who remains a genius in the eyes of his or her investors for more than a decade. Somewhere between the tenth and the fifteenth year of their geniushood, they start bleeding IQ points.

naked As in naked option, naked call, naked put. Those who elect to traipse around nude, either on the beach or in the stock market, run certain risks. Pick the wrong beach and you may be carted off to the hoosegow, or if you're not endowed with a Hollywoodesque body, you may face laughter and ridicule. On Wall Street, naked means having promised to sell something one does not own, as in the puts/calls game (see **put** and **call**). Piles of lucre, filthy and otherwise, can reward the person who cavorts naked in the markets, but the risks are huge and the consequences are disastrous when one is suddenly confronted with a demand to hand over what one doesn't have and can only obtain at ruinous prices. (See **selling short**.)

The nineteenth-century scalawag financier/swindler Daniel Drew (1797–1879) is credited with this bit of doggerel, which sums up the stock market version of the nude-in-public dream:

> He who sells what isn't his'n
> Must buy it back or go to prison.

natural monopoly Not necessarily found in nature, it is defined as a business that cannot successfully be operated in competition with like companies. The prime examples once given of a natural monopoly are electrical utility and telephone companies. (See **Vail, Theodore Newton**.) Telephone monopolies have been vitiated but hardly obliterated, while the ownership situation in electricity is chaotic. Since the network of high-voltage transmission lines, substations, transformers, and local distribution systems to the home cannot be duplicated by a rival electric company, the only part of the system susceptible to competition is power generation, and just recently, power trading. Until recent times, most jurisdictions have been willing to trade monopoly for government regulation. The hitch to that arrangement is that the cash pours into utility company vaults in such volume that there is plenty of moola left over with which to blandish the utility regulators. In a few places in the United States, the natural electric monopoly has taken the form of government ownership, which has worked reasonably well, but any institution supplying goods or services, not privately owned and therefore presumably bereft of the profit motive, is a stink in the nostrils of God, Who has a fine nose for smelling out socialism.

Newcomen engine This steam engine, invented in 1712 by the Englishman Thomas Newcomen (1663–1729), was the first shot of the Industrial Revolution. Although Romans had steam engines of some sort, Newcomen's invention was the first commercially successful steam engine and was used to pump water out of coal mines. It did not come as a bolt out of the blue, however, because, as with many another signal invention, people had been working on how to replace human and horse muscle power with steam power for three-quarters of a century before Newcomen, building on his predecessors' work, built his machine.

new economy In the 1920s the new economy was called "the new era," which in both cases means the good times will roll on forever as everything gets bigger, upper, and better. After certain untoward events in the stock market in the autumn of 1929, the new era was tucked away until the 1960s, when the professors brought forth "the new economics," which they claimed afforded the tools to "fine-tune" the economy, so that there would be no depressions, no panics, no recessions, and Americans would go to Club Med, stand on the beach, and tell themselves, "It can't get better than this." To the surprise of everybody but a knot of professional killjoys and paid naysayers, the new economy began to look like the old economy of the French government under Louis XV (1710–1774), which also practiced shop-till-you-drop economics.

The discovery that electronic inventions had canceled out the truth of everything that had been learned about business in the last three centuries again gave birth to the "new economy." Whenever the word *new* is used, proceed cautiously. The Internet is new; the economy isn't.

NGO (nongovernmental organization) Clara Barton, née Clarissa Harlow Barton (1821–1912), who seems to have been endowed with a force-five hurricane personality, is accorded her place in the devil's dictionary as the founder of one of the first and mightiest NGOs, the American Red Cross. Although Barton's accomplishments over a long, pioneering career are incontestable, she was forced out of the Red Cross and into retirement because of management troubles and questions about handling the money, questions familiar enough to us moderns.

Her life poses important questions. Can any large organization escape being a business of some kind? Is an NGO, such as the Ford Foundation, a business? Judging by the extremely handsome salaries and perks of their top executives, not to mention the billions in capital under their control, the case might be made that many an NGO is, from the standpoint of those running it at least, a business. They may not call it profit, but corporations like Ford grow larger every year and, because they operate under special laws set up for nonprofits, they are obliged to reveal only smidgens of information pertaining to their activities.

As the twentieth century drew to a close, the line between a business and such institutions as churches, museums, and universities got smudgier. Is Trinity Episcopal Church, the largest owner of real estate on Manhattan island, a church or a business? How does one categorize the New York Metropolitan Museum of Art, with its retail shopping outlets, large mail-order operation, and show biz special exhibitions? Organizations such as the United States Olympic Committee and the National Collegiate Athletic Association, with their big salaries, their perks, and their big-time, multibillion-dollar activities, are certainly business-like. While such institutions don't have stockholders, they do have stakeholders who do rather well, thank you, year after year. As universities shape themselves into multifarious organizations selling research and development services, earning money by patent exploitation, renting databases, and converting instruction—thanks to the Internet—from custom-made handiwork into a distance-learning commodity, even the distinction between education and business is blurring fast.

no-load Without commission or fee. However, no-load does not mean free. Free doesn't exist, so one way or another, there is a load there somewhere. You just can't see it.

nonrecurring charge One of those dipsy-doodle terms beloved of greasy accountants, snaky CEOs, and dust-in-your-face corporate public relations departments. It is used in connection with the announcement of a big financial setback or write-off (see **write off**). The words *special* or *one-time* or *unusual* are often used in place of *nonrecurring,* but the meaning is the same, to wit, suckers and speculators of every sort are not to take the bad news seriously, as it is a unique event, never to be repeated or happen again.

Noyce, Robert N. (1927–1990) Scientist/businessman and the epitome of what every parent wants a child to grow up to be, except, perhaps, Noyce's Congregational minister papa back in Grinnell, Iowa, who had strict ideas. Noyce was induced by his colleague Gordon Moore (see **Moore, Gordon E.**) to be first the founding president of Fairchild Instruments, and then again the founding president of Intel, because of his all-conquering charm, dynamism, and good looks. Tom Wolfe described him as a man with a Gary Cooper smile and a "halo effect," which made him a natural for developing the informal, low-hierarchy management that became a hallmark of the electronics industry in its wild, salad days.

Noyce was also the co-inventor, with Jack Kilby of Texas Instruments, of what may be the single most important invention of the last third of the twentieth century, the integrated circuit. The ever-shrinking, ever more powerful computer chip took the world away from steam, steel, and electricity and replaced them with electronics. Were the Nobel Prize conferred posthumously, Noyce would undoubtedly have shared it with Kilby, who received it in 2000.

operating earnings The same kind of crapola as the expression pro forma or EBITA. Operating earnings are not the same as operating income and net income. The two terms are strictly defined by GAAP, the acronym for Generally Accepted Accounting Principles.

opportunity cost Term of art meaning what it costs in income or profits foregone to invest money one way as opposed to another—for example, the difference between buying bonds and the return in rent after investing in an apartment house.

option/s Paying for the chance to buy or sell anything at an agreed upon price for a limited period of time. The price for the option is called the premium. If, for instance, you sell the right to buy one hundred shares of stock you own and the price doesn't go up, the buyer will not exercise his option and "call away" your stock. You get to keep your stock and the premium. On the other hand, if the price does go up, you must sell your stock at the agreed upon price, even if it is now worth much more, though you still get to keep the premium. The procedure is the same with options giving the buyer the right to sell a stock (see **put option**). Trading options for a living beats honest work if you have the nerves for it, and it does have a utility. People who trade options, like those who engage in other moment-to-moment stock market speculations, are similar to worms in the garden: lowlife, not very attractive animals without backbones but which keep the earth aerated and help with indispensable microbial activity. For the capital markets to work, stocks and other securities have to be easily bought and sold. It is the trader/speculator worms who make that possible.

option overhang　The number of shares included in unexercised stock options granted employees of a company. Exercise of these options can significantly reduce the percentage of the company owned by ordinary investors. Just another way a person can get whimwhammed, if a person doesn't keep a weather eye cocked.

organization chart　An object of mirth and many a supercilious wisecrack, the chart, at the chaotic dawn of modern business organization, was a clarifying godsend to managers who did not yet know how to manage. It offered businessmen of the 1850s a means of clearly setting out who did and didn't report to whom, who was on first and—damn it!—who was supposed to be on second. A publisher printed up the charts and sold them to eager businessmen for a buck a throw, and that, my dears, was in the days when a dollar was indeed a dollar.

The chart was the creation of Daniel Craig McCallum (1815–1878). One of a seemingly endless stream of gifted Scottish immigrants, McCallum was a structural engineer appointed general superintendent of the recently completed and utterly disorganized Erie Railroad, then the largest and longest in America. McCallum may have been the first businessman to take on a problem that plagues large organizations to this day, that of rapid and precise internal communications.

Not the least of McCallum's innovations was the marriage of two unrelated technologies, the steam-powered rail and telegraphy, to further internal communication, which is of great help if one doesn't want one's steam engines bumping into each other. Seventy-five years later, aeronautics and electronics would be similarly married, but now the interweaving of technologies in business organizations is too commonplace to merit notice.

our greatest natural resource Children. Other commodities much prized by American businesspeople and political speakers include oil, gold, natural gas, tungsten, silver, and molybdenum.

outside directors Men and women who do not work for the company whose board they sit on, but are paid to offer sage and disinterested advice to the management.

It's up to them to see the CEO is fairly compensated (no more than a billion a year) and observes the Biblical injunction: Thou shalt not cooke the books. Some directors do their job and some don't, as was famously demonstrated in the corporate scandals at the beginning of this century (Worldcom, Enron, etc.).

Although outside directors are supposed to be selected for their specialized knowledge and experience, more than one CEO has stocked the board with opera divas, washed-up politicians, society ladies, mistresses, and ex-jocks, who are happy to back the CEO in return for director's fees, private jet travel, inside tips, and other bonbons. CEOs also like to sit on each other's boards, with the understanding, "I'll screw your stockholders for you, and you screw mine for me."

outsourcing Sending work to wherever it can be done most cheaply. In the middle decades of the twentieth century, work was outsourced from New England to the Southern United States. As a result of hugely lower transportation costs, it became profitable to outsource work from the American South and elsewhere in the United States to points all over the globe. Has outsourcing hurt America? The statistics are so lousy nobody can say. Outsourcing should not be confused with outcompeting. Some jobs and businesses—for instance, airplanes, machine tools, printing equipment, electronic games, and automobiles—have moved to high-labor-cost countries such as Japan, Germany, and France because they make a better product at a lower price with higher-priced labor.

overcapitalization   Sometimes ungraciously called "watering the stock," it has been a financial hazard for business since the railroad bankruptcies in the late 1800s. A company is overcapitalized when it has created and sold more shares of stock in itself than the company would fetch if it were sold. The situation makes paying healthy dividends, if not impossible, often difficult and sometimes dangerous, because the company is paying out moneys it should be using to run itself. Business-people may have no choice when trying to combine and consolidate companies that must be reorganized, but overcapitalization makes them vulnerable to terrible drops in the price of their stock, with horrific conse-quences for stockholders and employees, as happened with the collapse of the overcapitalized dot-coms in the late 1990s.

over-the-counter (OTC)   If a stock is OTC, it's not traded on the major stock exchanges, but through electronic broker networks and via the old-fashioned telephone. Less expensive stocks are usually OTC, but some com-panies prefer going that route because they think their securities get a better break. Maybe the companies do, but the suckers don't.

Own-Your-Own-Home Movement   In the wake of the post–World War I housing shortage, the National Associ-ation of Real Estate Boards, with the help of schools, churches, and the usual exemplars of civic uplift, brought forth the Own-Your-Own-Home Movement for new, affordable, single-family, detached housing. In 1922 President Calvin Coolidge assumed the chairmanship of

Better Homes in America, as government and business combined to give birth to the pattern and style of living in twenty-first-century America, where 70 percent of the households own their homes or at least have a mortgage on them.

Pac Man Defense The corporate double gobble. So called when a corporation defends itself against a takeover by turning the tables and attempting to take over the aggressor. Envision two alligators eating each other up, starting at the tails, and you've got the picture. It is also a picture of idiocy and waste. The name comes from an electronic game popular some years ago.

Pan Am (Pan American Airlines) At one time Pan Am's name and logo were almost as well known as Coca-Cola's. The company, led by a monomaniac named Juan Terry Trippe (1899–1981), was put together by a small clot of rich WASPs, who knew each other as Yale undergraduates. Without their political clout, Pan Am would never have taken off in 1927 with a rich subsidy and a monopoly to fly South American routes, given them by the Coolidge administration. For years thereafter, Pan Am, known as "the chosen instrument" of the United States government, was the only American airline permitted to fly abroad. In return for the privilege, Trippe and his airline couldn't fly at home.

Pan Am and Charles Lindbergh, whom Trippe had hired as a celebrity front man and technical consultant, laid out and developed the major overseas routes, which worked out very nicely, thank you, as long as the airline had a monopoly to places like Honolulu. It was the airline of the China Clippers, on which Clark Gable and many another star flew off to movie adventures. In the years that Pan Am had its government license to rake in money, Trippe used it to push Boeing into the jet airliner business. On the debit side, the company was responsible for the Pan Am Building, the ugliest structure ever erected in New York City.

Pan Am is a textbook example of a one-generation dynasty. Arrogance, high costs, flapdoodle management, and change in the climate doomed Pan Am. In the 1930s and 1940s, the American government had used the airline to keep German airlines out of South America and away from the Panama Canal, but step by step the company's monopoly position was taken from it and, without domestic routes, it couldn't compete. In 1991, the last Pan Am airliner, named after Trippe, did a ceremonial flyover, giving a wiggle-wing salute, and landed in the arms of the bankruptcy bailiffs.

paper trail Accountant spoor.

par 1. Not Tiger Woods, but a good golf score for duffers. **2.** Something selling at its nominal value, like a hundred-dollar bond selling for one hundred dollars, which doesn't seem to happen often.

paternalism "And was Jerusalem builded here / Among these dark Satanic mills?" was the question posed by the poet William Blake (1757–1827), a question that tortured the conscience of more than one nineteenth-century American industrialist, and none more so than George Francis Johnson (1857—1948), the son of a teamster who left school when he was thirteen and worked his way up to a full partnership in the Endicott Johnson shoe company.

Johnson, denying that business had to be a perpetual struggle of capital against labor, stood out among the many executives who ran their businesses by humane standards, which now, more than half a century after Johnson's death, are unlike those of the twenty-first-century corporation. Johnson's ideal for an industrial development was a factory "out in the open country with the homes of the workers around it in a little village." Thus, the towns of Johnson City and Endicott, New York, replete with recreational facilities, utilities, libraries, schools, stores, and thousands of homes made affordable via mortgage programs, came into existence. (See **company town**.)

In 1916 Endicott-Johnson became the first company in its industry to embrace the eight-hour day; in 1919 it was comprehensive medical insurance for all employees and their families; the next year it was an astonishing move to divide the profits via a share-and-share-alike program, covering both executives and factory workers. Endicott-Johnson had a no-layoff policy, which the company was more or less able to stick to even during the

Depression, divvying up the available work. Not surprisingly, the company was able to ensure itself of a trained and loyal work force, which had no truck with union organizers.

While only a minority of companies were big enough and profitable enough to practice welfare capitalism, many did, if not always on a scale with Endicott-Johnson. Some of the practitioners were famous, at least in their time, such as George Eastman (1854–1932) of Eastman Kodak. Most were owner-proprietors, but there were exceptions such as Julius Rosenwald (1862–1932) of Sears, Roebuck, which was publicly held. (See **corporate paternalism**.)

Some companies' benefits were not so grand as those at Endicott-Johnson and might have been confined to subsidized cafeterias, baseball leagues, or musical programs. The motives for this altruism doubtless varied from a humanitarian urge to fear of unions, anarchists, and other sinister forms of syndicalism.

Company paternalism flourished from about 1890 to 1930, when the combination of business disaster and the hurricane of union organization all but ended the socially conscientious management.

pecuniary Of or pertaining to money. It comes from the Latin word *pecu,* which meant cattle before it became the root of pecunia, "money." Cattle, of course, are living things, and living things behave in a quirky fashion. Money does, too, and, like other living things, it can grow or shrink. As with cattle, pecunia takes looking after.

Pennsylvania Railroad (the Pennsy) Never missed a dividend for 123 years, which is some kind of record.

Then it went kerplunk in 1970, but compare that to some of our later corporations, whose stockholders are going to have to wait 123 years for a dividend.

penny stock   Stocks costing less than a dollar apiece. These days stocks selling under five dollars a share may be regarded as penny stocks. They are riffraff securities barred from the classier stock exchanges, so that you can only buy these no-accounts, long associated with mining and drilling adventures, in down-market joints like the Denver or Vancouver stock exchanges. Hoity-toity brokers will warn you against buying penny stocks, which, they are convinced (perhaps with good reason), are often floated by raffishly untrustworthy types. On the other hand, the odds that your small investment in Can't Miss Oil will pay off with a gusher are much better than your chances of winning Lotto. Also, the fun lasts longer. You buy your Lotto ticket and boom-boom, a couple of days later you turn on the telly and learn that you've lost. It can be months before your penny stock bursts; in the meantime, you have the fun of looking it up every day, and every so often you may experience the exquisite excitement of seeing your stock go up six or seven cents.

pension   Something your grandfather had. When the old boy retired from the We-Settle-Quick Insurance Company after thirty-seven years in the auditing department, they actually did give employees a watch and a pension. They may also have included medical insurance. Well, they don't do that anymore. Pension systems are expensive and, since they are legal commitments, they show up on the books as liabilities and drag down the price of the stock. Moreover, when inflation hits, retirees have been known to come back and make the company look bad by asking for raises in their monthly checks. Nowadays, unless you are a government worker or a member of the diminishing number of unions powerful enough to make pension programs stick, you get an investment retirement account of some kind and you're on your own, kiddo. Many companies with what is claimed to be excess funds in their pension systems have abolished them, switched their employees into 401(k)s, pocketed the "excess" money, and thereby made a tidy profit. It is also true that in some corporations the pension obligations generously granted by one generation of managers have all but left a shipwreck for the next generation. One more reminder that the United States is a nation in permanent turmoil over how to take care of the very young and the very old.

perk A shortened from of perquisite (medieval Latin for an acquisition), the word came into use in England in the 1870s with the explosion in the number of salaried employees. A perk is a nonmonetary emolument of luxurious character, including the Paris apartment, the company car, and the blonde doxy in public relations who staffs the boss's out of town trips. (See **compensation committee** and **benies**.)

Pickens, T. Boone (1928–) In the 1980s era of hostile corporate takeovers, he was one of the preeminent greenmailers. Part of his fierce reputation was owing to his name, which hints at picking flesh off T-bones, but this distant descendant of Daniel Boone owes his low repute to the Oil Patch aristocracy looking down on him as a pushy, uncouth Okie, which he is. He was one of a group of piratical financiers whose attacks on somnambulant managements was just the tonic many of those corporations needed.

Pickens got his start when he quit a low-level job at Phillips Petroleum and used his savings to start a business finding gas and oil deposits, an occupation which he was very good at. It was only after deciding to buy oil companies with proven reserves that he got into trouble. He went after a succession of large, indifferently managed oil companies, whose stock was selling for less than the companies would be worth if dismembered and sold at auction. While stockholders rejoiced at somebody coming along to resurrect their investments, the managements did not. "Mr. Pickens," said Fred Hartley, the president of Unocal, after T. Boone had begun to buy Unocal stock preparatory to a takeover, "has somehow created a speculative frenzy that has convinced his camp followers that there's easy money to be made attacking oil companies and to hell with tomorrow." More on target was Chevron's chairman, who remarked that, "Pickens does not break any laws doing what he does, but he breaks tradition." So the big oil companies put up their No Okies Allowed signs and chased Pickens away a much richer man.

Pinkham, Lydia Estes (1819–1883) A major businesswoman of the Victorian Age, Pinkham exemplifies how often new business enterprises spring up out of the social and economic facts of an entrepreneur's life.

The shambles that was the medicine of her time impelled Pinkham to study the curative powers of botanicals, and a good thing it was, because her husband, Isaac Pinkham, was a bust as a businessman. By the early 1870s, he had reduced the family to penury. In desperation

Lydia began selling what was to become one of America's best known trademark names, Lydia E. Pinkham's Vegetable Compound for "ladies' complaints." The logo with Ms. P's likeness on it made her face one of the best known in America.

The business was a huge success, which some attributed to her Vegetable Compound being suspended in a solution of almost 20 percent alcohol. That did not discourage leading members of the Women's Christian Temperance Union from endorsing it.

None was better at writing advertising copy than Pinkham, whose newspaper ads included little essays on everything from the life of the working girl to the Greenback movement. Her "Department of Advice" solicited letters from women seeking help for every imaginable problem, and, whatever the quality of the advice Pinkham gave these bewildered and isolated Victorian women, she answered every letter herself. That massive correspondence, which ought to throw a unique light on the daily lives of ordinary women and families of 130 years ago, has yet to be published. Only recently has history given Ms. Pinkham a break and conceded that both as a businessperson and a woman with a message she deserves a special recognition.

pink sheet So called after the color of the paper on which the cheapest penny stocks are listed along with the names of the brokers who buy and sell them. Newspapers disdain printing the buy and sell prices of swarms of low-class, no 'count, trashy stocks. Hence the pink sheet, and the yellow sheet for information on equally dubious bonds. It is satisfying to be able to buy hundreds of shares of a stock that cost less than a dollar, the only drawback being that they practically never pay off, but then again, neither do slot machines, and the people who play them give off every outward indication of having gotten their money's worth from the transaction. (See **over-the-counter**.)

pink slip Noun and occasionally a verb, but either way if you get one it means you are fired, sacked, rusticated, laid off, discharged, dehired, made redundant, given your congee, let go, cashiered, outplaced, downsized, terminated, given the old heave-ho, handed your walking papers, given the gate, demitted, kicked out, or thrown out the door. Why are there so many words for being pink-slipped and so few for being hired?

How a person gets fired depends on what box the person occupies in the organization chart. Top boxers get tens, even hundreds of millions, plus chauffeuring for life; in the lower, more numerous boxes, firees often get nothing more than five minutes to put the cactus and the picture of the children in a file transfer box before persons called "security" escort (it's always "escort") the doomed one to the parking lot; others, yet lower down, come back from their vacations and find their desks gone and their few, poor possessions transferred to the police Lost and Found.

Plastics The first and only plastic substance of the nineteenth century, celluloid, was introduced in the 1870s and, as used for such items as billiard balls, replacements for the stiff, high collars on mens' shirts, and imitation ivory for comb handles, it was an instant commercial success. By 1968, when the famous "plastics" scene in *The Graduate* played the nation's movie houses, the word had come to stand for cheap, flimsy, inferior, false, and generally third-rate. From the miraculous and wonderful, plastics had become a waste disposal problem.

Plastics came into their own in 1910 after Leo Baekeland (1863–1944), a Belgian immigrant and chemist-businessman, presented the world with Bakelite, a tough, iron-hard, lightweight substance that could be molded into a million shapes, and was. Bakelite was used for everything from insulators for power transmission to frying pan handles. As chemical companies began inventing other plastics, the plastic idea took hold of the imagination. Industrial designers, wooed by the plastics industry, created the streamlined, *moderne* look of the 1930s, as a Depression-era public came to believe that plastics were the key to a prosperous future where everything would "wipe clean with a damp cloth." Not only was the shape of things changing, thanks to what was coming out of the test tube, but so was the color. Thanks to plastics, America was changing from a drab society of all black autos into an eye-socking polychrome scene. In 1941 Plastic Man Comics arrived, and four years later at World War II's end, stocking-deprived women, crowding into hosiery departments, took part in what the papers called "nylon riots."

The ever-dropping prices of the ever-greater variety of materials not found in the wild enabled industry to package more than women's legs in plastic. Everything now comes in it. Business, so conscious and deliberate in the near term, has with oblivious disinterest bid fair to turn even the great American outdoors into a non-biodegradable trash land, ugly to man and lethal to animals. Even as the greeniacs beat business over the snout to stop its porcine habits, the partnership of business and plastics continues to usher in a never-ending procession of cheaper and better products. If we could just have the good stuff without the dreck.

point In quoting bond yields, a point is one percent. (See **basis point**.) In real estate a point—or, much more frequently, points—means you are paying through the pores. To give a point means paying back a loan for one percent more than the money you got. You agree to pay back a hundred dollars on a loan from which you only got ninety-nine dollars. You may pay points for "origination fees," ostensibly to cover the cost of appraisals, credit checks, and anything else they can think of, and for closing costs, which can be so numerous they get their own entry in the devil's compendium.

poison pill The deadly nightshade of corporate dinosaurism. Poison pills are gimmicks put into the bylaws of a corporation to make it all but impossible for the company to be gobbled up by another corporation against management's will. These cups of financial hemlock activate as soon as the enemy has gained control and generally involve automatic and costly benies being doled out to the shareholders and officers of the gobbled corporation. The benies may take the form of issuing new stock (see **watered stock**) or payouts, which add to the debt, or the hemlock may come in the form of the entire management of the acquired company leaping out the executive suite window, pulling the rip cords on huge golden parachutes and floating gently down to where a line of stretch limousines waits to take them off to play at celebrity pro-am golf tournaments for the next thirty years.

pools, pooling Agreements common in the 1870s between companies in the same industry—for instance, railroads, wallpaper, and pig iron—to divide markets and/or limit production to keep prices up. Theretofore, when business went south, the proprietor would lay off workers until trade picked up. He didn't make money, but he didn't lose it, either, but that changed with the installation of expensive equipment. The owner still had to pay for the machines, whether they were working or not. Hence pooling. In 1876 the Michigan Salt Association was strong enough to fine its members ten cents a barrel for salt sold in violation of the agreement, but most pooling agreements failed because of the participants' cheating. In the nineteenth century, overbuilt and floundering American railroads repeatedly tried to form pools to keep revenues high enough to avoid bankruptcy, but the temptation to cheat was too great, and by 1900 not a few of them were staring insolvency in the face. In the latter part of the twentieth century, the same problem beset OPEC (Organization of Petroleum Exporting Countries), which has seldom been able to hold together when demand slackened. Pools were soon abandoned in favor of the trust.

Pope, Generoso Paul, Jr. (1927–1988) In 1952 Pope, a graduate engineer from MIT, borrowed twenty thousand dollars with which to make a down payment on the *New York Enquirer,* a feeble weekly specializing in crime and the troubles in Northern Ireland. There was crime enough in Pope's family through his father—a mobbed-up political heavyweight, who owned *Il Progresso,* the biggest Italian-language newspaper, and a man suspected of having a hand in the murder of an antifascist politician—but the son had a legitimate talent. In short order, he changed the paper's name to *The National Enquirer*, changed the content, and perfected the supermarket distribution system, which saw the publication's circulation rise from fifty thousand to four and a half million.

predatory pricing Dinosaur behavior by large corporate reptiles. More specifically, the term refers to a big, well-heeled company dropping prices so low that it is doing business at a loss to force smaller and less well off competitors to bankrupt themselves meeting money-losing prices. As soon as the small fish have surrendered and disappeared, the big corporation puts the prices back up to their previous levels or pegs them even higher.

But all low prices aren't predatory prices. Andrew Carnegie, the nineteenth-century Pittsburgh steelman, was able to drive many a competitor to the wall by underpricing them, not by his gross financial reserves, but by consistently being the lowest-priced producer of steel. Carnegie would junk new, expensive equipment that was hardly used when he heard of something newer that would help him cut costs and increase production. Nobody undersold Andy.

Hence, the great predatory pricing conundrum. If the government accuses a corporation of dinosaur behavior, is it going after an inefficient pig organization whose ability to crush the opposition is the fat that enables it to sustain losses and force competitors out of business? Or is the government punishing the most efficient corporation and rewarding business success with fines and litigation? Punishing the efficient, who are few enough, protects the inefficient and sooner or later takes everybody to the poorhouse. Of course, in an age when some people put the protection of feelings before all else, we can choose the poorhouse over insensitivity.

preferred stock It's preferred because it always pays a dividend, at least it's supposed to. Sometimes the management goes back on the deal and skips the promised dividend to the preferred stockholders, but they are supposed to get their dough later on, unless they don't. Since there are more kinds of preferred stock than you can shake a stick at, the fine print needs reading. Nevertheless, preferred stock in a good company can be a sensible investment for people who are looking for steady income and would just as soon skip Wall Street's thrills and spills.

premium When you're young, a premium is a free trinket found in a Crackerjacks box. For older people in business, it is the amount of money paid to buy a stock above the going market price. In order to get 100 percent ownership of a company, a premium is often paid to the company's stockholders to induce them to sell. Premiums are also paid to greenmailers.

price controls A fine example of the triumph of hope over experience. From Franklin Roosevelt's administration to George W. Bush's, the American government has repeatedly, if fitfully, tried price controls, that is, the abrogation of free market activity by legislative or administrative fatwa. Roosevelt did it twice, once in the early 1930s, to prevent prices from dropping, and then in the 1940s to prevent prices from rising. Controlling prices soon results in shortages and people waiting for hours in lines. Next come black markets, cheating, and chaos. The results of price controls are the same under any and all economic and political systems, but for politicians who hope to buy time to do they know not what, it is a snap-your-fingers fix used to flimflam voters angry at sudden rises in price.

price discrimination Charging what the traffic can bear where and when it can bear it. Nothing bugs the hell out of people more than price discrimination, which means charging different people different prices for the same thing. The anger of a customer on learning that the person he or she is talking to paid less for the same drug, same airline ticket, or same automobile can reach the submurderous level and/or pressure to pass a law. Certain kinds of price discrimination have been illegal in the United States for decades. For example, it is illegal for a big airline to lower prices and sell tickets at a loss in order to drive a little airline out of business. (See **dump**.)

Other forms of price discrimination are legal and used everywhere in business to get the highest volume of sales. If you buy a hundred of whatever, each one will cost you less than if you buy one. Thus, hospitals pay wholesale prices and individuals don't. Nevertheless, that a drug used by old people costs less in Mexico and Canada than in the United States sends people into tizzies of indignation. Isn't equal treatment the democratic way?

Despite what politicians say, business doesn't have all that much to do with democracy. One of the ways businesspeople set prices is by figuring out who will buy, regardless of the high price, and who will buy only if the price is lower. Thus an AIDS drug may be very expensive in New York and quite cheap in South Africa. Tourist fares on airplanes are cheaper than business fares because business people must make the trip but vacationers won't unless the price is right. It ain't fair, and discrimination is a word we have been taught to hate, but it has its uses.

price-earnings (P/E) ratio The price of a share of stock divided by the company's earnings per share. Thus a stock selling for twenty-five dollars a share with earnings of a dollar will have a P/E ratio of twenty five, which for some is a bargain and for others a preposterously expensive security, there being no generally agreed-on definition of what is costly. Alas and alack! In recent years millions of investors have learned to their sorrow that finding out exactly what the "E" is may take some doing.

price fixing This is one crime for which a Republican administration will put a businessman in jail. GOPers, who ordinarily have a boys-will-be-boys attitude toward businesspersons cavorting, take it amiss when two or three companies that are supposed to be in direct competition close down the free market by agreeing to sell at the same prices or, which is pretty much the same, agree that one company or another will exclusively serve certain customers or geographical areas, thereby eliminating competition. Recent examples of well-known companies caught price fixing include Archer Daniels Midland and the fancy-dancey art and antique auction houses Sotheby's and Christie's.

price gouging Putting your thumb in your customers' eyes and twisting. Price gouging is the same as charging all the traffic will bear (a bad thing), which is the same as maximizing profit (a good thing). So, go figure.

price signaling   Price fixing by wigwagging. By unspoken agreement, the biggest company in a field sets a price and the small fry charge the same. In case the Justice Department's Antitrust Division gets antsy, evidence of conspiracy and price fixing is wanting, since the executives of the companies do not meet or directly communicate with each other. Airlines are often accused of price signaling, but then airlines are accused of so many other things that price fixing may not count for much with their furious clientele.

prime rate   An interest you will never get from your bank. The prime rate was once the lowest rate awarded to the most creditworthy customers, meaning very large and profitable companies whose business a bank wants. Nowadays, these same customers may get sub-prime rates while everybody else, unless enjoying some kind of government subsidy, gets prime plus, or as much more as the lender can charge. The movements of the prime have been the gauge of what money costs, but less significance is attached than in the past.

private placement   The sale of stocks, bonds, or other instruments that are not registered with the Securities and Exchange Commission. A private placement security is for investment only and not for resale to the general public. In theory a registered security that anybody may buy comes with a body of information telling the would-be buyer exactly what it is he or she is paying for. In practice, well, theory often deviates from practice, doesn't it?

pro forma   As in a pro forma financial statement. Take such a statement for an accurate picture of a company's situation when pigs whistle and ducks do foreign policy. Pro forma balance sheets, etc., don't represent what is but what management wishes were so. Other mare's-nest terms for nonexistent profits are *economic earnings, core earnings,* and *ongoing earnings.* There is another Latinism to be invoked whenever the phrase pro forma or some other deceptive term is used, and that's *cum grano salis*—with a grain of salt.

productivity   The word may be used in two ways: **1.** The ratio of production per worker per hour worked. This is a key, frequently cited statistic but a hard one to compile. The productivity of workers in a faucet factory is easy enough to calculate by counting how many workers are employed or how many dollars are invested in machines producing how many faucets. That's simple enough, but in a world of service organizations—be they hospitals, fast food restaurants, or consulting and engineering firms— quantifying the output to arrive at a productivity figure is tough going. Hence, economists can be overheard arguing about whether productivity is increasing and, if so, by how much. There were moments in the 1980s and 1990s when it seemed obvious to the eye that productivity was leaping ahead, but you might not have been able to prove it by the numbers. **2.** Productivity is also defined as how much you get in the way of production or services for the money invested. High productivity means low costs, which should mean, absent monopoly and such, low prices.

professional sports The first pro sports—horse racing, boxing, and baseball—were controlled by big-city politicians through health, safety, and blue law regulations. Not only did they make money, but boxing, for instance, provided political machines with election day muscle. Horse racing was a rich source of jobs. In the 1860s, New York's fabled boss, William Marcy Tweed, had the New York Mutuals baseball team on the city payroll. The board of directors of the National Association of Professional Baseball Players, the first professional league, was chock-a-block with pols, including one sheriff, a couple of aldermen, two judges, and six state representatives. Legend has it that turn-of-the-nineteenth-century Boss Cox of Cincinnati threatened to ram a street through the outfield unless he was cut in for a piece of the baseball team's action. The origins of the New York Yankees are to be found mixed in with Tammany Hall, the organization that controlled Manhattan's Democratic Party for generations. As late as the year 2002, The Yankees' top man had once been convicted of federal election law violations.

profit The name of the game. They can trick up the definition, and believe me, they do, but profit comes down to being what's left in the way of money after all expenses have been paid. (See **earnings**.)

program trading The buying and selling of stocks by a computer according to a preset formula. Sounds automatic and infallible, but people write the instructions for the computer to follow and, of necessity, those instructions presume that today's market will be more or less like yesterday's market, thus ensuring that when something altogether new erupts, the program trading will go flooey with God knows what results.

prospectus An impenetrable document legible only to the initiates of the securities industry, which would-be purchasers of new stock issues are incessantly exhorted to study, and which they seldom seem to do. A prospectus, containing the most important information about any new issue of stocks and many other kinds of investments, must be approved by the Securities and Exchange Commission before a new issue may legally be offered for sale to the general public. If it subsequently turns out that a prospectus should have been received as a work of fiction, the authors are subject to being thrown in the slammer and/or reprobated by lesser punishments. This almost never happens, which may mean that (a) virtually every prospectus is what it ought to be or (b) quite a few people are getting away with swindles undetected. Only the devil knows the truth of the matter, and he's not talking. (See also **red herring** and **form 10-K**.)

protective tariff Duties on imports imposed not to raise money but to raise prices on foreign goods. Who is protected from what? Domestic providers and their employees are protected against competition, which is fine and good for them but not for domestic buyers. Thus, even when the United States is in one of its periodic Buy American paroxysms, any given protective tariff will have as many opponents as proponents.

Dating from 1816, the protective tariff is one of the earliest federal government interventions in the free market. In 1828 with the enactment of "the tariff of abominations," protectionism became, like abortion, one of those perennials of American political controversy, never to be resolved. Free trading globalists despise the very idea, but for many decades American industry was aided in its growth and development by tariff walls so high you couldn't get a foreign-manufactured safety pin in the country.

Health, safety, and labor standard regulations such as the minimum wage are used to camouflage what are in reality protection gimmicks. Politics can be used for the same ends. Thus, one can never be sure whether it's Cuba's communism or low prices that keep its sugar safely out of the United States.

proxy fight A struggle between two factions to elect a majority of the members of a corporation's board of directors. It is so called because the fight revolves around which side can collect the most proxies from shareholders—that is, authorizations to vote their shares. Corporate elections are not democratic one man/one vote affairs; they are, instead, one share/one vote elections, thus giving the owners or controllers of large blocks of shares a greater say in the outcome than the owner of a piddling hundred or two hundred shares. Nonetheless, with hundreds of thousands of shares outstanding, getting the proxies is an expensive and difficult undertaking.

Proxy fights date back more than a century, which is to say from the time that shares in companies became widely traded on the stock exchange, out of the hands of a small group of founders (see **corporate governance**). These battles are rare, expensive, and usually very bitter.

prudent man rule The rule by which people in positions of trust (see **fiduciary**) are judged in handling other people's money or property. Did the person take care of the money as a prudent man would? This is the cover-your-ass rule for trustees and can be loosely translated into: Did you invest the money the way other idiot trustees did, and if the answer is yes, you are off the hook even if you lost 90 percent of the dough. The line between prudent and stupid can be very faintly drawn.

Public Company Accounting Oversight Board (PCAOB) Although the name sounds as though it was thought up by speech therapists, this governmental entity was created in 2002 as part of the Sarbanes-Oxley Act by a reluctant Congress in reaction to public displeasure, not to say fury, at the part played by crooked accountants, notably Arthur Andersen, in the corporate peculations summed up by the name Enron. With its members appointed by the Securities and Exchange Commission, the Board's duty is to keep the accounting industry honest, just as it is the Drug Enforcement Agency's duty to keep America weed free. Unlike the DEA, the PCAOB's costs are borne by fees assessed on the accounting industry, which it regulates. That being the case, the board describes itself as a "private-sector, nonprofit corporation," and if that turns out to be true, the industry will be regulated with a light hand.

public education The industrial processing of the young.

public relations Press agent, publicist, flak. That this occupation has so many names tells you something about it. The originator of the schpin und schmooze business is probably a chap named Ivy Ledbetter Lee, (1877–1934). Lee was the first proponent of the Tylenol option for corporations teetering on the edge of a public relations catastrophe, that is: tell it all and tell it quick. Well, maybe. The poet Carl Sandburg called him a "paid liar," and Upton Sinclair dubbed him "Poison Ivy."

Ivy changed the innate reaction of businesspeople to clam up and hide when the untoward occurs. The usual response of the railroads to accidents and grade crossing deaths was to try to keep them out of the newspapers. Ivy Lee's first success was in handling a Pennsylvania Railroad accident by rushing reporters to the scene and thereby garnering goodwill and good publicity for his client.

Lee was retained by some of the largest corporations and richest people of his era, none more so than the Rockefeller family. It was often said that he coached John D. (see **Rockefeller, John Davison**) to give away dimes to the people he met. (The dime was worth a good deal more then, and most people had precious few of them.) The story isn't true, but he did get Rockefeller to let him publicize this possibly endearing custom.

It tells you something about the art of public relations that Lee died in the midst of a storm of misunderstandings. Congressman Hamilton Fish, Jr., denounced him as a Communist propaganda agent, even as newspapers across the country were beginning to attack him for performing similar services on behalf of Adolf Hitler. Neither accusation was true, but regardless of what Ivy Lee and the late Jay Cee may have said, the truth is not always the best policy, although if they find you out, lies aren't so good, either. Take it from the devil. He knows.

puke point Another one of those delicate Wall Streetisms. This point is reached when the market has gone so far south you want to vomit up your stocks, sell them, and walk away.

Pullman, George Mortimer (1831–1897) Starting out in life as a cabinetmaker and contractor, Pullman made railroad travel, which had been pure hell, a comfort and a joy. First came his sleeping car, then the parlor car and the dining car, all done *deluxe,* the Pullman hallmark. A gung-ho salesman and promoter, he talked the railroad into raising bridge heights and such to accommodate his extra-large cars and, more remarkably, he did not sell his cars to the railroads but attached them onto their passenger trains, complete with the service of African-American personnel, whose proficiency was legendary. Pullman changed travel from a torturous ordeal to a luxurious pleasure, thus opening the way for the tourist/vacation industry.

Pullman, Illinois Erected by George Pullman in the early 1880s, on the outskirts of Chicago next to his new factory, the place was the most famous company town in America, if not the world. A planned community with its artificial lake, little parks, and other facilities, the architectural style was red-brick American Queen Anne, done with taste and without monotony. In the unanimous opinion of its visitors from here and abroad, Pullman was a delightful, groundbreaking example of how good planning could blend industrialism, aesthetics, and wholesome community life. Nonetheless, the place was the site of one of the major disasters in business history.

The twelve thousand residents were all employees of the Pullman Palace Car Company, to whom they paid rent. As in many modern developments, Pullman allowed for no changes, but he went further. All the houses were subject to inspection, all land was owned by the company, not even churches were allowed to build on their own, liquor was banned, and a curfew was maintained. This was a formula for trouble in good times, but after the panic of 1893, prosperity vanished, wages were cut, and the union struck. Before the strike was over, the residents of Pullman were evicted and reduced to beggary, five people were killed, and hundreds were arrested as the strike spread to Chicago, where the railroad yards and warehouses were burnt down, at a cost of millions, and the president ordered in the United States Army to stop the violence.

As if proof were needed that nobody ever learns anything, fifty years after Pullman, the government was trying to run public housing as George had tried to run his model town. The Pullman experience made business chary of heavy-handed paternalism, although it did not back away from attempts at planning the physical and social environment.

pump and dump A practice as old as Wall Street, perhaps older. First one pumps up the price of the stock by floating optimistic unfounded rumors and promoting it on TV shows and in hot-tip columns and newspaper stories. Then, as soon as the price reaches a point of satisfactory absurdity, one dumps it, pockets one's profits, and walks off in search of an opportunity to repeat the procedure. Pumping and dumping is vaguely illegal, as is parking in front of a fire hydrant. Needless to say, the jails are not full of such transgressors.

pumping or **portfolio pumping** Sometimes more aptly called "window dressing." By any name, it means attempting by trickery to drive up the value of a mutual fund in time for the next quarterly report. Fund managers carry off this financial optical illusion by dumping large wads of extra cash into the purchase of a stock their fund is already heavily invested in. This move is intended to kick up the price of the stock, thereby making the fund's overall quarterly numbers look better. After a short period, the stock, unable to maintain its new price level, falls back, thus costing the fund money, but by that time new, would-be investors should have been euchred out of their money. Pumping is against the rules, but proving it is difficult because you have to show that the fund manager was larcenous, not simply stupid.

purgatory A place where one must pay, and the emphasis is on the word *pay,* for one's sins before journeying on to taste celestial delights. Purgatory, which did not exist during the first one thousand years of the Christian religion, comes into existence at the time the first merchants gathered in early cities. These same merchants instituted a next-world banking system by which they could pay others to say prayers that would be credited to their post mortem accounts, thus shortening their stays in purgatory. A form of otherworldly money called indulgences was good for lightening purgatory sentences. These indulgences were bought and sold until this form of trade got entirely out of hand and was suppressed. But purgatory is still going strong in certain quarters, and the devil, ever amenable to a good proposition, has been receiving petitions, accompanied by small though suitable presents, from an ever-lengthening line of modern CEOs.

put or **put option** The other side of the seesaw that is put and call options. A call option gives the buyer the right to obtain shares of stock at a set price for a set time, and the put option is the right to sell a stock at a set price for a set time. Getting puts and calls straight drives anyone who isn't a professional crazy. The buyer of the put is gambling—if one is allowed to use that word in connection with the stock exchange—that the stock in question will have dropped in price, so that he can sell it for more than it's worth. For example, Dick pays Jane a dime for the right to sell Jane one share of IBM stock for one dollar at any time before the end of June. IBM goes down to fifty cents a share. Dick buys one share of IBM for half a dollar from somebody else, but Jane has to buy it from Dick for a dollar. Dick's profit is fifty cents minus the dime he paid Jane for the put, or forty cents. Spot hears about this deal and runs like crazy. (See **selling short**.)

Q ratio Businesspeople and their pilot fish, the economists, love ratios (see **P/E ratio,** for instance). They divide some things into other things, in the belief that the answer will provide a critical understanding of the business. The Q ratio is what you get when you add up the value of all of a company's outstanding stock and divide it by what it would cost to replace or buy the company's assets. The guy who thought up the Q ratio, James Tobin, won a Nobel Prize in economics, so it must be hot stuff, although there are some ill-disposed persons who, insisting that economics is more witchcraft than science, have little use for ratios. In truth it takes more than a little long division to get a line on a company's health.

qualified plan One more on the ever-growing list of tax sheltered plans set up by Congress for retirement, education, medical services, home buying, etc. It remains to be seen how much the tens of millions who have money in the plans will get from them, given the brokers' and account managers' fees, the ups and downs of the stock market, and original sin.

quality control Oh, let's free quality from control. Take off the wraps and let quality rip.

Radio Corporation of America (RCA) More than any other entity, this company, now part of General Electric, gave birth to radio and television broadcasting in the United States. RCA had its beginnings with Guillermo Marconi, the inventor of wireless telegraphic transmission. In due course the Marconi patents were pooled with those owned by AT&T and General Electric to form RCA, a company that probably wouldn't have amounted to much had it not been for its office boy, a kid named David Sarnoff (1891– 1971). Sarnoff's is one of those life stories they tell about on patriotic occasions. He came here from Russia at age nine, sold newspapers, sang in the synagogue, and ultimately hooked on with Marconi, teaching himself Morse code and studying electronics at night.

As he worked his way up at RCA, Sarnoff became the prophet of the business and the industry, the one who convinced his superiors that the future lay not with tapping dots and dashes out with a telegrapher's key to the ships at sea but with "broadcasting" voice and music. Sarnoff put RCA in the business of manufacturing radio sets, and it was he who put together the first radio networks and later invested millions in developing television, and then color television. But after the first hugely profitable years, RCA fell behind the competition, partly because Sarnoff was much better at starting things than running them, and partly because in his time it was not yet apparent that with electronics you'll make more money with the software (programming) than with the hardware (making TV sets).

Toward the end of Sarnoff's career, the company began to wobble as it meandered off to buy other companies (rugs and food) that it had no reason to think it could run; then it got into computers, another industry in which RCA was well equipped to lose money. Finally, Sarnoff committed the daddy sin. He put his son in the top job.

With all his flaws, Sarnoff invented this industry. An idealist, he was the guy who put the Metropolitan Opera on the air and brought Arturo Toscanini, the classical music maestro of the era, to NBC and gave him the wherewithal to assemble an orchestra that, it is said, was without peer then and still is now.

rapers and pillagers The extractive industries, coal, oil, metals, and lumber. The archetypal raper-pillager is Frederick Weyerhaeuser (1843–1914), who took it on the lam out of his native Germany to escape conscription and arrived in the American Midwest suffering from a raging entrepreneurial fever. There was a moment when it appeared that Weyerhaeuser would end up owning every tree in North America, so many millions of acres came under his control, along with the lumber and paper mills, the transportation facilities, and the sales organizations. Weyerhaeuser, a chap who could see both the forest and the trees, moved into the Pacific Northwest and bid fair to denude the region. His last words were reported to be, "Cut 'em low, boys, cut 'em low." As he was cutting 'em, he was also replanting at least some of them, and his companies may have been the first to get into reforestation.

In the old man's time, everybody believed the resources would last forever and it was the natural thing to dig, drill, or cut 'em out and move on. Weyerhaeuser was successful because he supplied products people needed and wanted, and they were willing to tolerate devastation to get them. In the twenty-first century, the toleration quotient has shrunk but so has the demand for dead trees, as new materials, recycling, and more efficient manufacturing processes stay the woodsman's ax.

receivables or **accounts receivable** Merchandise or services ordered but not yet paid for by a company's customers. Many and devious are the accounting games played with receivables to rosy up a picture of a firm's financial situation. (See **channel stuffing**.)

recession Six straight months of no growth or worse, according to the number-loving school of economists, though the definition found in an old joke may be more accurate: It's a recession when your neighbor is out of work, and it's a depression when you are. The use of what TV business programs call "the R word" to describe hard times goes back to 1929 and might have been employed because it sounded less ominous than "depression."

There are almost as many words in English for business downturns as the Eskimos have for snow. The mildest is *slowdown,* followed by *slump,* which can lead to *meltdown. Panic* is too frightening, and after the 1930s, *depression* was put back in the warehouse, never to be uttered or thought unless and until the economy hits ten on the Richter scale.

Reconstruction Finance Corporation (RFC) Created in 1932 under President Hoover (see **Hoover, Herbert Clark**), the purpose of the RFC was, in modern parlance, to "bail out" companies on the verge of going under, as the entire nation slid toward the implosion of the banking system and the Great Depression. Alas, the RFC was put under the direction of such conservative businessmen that they never got the bailing operation underway. A pity, since it might have helped. The Corporation was continued under Franklin Roosevelt during the Depression years and World War II, when it was used to provide quick financing for war plants, etc. It was finally killed by the Eisenhower administration, but the precedent of government arranging the injection of capital into businesses whose demise is too painful to contemplate was established.

red herring The slang name for a preliminary draft of a prospectus that carries a red ink disclaimer on its front page, warning that the contents ain't officially approved. Alas, the sobriquets of most documents required by the Securities and Exchange Commission are rather more drab and less memorable.

redlining The practice by banks and insurance companies of refusing to make mortgages and other kinds of loans in minority areas. So called because these no-loan zones were once delineated by red lines on the map. Like everything else that is deprived of capital in a capitalist society, areas thus financially asphyxiated fall to wrack and ruin. It is also against the law.

reputable firm, or, alternately, **old-line firm,** and sometimes even **white-shoe firm** These are holdover terms from an age when there was some—the devil cannot say how much—correlation between companies with such reputations and honesty and competence. Generally speaking, what a company did or was yesterday says nothing about what it is today. Companies can change overnight. Some have been known to make a quick killing on a great reputation by cheapening the product before customers realize it ain't what it used to be. It is said that is what the Maytag company did with its once highly regarded washing machines.

research and development (R&D) In 1875 Charles B. Dudley, a chemist with a PhD from Yale, may have become the first research scientist regularly employed by an American corporation. The English and the Germans had already put scientists, particularly chemists, to work, and their example seems to have gravitated across the Atlantic into the noodles of American businessmen. About the same time as Dudley went to work for the Pennsylvania Railroad, Andrew Carnegie (see **Carnegie, Andrew Morrison**), not one to let the grass grow between his toes, imported Ernst Fricke, a chemist from Germany whose work paid off so quickly for the great steelmaster that old Andy was to say, "What fools we had been! But then there was this consolation, we were not as great fools as our competitors."

R&D in the modern sense was some time in the making. Dudley and Fricke were put to work studying materials used by their respective industries to improve their quality and utility, not to develop new products. Acceptance of full-time laboratories and staff came fitfully to late-nineteenth-century manufacturing executives, who were reluctant to spend money that did not immediately return a profit. Fear that competitors would take out patents that might put them at a disadvantage pushed some companies into research. American Telephone & Telegraph (the Bell System) looked for new, patentable technologies to keep smaller competitors out of the long-distance business. Sometimes the customers or the sales department pushed a company into R&D. After one of its salesmen had sold a textile mill a manufacturing system powered by motors that did not yet exist, General Electric had to invent the equipment.

Scientists also had to be convinced that good work could be done in a commercial laboratory. In 1909 Irving Langmuir (1881–1957) went to work for the General Electric, where fundamental and applied science was combined in one lab for the first time. Not only did Langmuir succeed in making major improvements to the light bulb, he also won the 1932 Nobel Prize in chemistry. He would not be the only Nobel Laureate to come from corporate R&D.

It takes a CEO with a fine touch to know what needs inventing and to have a feel for what is actually inventable. From a broader perspective, the society as a whole is the loser if R&D talent and money are used to reinvent what's already invented for patent protection purposes, a game that pharmaceutical companies are notoriously prone to play.

resources When used without a modifier like *intellectual* or *natural,* it is a finicky substitute word for *money.* For example, "We need more resources to help the spiritually depraved." People who say "resources" because they can't spit out the word "money" are probably after yours. Check your wallet.

restricted stock or **letter stock 1.** Stock you can't buy. Restricted securities are those that have not been registered with the Securities and Exchange Commission and therefore may not legally be offered for sale to the public. Buying and selling restricted stock is a private transaction between two parties who presumably know what they're doing. Registered stock sold to the public at large comes with a prospectus, which is supposed to provide you with the essential information needed before deciding to buy into a company, assuming you can penetrate the non–Indo-European language this document is ordinarily written in. **2.** Stock given employees of a company as part of a pay package which cannot be sold for a given period of time or must be sold back to the company when the employee leaves.

Reuther, Walter Philip (1907–1970) The most influential labor leader of the post–World War II period. As president of the United Automobile Workers, he pioneered contracts with rich health benefits, pensions, vacations, and a guaranteed annual wage. This kind of private-welfare-state contract became the norm in the highly unionized, major manufacturing industries, which, in the United States and other advanced nations, now lack the money to live up to them. At the peak of the Cold War, such labor agreements served to argue that the real "workers' paradise" was in America, not in the Soviet Union, but as Communism fell to pieces, competition, new technologies, and changing demands put a crushingly heavy burden on many companies. In some cases—such as those of a number of airlines and LTV, a big, basic steel manufacturer—the Reuther legacy was one of the final elements putting the company into bankruptcy. Although the Reuther approach has been superceded by changed conditions, business and the nation struggle to find a formula to replace it.

risk Although there is endless palaver in business schools and at award banquets extolling risk takers, business people fear and flee risk. The business equivalent of the fountain of youth is the risk-free deal, and they are few and far between. Even monopolies and cartels, attempts to eliminate risk and therefore guarantee profits, are less than foolproof. The business world is crawling with gimmicks, formulae, and complicated arrangements meant to reduce or eliminate risk, and some are successful up to a point. Past that point, there is always the government, if a company's lobbyists can find the right politicians to buy and keep them bought. A famous case in point is the pharmaceutical industry in the United States, which has been able to put a floor under its prices with government assistance.

road warrior From pre-Revolutionary Yankee peddlers to our own day, business has required some of its people to travel ceaselessly through long and exhausting careers.

With the coming of the railroads, the commercial traveler became a ubiquitous figure who played the part of the traveling salesman from the big city in the farmer's daughter jokes Americans once loved to tell each other. In the era of the Pullman car and the cigar, these knights of the road brought news of changing fashions and big-city ways, as well as goods and services, to a rural majority that has vanished into the realm of folklore. Cheap airline travel may have multiplied the number of road warriors out there playing frequent flier games, but their sense of solidarity and their impact on the society is gone.

robber baron (*antonym,* captain of industry) A term used with more passion than discrimination to mean the boss of any great profit-making enterprise. Its corollary is *labor boss,* a name used by the admirers of captains of industry for any high-ranking union official. The expression *robber baron* may have first been used in this way by Republican Senator Carl Schurz (1829–1906) of Missouri. The name derives from those chaps in the castles on the River Rhine who paid for their fancy digs by extorting money from travelers unlucky enough to fall into their power.

The phrase's enduring use is owing to Matthew Josephson's book by that name, published in 1934 in the depths of the Depression, when businessmen were about as popular as Communists during the Cold War. The book drives today's more probusiness historians up a tree, but, with its flaws, it still has something to say to modern readers.

Robinson-Patman Act Enacted in 1936, the act contained a tangle of provisions aimed at protecting small retailers against chain stores with their lower prices and greater merchandising power. The law was to be administered by the Federal Trade Commission, no simple task, given the impenetrable fuzziness of much of its contents. Robinson-Patman was but one episode in the long, long struggle pitting local interests and community values against the greater efficiency and competitive superiority of national organizations.

Rockefeller, John Davison (1839–1937) The man who put King Midas in the shade. At a time when the average American was earning about ten dollars a week, Rockefeller was a billionaire, although big, big, big wealth is always hard to pin down exactly. In terms of relative worth, he may have been the richest man who ever lived, and in his own lifetime he may have been the most hated. No doubt about it, this boy was a rough customer when it came to slitting competitors' throats, monopoly tactics, and sneaky, sly tricks that make people especially furious.

Whether or not he deserved the obloquy directed at him, John D., in the course of building the Standard Oil (Exxon) empire, was the author of a series of organizational inventions leading not only to the creation of the modern corporation, but also to high-volume, low-cost production, distribution, and merchandising networks unheard of until then. More than a century before the word *multinational* had been coined, Rockefeller had brought into existence an organization that took oil, refined it, and sent it out across America and abroad, to fuel the lamps of the world. It has been said that, thanks to Rockefeller's inexpensive kerosene, for the first time in history human beings could hold back the night.

rollover The term involves the renewal of some kind of financial instrument. It may be a loan or mortgage or a 401(k) plan. Rollovers may or may not be on the same terms as previously.

Rosenwald, Julius (1862–1932) Apparently Rosenwald didn't put much stock in the great talents he displayed during his years at Sears, Roebuck since he destroyed his business papers, leaving only his equally remarkable record as a philanthropist. Rosenwald took over from Richard Sears (1863–1914), the firm's chaotic founding genius, to develop the various systems that made it possible for a retail house to handle theretofore unimaginable volumes of business. There is a straight line between him and Sam Walton (see **Walton, Samuel Moore**) in the never-ending effort to cut distributional costs in retail trade. Rosenwald, beside being an exemplary employer, who eschewed layoffs and pioneered health insurance and profit sharing, was probably the first businessman to build a consumer product testing laboratory, which gave Sears its reputation for tough, quality merchandise. If Rosenwald wasn't the ideal businessperson, he will do until such happens along.

Rouse, James W. (1914–1996) Rouse may or may not be responsible for restaurants with exposed brick walls, but without a doubt he gets the credit or blame for "festival marketplaces," of which the first and most famous is Boston's Faneuil Hall, the ancient, unused, Greek Revival warehouses that he rejuvenated into a colorful retail center drawing in immense crowds. Soon every city was following suit, with places such as Harborplace in

Baltimore and the South Street Seaport in lower Manhattan, two other famous Rouse projects.

A pioneer in the development of suburban closed malls, in the 1960s Rouse built Columbia, Maryland, a planned city of 56,000 people, 20 percent of whom were African-American. (See also **Levitt, William Jaird**.) Rouse had a genius for doing good and making money at the same time. Combining real estate development with what used to be called uplift, Rouse also started the Enterprise Foundation, whose purpose was housing and community organization for poor families. By the time of his death, it had created tens of thousands of new homes.

Rudkin, Margaret Fogarty (1897–1967) After the 1929 market crash, Margaret Rudkin's stock-broker husband incapacitated himself falling off a polo pony and her son came down with an asthmatic allergy for which the doctor prescribed moving the family to Arizona or feeding the child costly, additive-free bread. Broke and marooned on her Connecticut property named Pepperidge Farm, Rudkin opted for baking bread, which she did so well she began selling it to her neighbors. In the money-scarce years of the Great Depression (1930–1940) she was soon selling fifty thousand loaves a week and charging twice the price of ordinary commercial bread. Rudkin was famously finicky about ingredients, even milling her own flour, but her strategy was successful. The Pepperidge Farm brand had created an unassailable niche and a national reputation for pure ingredients and superior taste. Since it had a short shelf life because it contained no preservatives, Rudkin took back the unsold loaves of Pepperidge Farm bread and made them into croutons.

Thus did she and her company prosper until she sold it to Campbell Soup Company who did what so many big companies do when they buy themselves a good thing: they let what was special with the brand go slack until it lost its niche and became just another loaf on the supermarket shelf.

Sallie Mae or **SLM Corporation**   Another government-sponsored enterprise, or GSE. This one, originally called Student Loan Marketing Association, buys student loans from the original lenders and converts them into bonds, which it sells and makes oodles of money. GSEs drive the competition wild because of their unique privileges and immunities from taxes and certain kinds of regulation. Defenders say they are providing a unique and necessary service; critics reply that GSEs are constantly moving into areas of business that are far beyond their charters and, because they make so much money, are nice warm and dry places for relatives and friends of lawmakers and other officials who protect GSEs. The devil says that he doesn't believe that people in high places would stoop to forcing anybody to play favorites. Ah, the tongues of malice, what wouldn't they say?

sanitary napkin A nice example of the interactions between business and social change. This is a product that enables women to move from place to place outside the home more easily and comfortably than was possible when they had to fashion napkins out of fabric scraps or birdseye, a material also used for diapers. It was hardly coincidental that, shortly after women began to be a familiar sight in offices in the mid-1880s, the Montgomery Ward catalog began offering sanitary napkins. In 1920, as women got the vote and assumed an ever-growing number of positions in the workplace, Kimberly-Clark commenced marketing Kotex. By the mid-1930s tampon products had arrived, and sanitary napkins had moved from being a dainty and pricey product for middle- and upper-class women to a necessity for women of all classes.

With all its convenience, it is a major disposable, non-reusable product making its contribution to the society's waste problem.

Sarbanes-Oxley Act (SOX) A law that makes top executives of companies criminally liable for putting out false information, prohibits board members and officers from lending company money to themselves, bans various kinds of conflicts of interest, requires new kinds of financial information to be made public, and brings into existence something called the Public Company Accounting Oversight Board. Considered the largest extension of government supervision of corporations whose stock is sold to the public since the creation of the Securities and Exchange Commission in 1934, SOX resulted from the seismic collapses of famous names like Enron, Worldcom, and Arthur Andersen. It is said that these are the largest and most earth-shattering scandals in American corporate history but, while indubitably extremely naughty, that is the way the most recent scandal is always described. The usefulness of SOX will be debated for a long time. It's true the law had to catch up with modern times, but sooner or later, every lock gets picked.

Section 7a Also called Labor's Magna Carta, section 7a of the National Industrial Recovery Act of 1933 gave working people the right to organize themselves into unions. Under Federal protection, union membership leapt upward in the 1930s, opening up the role organized labor would play for much of the rest of the century.

Securities and Exchange Commission (SEC) It is worthy of note that the first federal government office of consumer product safety was set up in 1934, in reaction to the 1929 stock market debacle, for the benefit of purchasers of stocks and bonds. Protection against dangerous or fraudulent merchandise such as automobiles or children's pajamas came into effect several generations later. The SEC lays down the rules under which securities are publicly bought and sold. Violation of the rules can, it is written in some dusty old book, result in the rule breaker spending time in the hoosegow, but this rarely happens, and when it does it doesn't happen to the people who run the big outfits. When the big stock market people are reined in, they are customarily given small, tax-deductible fines and asked to sign what are called "consent decrees" promising not to do whatever naughty thing it is that they have done, while stating that they're not saying they ever did it in the first place.

Whether the SEC offers effective protection to consumers or makes them easier to gull because they rely on government protection that isn't actually there is a matter of conjecture. The energy and dedication with which the SEC pursues slimeballs, slickheads, and swindlers ebbs and flows, depending on who controls the White House and Congress and therefore the money and authority the Commission has to work with.

The red hots of the right believe that any grant of power to the SEC is an unnatural government intervention in the private sphere, which is dangerous bosh. Since Roman times, if not before, one of the paramount duties of government has been to ensure honest markets, whether that means accurate weights, unadulterated merchandise, or reliably described securities. Free markets cannot exist without policing.

securitization The conversion of ownership of any kind of property, from a parking slot to a three-hundred-passenger airliner, into some of form of bond or stock that may then be sold to the public. The opportunities for naughty games by betraying investors' confidence ought to take a swindler's breath away, but, when legitimately handled, which is most of the time, it's both profitable and an excellent way of spreading risk so that when things do go awry the resultant losses aren't too big for any one institution or person to bear. (See **asset-backed security**.)

self-dealing The act of feathering your own nest by using your position in a company to make a loan or contract in which you are the major beneficiary. Bankers are famous for self-dealing, typically by lending money to companies in which they themselves own a significant chunk of the stock. This is a jailable offense, but many business crimes are situational. What is plainly dishonest at one time may be above criticism at another. Bankers before the Civil War commonly self-dealt, but banks then were not a business where anyone might walk in and open an account. Banks of that era drew their money from a small circle of entrepreneurs, who made loans within the circle and not to strangers with unknown credit histories. As banks changed from being mutual assistance societies for raising venture capital to being public institutions, self-dealing fell from being the raison d'être of the institution to becoming a crime.

self-improvement An American trait dating back to the earliest days and owing its existence, at least in part, to the problematic availability of decent schooling. From the 1850s onward, courses and training programs came into existence to teach specific business skills, but it was in the twentieth century that businesspeople were told success lay in remaking the inner person to bring forth a new outer person. For the price of a book or a seminar, an injection of transformative, motivational pep would vouchsafe wealth and a perch atop the power pyramid.

In 1936 Dale Carnegie (1886–1956) published *How to Win Friends and Influence People,* and soon thereafter came Dale Carnegie schools, lectures, and newspaper columns, as his gospel of enthusiasm took root. A year after Carnegie's great success, Napoleon Hill (1883–1970) hit it big with the publication of his *Think and Grow Rich!* thanks to a sale of twenty million copies to as many hopeful businesspeople.

The self-improvement industry goes merrily along to

this day, as a cavalcade of athletic coaches, crackpots, generals, psychologists, mountebanks, and unemployed cardsharps give businesspeople the oomph needed to take risks, to persevere, and to find the extra ounce of energy and determination that can lift a person from the ranks of the ordinary. Most of this stuff is intellectually disreputable and not far removed from rubbing amulets for luck, but I've also seen doctors of philosophy knock on wood to ward off evil.

self-made man Parthenogenesis is unknown in vertebrate biology and business. Regardless of how many great men may seem to be striding through boardroom and legend doing solo acts, it is rarely so, but the belief that you are captain of your fate has been an enduring motivator for businesspeople. The idea that a man or a woman who has the moxie can make it on his or her own is exceedingly helpful, both for individuals and business in general. Much work in business is tedious, difficult, mind numbing, and, if you step back a pace or two, pretty stupid, but it needs doing by enthusiastic people. Moreover the rewards are often problematic and distant, so the faith that drive and gumption will be rewarded with the golden banana is indispensable for creating a bright-eyed and bushy-tailed staff.

Legendary examples of self-made men abound. (Fairy stories about self-made women are harder to come by.) An earlier era swore by Andrew Carnegie (see **Carnegie, Andrew Morrison**) as this one does by Steven Jobs of Apple Computer. Carnegie, a man of immense business gifts, force, and focus, was the beneficiary of members of his ethnic group, the Scots, who gave him the breaks even the most talented need. The myth of the computer genius doing it on his own in the family garage is personified by Jobs, who is, perhaps, a genius—but in merchandising, not in computers. The credit for the technical side of the Apple goes to another man, Stephen Wozniak. (See **Alger, Horatio, Jr.**)

self-regulation Reliance on scout's honor in place of government supervision of businesses for safety and honesty. Although noninterference is derided by nature's pessimists as absurdly Panglossian, experience has shown that businesspeople will almost always put the interest and the good of others ahead of their own. To entice them along the path of virtue, executives are recipients of numerous annual awards extolling them for refraining from poisoning their communities, cheating their customers, or stealing from their stockholders.

self-service You have Clarence Saunders to thank for self- or no-service shopping. Saunders opened the first self-service retail establishment, a Piggly Wiggly store, in Memphis, Tennessee, in 1916. Self-service retail saved labor costs and freed the management from such things as home delivery and credit, but for the system to work on a grand scale other elements were needed. Somebody had to invent the shopping cart and the bar code. The buying public had to accept a no-haggle, single-price policy, and, since there were no clerks to answer questions, the customers had to know exactly what they wanted before they walked into the store, a problem solved by national advertising and brand recognition loyalty. Self-service didn't begin to pick up a full head of steam until the 1930s, when large stores with big, adjacent parking lots commenced popping up in the suburbs.

selling short   People who engage in short selling are not held in good odor; they borrow stock and sell it high, expecting it to drop low, so they can buy it back and replace it at the cheaper price, thereby making a profit. Of course, if the stock goes up, they have screwed themselves, a cause for smirks on and off the trading floor inasmuch as the short seller is looked on as a killjoy and a spoilsport, a person who gains from others' losses and lacks that faith in the market's inevitable rise that gives business its ever-persevering oomph.

SEMATECH   A not-for-profit research consortium whose cacophonic name is derived from Semiconductor-Manufacturing-Technology. In the mid-1980s, the government and the American electronics industry went into a panic fugue as they saw the domestic chip industry lose out to Japan. To reverse the direction of things, the antitrust laws were put in cold storage and, under federal government money and orchestrations, competitors such as Agere, Advanced Micro Devices, Hewlett-Packard, IBM, Infineon, Intel, Motorola, Philips, and Texas Instruments combined to develop manufacturing techniques and superior products designed to reclaim American preeminence. To the stupefaction of skeptics, it worked. Whether something like that could be done again twenty-five years later is questionable, since, in the meantime, these industries have so internationalized themselves you'd be hard-pressed to say what is American, or Japanese, or Dutch, or Taiwanese, or British.

SEMATECH goes to show how infinitely varied are the ways government subsidizes private enterprise, from outright cash grants, to tax breaks, to cheap electric rates, to building ballparks for professional baseball teams. No compilation of all the subsidies exists, and no one can say what their effects are—which are simply corrupt gifts, which create and/or hold jobs, and which encourage inefficiency, high costs, and low productivity. What's known for sure is that everyone is against every subsidy except the one they're getting.

service economy A good idea.

share or **share of stock** A portion of ownership in a company. Share owners are entitled to dividends when and if the management decides to bestow them on those who are, very theoretically, their employers. However, in our era, paying dividends has gone out of fashion. Today people buy and hold stock not primarily for income, but in hopes that its price will go up and they can sell it at a profit. That sounds good and is good if the shareholder actually sells when the stock goes up. Many hold on, however, believing it will go up higher. Then it goes down.

Modern shareholders also have to put up with having their shares devalued when management prints gigantic amounts of new stock (see **diluted shares**), issues stock options, or pays out too much to buy other companies.

Should the company in which you own stock founder on the rock piles of finance, be prepared for a wipeout. In bankruptcy and consequent reorganization proceedings, stockholders often suffer monumental dilution or complete cancellation of their stocks as the company's creditors and their bankruptcy lawyers move in and take over ownership of anything and everything of value. (See also **corporate governance**.)

short interest A term of art employed by the pros on the stock exchange floor, who wear gray jackets and look as though they smoke cigars. The short interest is the total number of bets made that a given stock or stocks will go down in price. Although it may seem like un-American pessimism, you can make money betting that the price of a stock will decline. A high short-interest number is considered a harbinger by some that a stock that is presently taking a nosedive will soon go up. And sometimes they're right.

show business The term *show business* was probably coined by P. T. Barnum (1810–1891) who, if he didn't invent the industry, did perfect the hype that creates celebrities and launches theatrical events. Barnum established the line in business that divides honest misrepresentation, disarming bunkum, and the entertaining deceptions of the medicine show from the kind of dishonesty that invites necktie parties and other manifestations of customer dissatisfaction.

Siegel, Benjamin (Bugsy) (1905–1947) Real estate developer. Though he wasn't the first businessman to build a hotel-casino in Las Vegas, when Siegel began work on the Flamingo in 1946, he was creating the first of the non–dude ranch, glamour hotels swarming with gaudy luxury, Hollywood stars, and the other elements that have made Las Vegas a flashing light in the world tourist atlas. The financing of the Flamingo was provided by racketeers such as Meyer Lansky, Lucky Luciano, Santo Trafficante, and Moe Dalitz. Additional investors apparently included general contractor and New York

Yankee baseball team owner Del Webb and elements of the Mormon Church.

In the shortage-plagued period that followed the Second World War, Siegel showed himself to be an effective executive who could get the job done by lassoing critical materials and labor. Money for the project was sometimes brought in cash in suitcases from the East by Dandy Phil Kastel, an employee of the storied political fixer Frank Costello. The project was wildly over budget, there were strong suspicions that money was being skimmed into a Swiss bank account, and the investors, despairing of getting their money back and not wishing to call upon the uncertain justice of Nevada's law courts for an accounting, resorted to a method of dealing with wayward associates not studied in business school. They had Siegel murdered.

The manner of Siegel's passing does not diminish his stature as a major figure in American real estate, nor should his business connections with gangsters and religious organizations cloud over our appreciation of a businessman who, for practical purposes, founded a city that has astonished the imagination of the world and produced riches rivaling all the precious metals discovered in the mountains of Nevada.

Silicon Valley Before it was the electronic Golconda, it was the Santa Clara Valley southeast of San Francisco. Silicon Valley was founded in 1956 by William B. Shockley (1910–1989), when he leased a converted Quonset hut and tacked up a sign announcing the existence of the Shockley Semiconductor Laboratory. Shockley, after sharing a Nobel Prize with two other men for the invention of the transistor, had left his job at AT&T to strike out on his own. Though his own company fell to pieces thanks to his abominable people skills and don't-bother-me tunnel vision, it was Shockley who chose the place and brought in the people who made the name Silicon Valley synonymous with the technology that changed the way the world does business.

single-price policy In the middle years of the last century, a certain stripe of Americans knew their country was superior to all others because foreigners haggled over price while gesticulating with their hands. In an American shop, the price was written plainly on a tag, or at least it was after 1846, when the single, we-don't-bargain-we-don't haggle price was introduced by Alexander Stewart, the proprietor of New York's largest and most fashionable dry goods store. Other department stores followed suit, not because they were out to screw the customers, but because clerks, in order to bargain, would need to know a lot about the merchandise and the business and have the ability to size up the customer. Getting help is one thing, getting good help is another. "They are simply machines working in a system that determines all their actions," the proprietor remarked of his clerks.

For the haggled price to return, another means of selling had to be devised, and it was. The coming of the Internet lets unlucky customers pit their negotiating skills not against a stupid clerk but a smart computer program.

sinister doings For much of the last half-century, a small but energetic body of opinion has had it that powerful and hugely rich persons have been weaving a plot to take over and run the world. Many years ago the conspirators were called "the Bilderbergers," so named because they were said to have first met in a Dutch town of that name; next, in the 1970s, the plot centered around the Trilateral Commission, and lately it is reported to have moved on to Davos, Switzerland, where the mighty of the world annually congregate to asphyxiate themselves in speeches redolent with whatever is the generally accepted wisdom of the moment. The Bilderbergers, the Trilateralists, and Davosians are more or less guilty of fostering an antipatriotic cosmopolitanism that hopes to see one system of commercial laws and other business arrangements imposed around the globe, to the humiliation of the Stars and Stripes.

sinking fund Money put aside by a company or governmental entity for the exclusive purpose of repaying a debt. It is a no-no to raid the sinking fund, but the discussion is academic since most corporate entities can't stand the thought of putting cash into an account they may not get their hands on. Thus sinking funds, while not nonexistent, are in the rara avis category.

Slater, Samuel (1768–1835) A man whom modern Americans might describe as an intellectual property thief. In violation of British law, Slater brought the secrets of the then new textile technology to the United States. Encouraged in his illegal activities by several American states, which put ads in the British press offering money to anyone illegally smuggling the know-how of power looms and spinning out of Great Britain, Slater memorized the information that he would use to fire the opening shot of the Industrial Revolution in

America. He arrived in this country in 1789 and, within a few years, had the nation's first factories up and running. Factories, prior to Slater, did not exist, nor did the modern concept of a job. At first, Slater hired entire families, which proved to be neither convenient nor practical. He abandoned that practice in favor of hiring young women, who were housed in closely supervised dorms. The breaking down of what we call the traditional family by a nascent business culture had begun. (See also **breakfast**.)

slavery For business purposes, which are only intermittently coextensive with morals, slavery is labor obtained at below the market rate, which should give the slave owner an advantage over competitors employing free laborers. The slave advantage ought to have generated profits that could have been invested in new plant and equipment, but it rarely worked that way, and such extra profits as the South might have had from its cheap slave labor, it appears to have wasted on high living. Cheap labor became a disincentive to invest, while the more expensive and difficult to control labor in the free states was a spur to replace people with machines.

Slavery continued in slightly disguised form after the Emancipation Proclamation, through leasing convict labor to businesses, the best-known example of which is U.S. Steel's using slaves in its Alabama mining subsidiary. This form of involuntary servitude was finally abolished in 1928. No actions in court have been taken against the companies that profited from post–Civil War slavery, but, if German companies using slave labor in the Nazi period are liable for back pay and damages, there is an argument for the same to apply to American companies.

Sloan, Alfred Pritchard, Jr. (1875–1966) The archetypal business executive, his portrait in oils seems to hang in the boardroom of every well-run corporation. Sloan, as much as it can be said of any single individual, is the businessman who built General Motors into the largest, most profitable, and most prolific manufacturing corporation there has ever been. At the apogee of the age of heavy industry, there was Sloan's General Motors with its thousands of products ranging from refrigerators to diesel locomotives, its hundreds of thousands of employees, and its millions of customers around the globe.

Sloan is not remembered as a leader or a man of vision or any of that crap, but as the pluperfect manager, a deviser of systems, an extraordinary planner, and the perfecter of organizations. As such, Sloan and his works are still closely studied, although the General Motors of his day is an anachronism now. His memory is cursed by all those who hate "Detroit" and what it has stood for, practices such as the annual model change. Sloan answered that as the models changed, the cars got better and better, which they did. As to the noxious side effects, Sloan had the tunnel vision inseparable from business success: There's only so much one man can do. Smog was not his problem.

small business A type of enterprise everyone is in favor of and nobody can adequately define. It has been delineated by the number of employees, by type of ownership— mom and pop, and family farm being the most favored—by whether or not it's dominant in its industry, and by smell, feel, sentimentality, and the number of votes to be cadged from it. Small business is patriotically American, a generator of new jobs, and a veritable furnace of creativity and individuality. Flag waving aside, there is a modicum of truth to such propositions, although it is not true that small business, by virtue of being less bureaucratic, is more flexible and quicker to react to changing conditions. Small businesses go under at a frightening rate, and one of the reasons is their inability to adapt to new ways and conditions, just like creaking old giants such as the defunct International Harvester or Polaroid. While failure to compete successfully against the behemoths has dropped many a little guy, many others make their livings by selling specialty items or providing specialty services to big businesses. Moreover, from some acorns more than a few big businesses have grown: Boeing, IBM, Microsoft, Dupont, and Procter & Gamble are corporate names that began small.

Until the 1880s almost every enterprise was small. The first hue and cry for saving small business revolved around rescuing the independent retailer from chain stores and mail-order houses (see **catalogue merchandising,** along with the **Robinson-Patman Act**). Protected or not, a huge number of small businesses are to be found, and, whether their return on capital would please a Wall Streeter or not, the small enterprise is not about to go away.

Small Business Administration Dwight Eisenhower signed the legislation creating this organ of government in order to help small business, ostensibly the nation's largest source of new jobs. Since "small business" is whatever you care to make it out to be, all claims of this sort are easily proven and just as easily refuted.

What's certain is that its fifty years of existence have been of little or no help to business of whatever size. Its history is of unending scandal, which has seen administrators, Congressmen, and businessmen sent to jail. Nevertheless its appropriations have grown, decade after decade, as African-American, Hispanic, and feminist groups, not to mention ordinary banks and other businesses, have found ways to carry off cash and other trinkets from the SBA to their respective lairs.

Although often in the past two-plus centuries, government has been of inestimable help to business and private enterprise, direct grants and loan guarantees to private entities invite corrupt outcomes. This is as true today as it was with the Lincoln administration's subsidies to the railroads. The best or at least the most prudent loans are made by people lending their own money.

small-cap Not the American translation for petit chapeau, but the short name for small-capitalization business—a business worth $500 million or less. Below small caps are microcaps. They are not mushrooms but companies worth less than $50 million. Needless to say, there are medium- and large-cap companies, whose worth is up in the billions.

social responsibility A term of uncertain meaning, intermittently used by ministers of religion, editorialists, malcontents, political dyspeptics, and ethicists. Companies said to be acting with social responsibility are praised, and those acting in a socially irresponsible way are severely tut-tutted. Although corporations are persons (*personae fictae*) enjoying the same rights as you and me under the law, they are not people, and hence they do not have a conscience or a moral code. The people running them may or may not have consciences, but it is of little matter.

soft landing Getting off a boom without the country going into a bust. It is a fixed item of belief for those who hold that volcanic eruptions and earthquakes are controllable that the economist wonks in the government are able to bring off pleasant, soft landings. Let's hope they can, but you might not want to do away with your seat belts quite yet.

software Invisible algorithms on a CD or buried in a computer or floating in electronic space on an Internet server, software programs often cost huge sums to invent and perfect. These up-front capital costs are not unlike those of an electrical generating company, which also must spend millions on an electric plant before it sees a dime in revenue. The difference is that with electricity it costs millions more to distribute it. Software, once it's found its buying public, costs next to nothing or nothing. Nevertheless, software companies charge a pretty penny to recoup their costs and—Hark! A blast of brass in the background!—make a profit.

sophisticated Variously, a word for a person who prefers martinis without vermouth and dances like Fred Astaire or Ginger Rogers, or a fancy-pants word meaning "complicated," used by people who wish to convey the impression that they understand that which they probably don't.

sound *(adjective)* The all-purpose business comfort word derived from the Middle English word for healthy and used ad nauseam in such phrases as "a sound company," "a sound investment," or "the economy is fundamentally sound." When you hear the last one, head for the hills.

spam (not Spam) When capitalized, the word refers to a form of human alimentation composed of the Devil knows not what ingredients. Uncapitalized spam is a free knowledge distribution service via the Internet, offering recipients opportunities to get in on the ground floor of new businesses and procure pictures of unclad persons doing the most unusual and entertaining things with various organs and orifices. The word *spam,* in this use, is supposed to derive from a Monty Python episode that takes place in a restaurant where capital S Spam is served to the patrons regardless of what they order.

special-purpose entity or vehicle A term briefly in vogue during the famous Enron scandal of 2002. The entities in question were quasi-secret, complicated partnerships designed to hide the company's debts. SPEs had the added advantage of unethically and possibly illegally enriching officers of the corporation. While there is no limit to human ingenuity, the discovery of the existence and size of the special-purpose entities made the hearts of some of Wall Street's most accomplished varlets skip a beat.

specialist Wall Street lingo meaning a member of the stock exchange who makes sure that the prices of the stock or stocks he specializes in do not jump up and down wildly. (See also **market maker**.) The specialists' operations are necessary to maintaining an "orderly" market, the desirability of which is an anal fixation of the securities industry. Prices are supposed to flow—downward if necessary, upward if at all possible—but flow, not leap, hop, or jump. From time to time, specialists are accused of hanky-panky, that is, manipulating the price of stocks to their advantage, but since it has been established beyond doubt that members of a reputable stock exchange live on an ethical plane otherwise attained only by licensed ministers of religion, such accusations are manifestly false. It is also maintained that a computer can do a specialist's work faster and more honestly but, as the world has come to know, computers are only as honest as the people who program them.

statistical quality control There are those moments, no matter how brief and how rare, when it does appear that the world may have become a slightly better place. Those moments sometimes occur when you buy something that not only works, but continues to work. For this you have statistical quality control to thank, at least in part. It is a method of statistical analysis that tells management if the defective items coming off the production line are rare deviations from a perfect norm or the sign that something is wrong in the design, the material, or the production process, and therefore improvable.

stock certificate Gorgeous pieces of paper on which were engraved such scenes as water nymphs cavorting, steam engines, mighty oceans, gold miners with pickaxes, or the St. Louis skyline as it appeared in 1913, made to testify to a named person's ownership of a specific number of shares in a company. If the company went bankrupt, the owner at least had the pleasure of framing the certificates. Alas! With billions of shares of stock trading every day, the old-time certificates have all but been retired to nostalgia-land.

stock option The chance to buy a given number of shares of stock at a fixed price at a time of one's own choosing. If the stock doesn't go up in price, you don't exercise your option; if it does, you clean up. Profit without risk, but not without its critics.

Stockholders complain that the promiscuous use of options diminishes their ownership share of the company, as thousands of new shares may be created when and if the options are exercised.

In the last quarter of the twentieth century, paying a chunk of executives' salaries via stock options became a famous method of compensation. The danger to the enterprise is that CEOs, hungry to cash in, have been known to do shortsighted things in order to whip up the company's stock. And since stock options are not carried on the books as a cost of labor, a company ladling them out like handouts in a soup line can make itself look more profitable than it is, until the options are exercised. How much a company potentially owes through unexercised stock options may only be apparent to someone going through the back of the annual report with a jeweler's loupe.

stock split Taking back a share of stock from its owner and replacing it with two or more shares, i.e., splitting the stock. If it's a two-for-one split, each share will be worth half of what it had been worth, but there will be more of them. Companies split their stock when they believe the price per share is too high and is scaring off would-be buyers. It can also go the other way with a reverse split, in which case a company might exchange four or five shares for one share, thus raising the price per share. Since shares selling at too low a price are considered just a tad mezza-mezza, the purpose of this maneuver is to get the price per share up into a respectable price range appropriate for a non–fly-by-night corporation. (See **penny stock**.)

subprime or **nonprime,** also called **B or C loans** Names for higher interest rates for people and businesses with less than prime financial balance sheets.

Some subprime-rate loans are so very subprime that they are called predatory loans by defenders of the poor, the aged, the innocent, and the stupid. These subprimes, which are often mortgage loans, are loaded with financial land mines, like extra fees and expensive insurance policies protecting the lender. Predatory loans may be of short duration and may come with a balloon payment, thus forcing the home buyer to refinance at unnecessary expense.

The defenders of the financially flimflammed have been agitating for years for protective legislation, and, while there is no doubt that many of their wards have been egregiously hornswoggled, often with heartbreaking consequences, new laws have been hard coming since some of the nastiest subprimes are wholly owned subsidiaries of large and respectable financial institutions, folks who have a magic way with legislators. A second problem is that which adheres to much protective legislation: how to draft it so the law doesn't make it more difficult and more expensive for poor people to get loans.

summit A meeting of two or more pompous, powerful persons. Not yet in our vocabulary is the verb *to summit,* but just you wait till you hear someone say, "We summited together last night and the earth moved."

supply-side As in "supply-side economics," the doctrine that the lower the taxes, the greater the general prosperity. The doctrine's advocates aren't nihilists, so they don't espouse doing away with taxes, but they believe that low taxes, a subjective concept if there ever was one, are optimal taxes. Supply-siders especially deplore capital gains taxes and government regulations, believing as they do that managers and investors know best. Supply-siding was given a try during the Reagan administration, when taxes were cut with splendid enthusiasm, but they're still screaming at each other over whether or not supply-sidism had the desired effects. Since these kinds of doctrines can't be tried out in vitro, with no other intervening conditions messing up the experiment, it is impossible to prove their validity in anything like a scientific sense. There are no absolutes, but there certainly are times and circumstances when even a jackass can see that tax cuts and deregulation would be helpful. But anyone who believes you can run a society on the basis of any one-cylinder theory is, if not a jackass, a zebra.

swap and (are you ready for it?) **swaption** If you don't know what a swap is, you're better off. Anything by way of a security or currency can and is swapped, although bonds and currency appear to be swapped the most often. This is tricky stuff whereby one entity exchanges a bond with a particular interest rate and/or other features with another entity whose bonds have other features. All of this is done for arcane but legitimate motives and sometimes for nefarious reasons, such as trying to foil the tax collector.

A swaption, if you can stand it, is buying the right to make a particular swap within a given period of time.

synergy The word comes from an incomprehensible theological proposition having to do with human will and divine grace working together. Applied to business, it refers to a miraculous action that makes the total value of a company greater than its corporate parts. The word is often invoked by executives defending corporate mergers that defraud the stockholders and lack any rationale other than enrichment of top management, their lawyers, consultants, and investment bankers. Whenever the word is used, you may be sure the speaker is either a knave or one of those human water bubblers who know not whereof they speak.

System/360 In April 1964, IBM announced the introduction of its group of System/360 computers, which changed the electronic business in ways that would endure for the rest of the century and beyond. The company had bet the farm on System/360, so named because the 360 computers could handle the full circle of computer needs, from science to the military to commerce. Had the System/360s tanked, IBM would have fallen back to being just another large company; however, the line was such a success the company has remained the nation's premier electronic corporation to this day.

So successful was the 360, it spawned other industries and companies. These computers could talk to each other (see **compatibility**) and could handle programs then running on older machines. This led in short order to the separation of the hardware manufacturing business from the writing and selling of software (see **Gates, William Henry**), except in rare instances like IBM, which has continued to do both.

systems management The pharaohs built the pyramids with a couple of architects, a bunch of plantation foremen with cat-o'-nine-tails, and a huge army of mostly naked guys doing exactly what they were told. Doubtless there are businesspeople today who'd like to run projects the same way, but it can't be. No single company can handle a major project today in-house. The greatest of the self-contained corporations was General Motors at its zenith (see **Sloan, Alfred Pritchard**), but that era is long gone. Big projects in our era, such as the space station or Boston's central artery, require dozens of companies and technologies in webs of complexity that we who don't do it can't understand. Those who do it are modern systems managers, and you can be sure they don't succeed by using bullwhips.

target price The price the analyst, broker, or financial adviser expects a stock to reach. The use of the word *target* makes the suckers think of bows and arrows, aiming well, and hitting the bull's-eye. But the term should be considered more of a prayer than a factor in making a sane business decision.

Taylorism or **scientific management** The brainchild of Frederick Winslow Taylor (1856–1915), the world's first efficiency expert, who invented time-motion and its worker-hated intrusiveness. Both he and his vocation seem to have pissed off most of the people he came in contact with. Nevertheless, he was a gifted engineer who possessed a vast practical knowledge of the complexities of machine-shop work. He patented a number of significant inventions in the field, but his lasting contribution was the systematic study of the relationships among worker, tools, material, and the task being performed. Factory workers had him to thank for such things as the despised "speed-up," and all sorts of clever pay schemes designed to get more work out of the people in the shop for less money. He also deserves much of the credit or, if you like, the blame, for laying the foundations for the assembly-line manufacture so brilliantly exploited by Henry Ford (see **Ford, Henry I**).

technology transfer It is an American conceit to believe that it cooked up the technological parts of the business civilization all by itself. From the first industrial establishments (see **Slater, Samuel**) to the development of the computer, the United States has borrowed technologies from other nations, particularly the United Kingdom.

Since it dawned on the dunces who run national governments that technology, in the right hands, produces more wealth than all the gold in all the mines in the world, they have sought to keep technical knowledge locked up within their own borders. In the late eighteenth and early nineteenth centuries, the British, who were far ahead of everybody else, went so far as to forbid men who had such knowledge from leaving their island. Modern American officials are hysterical on the subject, although history teaches that it is all but impossible to keep this kind of knowledge out of the hands of people who want it. Trade, spies, professional journals, and international scientific conferences make keeping secrets very hard. The mere knowledge that people in one country have figured out how to do something may be all people in another country need to dope out the technology themselves.

The existence of advanced technical ideas and inventions, in and of itself, may mean little. Leonardo da Vinci filled his notebooks with ideas for which no supporting technology existed. Thomas Watts's (1736–1819) steam engine, which made railroads and a thousand other things possible, could not have worked without the precision pistons bored by the great ironmonger John Wilkinson (1728–1808).

Sometimes technology needs to move to another nation to be perfected. The modern rocket was invented and ignored in the United States, as was the jet engine in Great Britain. It took the Germans to develop both technologies, which were then transferred back to the United States at the end of the Second World War.

temps, tempos, or **temporary workers** The figure of the itinerant worker was a familiar one from the earliest times, and never more so than now. Once upon a time temporary work was what you got until you could find something "more permanent," but no occupation is entirely permanent. From migratory farmworkers to the hoards of adjunct college professors, millions are effectively on their own, left to make whatever arrangements they can for health insurance, retirement, and vacation time.

the customer is always right A phrase written in the runic alphabet chiseled on a stone found outside of Bird of Peace, Pennsylvania. The carving dates from the eighth century, but modern archeology is not yet able to explain its meaning.

the market As in ejaculations such as "The market was telling investors today that. . . ." and "The Market gave a big thumbs-up today to. . . ." The stock market, treated as a living, breathing sentient being with a very sensitive nervous system and irritable bowel syndrome.

the simple life The simple life, a green existence of a few possessions, wholesome food, and a garden on the inconspicuous edge of the business society, is a luxury available only to the comfortably situated.

thinking outside the box An expression used by biz idiots incapable of thinking in the box, out of the box, over the box, or under the box. Anyone who'd say that doesn't know where the box is or what's in it.

thinly traded A thinly traded stock or bond is only bought or sold from time to time. Some securities are seldom traded because they are dogs, but usually the term is applied to securities that are perfectly fine or even very good but which are few in number. A truly liquid market requires a huge volume of shares being offered for sale.

ticket scalper One who has the temerity to buy tickets to shows or airlines or anything else and resell them at a profit. Buying low and selling high has earned many a man an invitation to dine and an ambassadorship to Fiji or the Court of St. James, but not if the trader is trafficking in tickets. Tickets, for reasons I have never seen explained, are to be sold and resold at the price printed on them, unless—this may be a clue—the seller is a licensed ticket agent. The system has zero social utility but doubtless yields respectable profits to the agents and the politicians into whose hands the agents place their bribes for being granted their agencies.

time On Sunday, November 18th, 1883, the railroads of the United States reset their clocks to conform to the standardized time zones we are familiar with today. Previously, freight and passenger trains had been running on schedules figured in no less than forty-nine different times. Not too long before, every village and hamlet could and often did have its own time, but in a prebusiness age, only soldiers and mariners had need of horological conformity and exact precision. Time as we understand it did not exist. Even the expression "on time" seems to have come into existence at the dawn of the railroad age. The business society aborning in the nineteenth century depended on punctuality. Getting there early was not the same as being at your workbench at seven sharp.

In Shakespeare the characters ask each other what hour it is, but in the business society, we must know to the minute. By the 1870s it was possible to keep wall clocks accurate to the minute by sending them signals through the telegraph system, and for a while supplying this service provided astronomical observatories with a little side money. That was fine for offices, but self-employed workers needed their own timepieces, and these Eli Terry (1772–1852) set out to provide when he undertook to mass-produce clocks with wooden works. An apprentice of Terry's subsequently was able to make brass clocks, but what was really needed was an inexpensive watch, so the members of the business society could take their time with them. Only after the costly perfection of precision machine tools was the Waltham Watch Company able to provide such a watch. By the mid-1860s they were making pocket watches by the hundred thousand, and then the Ingersoll company came out with the dollar watch, and timepieces, once so rare and dear that only the rich could have them, were being sold by the million.

tombstone or **tombstone ad** The name for a newspaper ad announcing a new issue of stock. The names of the companies with the biggest stake in the underwriting are in the largest type, and the smallest are at the bottom in the smallest type, making the ad look like a tombstone. The ads are impressively dignified, giving off the suggestion that they are the work of frock-coated gentlemen of stern probity. Alas, some of the old boys are not.

too big to fail The belief that some companies are so large that they must not be allowed to go under, regardless of how stupid their management, how few their customers, how huge their debts, how larcenous their executives, and how inefficient or obsolete they've become. Railroads, banks, airlines, steel companies, and the stock market have all been designated as too big to let go of, at one time or another. Occasionally a persuasive case can be made for too big to fail, but the old Soviet Union and pre-Thatcher England demonstrated that too many too bigs, and the whole goddamn country can turn its belly toward the sky and cease to move its little gills.

toxic waste Wall Street being waggish again, ladies. This playful term applies to securities backed by the riskiest of junk bonds. Although Michael Milken, the jailed bond speculator, was able to show that many low-rated or non-investment-grade bonds were in fact a good deal, some are just as bad as they smell.

tracking stock (See also **classified stock**.) A share of tracking stock is a share of nothing. In theory it tracks the company issuing it, but when you buy it you don't get an ownership share of the company. You only get a dividend, if there is a dividend to get, and often there isn't one. Tracking stock is sometimes called "alphabet stock" because it's denoted in the stock tables by a letter in parentheses to distinguish it from the company's ordinary stock. If none of this makes sense, please remember Hoffman's Law #2: The greater the complexity, the greater the profit. Not for you, dear reader, but for the dealers.

trade associations Although they've been around forever and number in the thousands, trade associations are next to invisible. Organizations whose memberships consist of companies in the same line of business, they are either vital contributors to an industry's common good or a conspiracy in restraint of trade, depending on where you have your money. Is the Dairy Association a group of well-meaning persons encouraging strong bones and healthy teeth, or a bunch of conniving operators manipulating Congress for subsidies and permission to fix prices?

Trade associations do much of the heavy lifting in national and state legislative lobbies and maintain day-to-day contacts with government regulatory agencies. In addition to promoting an industry's products and helping develop and spread the news about new technologies, they provide a forum for setting standardized technical specifications covering everything from bolt sizes to electronic arcana.

trade barriers Government action or customary practice that favors some people in selling products or providing services by making it hard or impossible for others to enter the business. Customs duties are the most obvious form of trade barrier, but health and sanitary regulations, environmental restrictions, and labor rules also do nicely as a pretext for favoring some over others. Limitations under these categories can be urgently needed, richly justified regulations, but the line between necessary measures and business-crippling favoritism is not easily drawn, as endless trade wars, lawsuits, boycotts, and retaliatory tariffs testify.

In the early 1920s, when women first began cutting their hair, organized pressure from barbers succeeded in getting laws passed in some states forbidding beauty shop operators from taking up scissors and comb. A 1924 beauty shop publication reported that one "Madame Florence De Guile, President of the National School of Cosmetology and proprietor of a fashionable beauty parlor," received thirty days in the city workhouse for "cutting hair without a license."

transparency The degree to which barriers to international trade are clear and measurable to people seeking to do business or invest. A modern business cannot long be run if the authorities are rapacious, the laws incomprehensible, and the books of other companies unfathomable. Transparency, or the lack thereof, is an ever more crucial matter as business becomes the daily life of an ever-growing fraction of mankind. When a company's true condition is made opaque by incomprehensible jargon or deception, customers, vendors, and lenders are tricked into putting themselves in jeopardy. Investors, instead of knowing what they're buying, end up with a mystery stock. Condescending American officials and business executives have been given to trotting about here and there lecturing the natives on the need for transparency, which exists everywhere, apparently, but in the United States, where the business world in 2002 was racked with transparency scandals.

Transparency International   A worldwide, nonprofit organization set up to reduce bribery and other corrupt practices that inhibit trade. It puts out a Bribe Payers Index of major exporting countries, "ranked by the propensity of their companies to bribe while doing business abroad," and a Corruption Perceptions Index, a ranking of the least and most corrupt countries from the point of view of those doing business in them.

For reasons clear only to God and the sociologists, there is a high correlation between nations with excellent indoor plumbing and honest public officials. Thus it comes as no surprise that Denmark is first, quickly followed by other famously anal retentive nations, Finland, New Zealand, Sweden, Canada, Iceland, and Singapore. The United Kingdom comes in at thirteen, and the United States at eighteen, a nose length ahead of Chile and Israel. Why the United States should rank so high is not explained.

traveling salesman   See **road warrior**.

Trilateral Commission   See **sinister doings**.

Truman, Harry S.   (1884–1972)   Unsuccessful small businessman. Having failed in the private sector (farming and retail men's clothing), he switched over onto the public teat, where, by most accounts, he did better.

trust, trust officer 1. Faith in another human being, usually misplaced. **2.** A bewildering variety of trusts exist, all of which have as their central idea that someone is paid to handle somebody else's money. For example, a company may create a trust administered by a bank to run its pension program or oversee payments and such on bonds a company has issued. The classic trust is the one created by the father who made the money, because he believes his children are too dumb to take care of their inheritance, or that they'll drink it up and leave nothing for the grandchildren. Such trust funds are run by bank trust officers, who have a stinky reputation for being, of all things, untrustworthy. Stories abound of bank trust officers who left the money in securities that were eaten up by inflation, or in stock of companies that went the way of the California condor, or who simply, via one form of self-dealing or another, stole the contents of the trust. More than one heiress has gotten a bolt-from-the-blue call from a larcenous trust officer appointed by dear, defunct daddy, telling her that she is flat broke and will either have to get married or go to work. **3.** Late nineteenth- and early twentieth-century word for monopoly, of which the connotation was entirely pejorative. **4.** A specific form of business organization used in the late nineteenth century to stop "cutthroat competition" and/or satisfy the greedy urgings of the counting house. First perfected by John D. Rockefeller in the early 1880s with his Standard Oil Company, a trust was created when the owners of all or most of the companies in a given industry surrendered their stocks or rights of control and got back in return what were called trust certificates. Having done away with the competition in their industry, the certificate owners elected trustees, who were empowered to control the production, set prices, divide markets, and pay out the monopoly profits. In short order, the nation beheld the tobacco trust, the lead trust, the whiskey trust, and so forth; in even shorter order, in 1890 the famous *Sherman Antitrust Act* was passed, thus ending the trust but not efforts to mitigate the effects of competition on profits. (See **pools** and **holding company**.)

tulipmania See **bubble**.

twenty-four/seven (24/7) Pluperfect go-getter term for "we never close, we never rest." We are, in that odious, insincere phrase, there for you, my dear customer. The spread in the use of 24/7 confirms the long decline in familial rituals such as eating or enjoying leisure together. Thus doth business shape culture. Save in restaurants and on Thanksgiving, Americans are, thanks to the rush-rush life of 24/7, increasingly eating standing up as they poke around the fridge and pop goodies into the microwave. Indeed, business, noting the change it has wrought in immemorially old customs, often uses the word *grazing* instead of *eating* to describe the act of taking on nourishment.

As of this writing, in Euroland, where the standard of living is approximately the same as that in the United States, 24/7 mostly has been rejected. The stores do close, the factories stop—often compelled to by law—and people go take their rest. In the United States only Sabbatarians, that is, religiously motivated persons, struggle to have at least one day of the week when the noise and the striving cease, and the worried and the driven can look up from their monitors to see a bird or touch a flower or hear the voice of God. A shift to a 24/6 society is opposed by the elements who know that idle machines cost as much as busy ones (see **work ethic**).

underground economy Any business, and that's a hell of a lot of 'em, that cannot survive without violating law and regulation. This definition excludes most forms of common, garden-variety piggery, namely businesses that would make money if they abided by the rules but make more money if they don't. Doing business off the books by hiding tax liabilities is probably pandemic among very large and very small enterprises, but should its practitioners be considered true members of the underground economy or merely fellow travelers? There is a gray area here. What about an undocumented or illegal alien without a green-card working permit who runs a small carpentry business?

The illegal drug business belongs in the underground Dow Jones. Besides bread, milk, and gasoline, illegal drugs are the only consumer commodities available 24/7 everywhere. To serve its millions of customers all the time, the industry must have an elaborate and highly visible distribution system whose protection has to involve large expenditures on law enforcement officers, prosecutors, and judges. This large cost of business is offset by not paying taxes and charging healthy markups.

Light manufacturing of such things as clothes, lampshades, and junk jewelry makes up a significant component of the underground economy. These businesses are carried on in violation of the wage, hour, and safety laws, and their proprietors are seldom invited to the better class of civic awards banquets. This shunning, as the Pennsylvania Dutch say, doesn't seem to be much of a deterrent to this class of entrepreneur. Those who find child or sweated labor abhorrent have an uphill struggle, as the victims need the income, which is more than they can make doing anything else.

underwriting To take the risk in return for a fee or a cut or a chance to cash in. **1.** An insurance underwriter checks out an insurance application as to how risky it is and whether or not to accept it. Sometimes insurance underwriters will sell part of a policy to another underwriter to forestall a huge payment if a big claim comes in. **2.** In finance an underwriter is the same as an investment banker.

unfair competition **1.** See **dump**. **2.** Anybody who is stealing my market share. **3.** A cheaper product than mine. **4.** A new and better product than mine.

unfair labor practice laws The federal rules and regulations relating to the conduct of management and unions in their dealings with each other. The whole business is a relic of another time, as the United States moves toward being the first technically advanced society without labor unions. Union-free businesses today need only be concerned with other laws on the books, such as requiring that employees be paid for all, not some, of the hours they work, and so forth. To what extent these laws are obeyed is a matter of conjecture. Infractions come to light when employees complain, something they do after learning they have come into a large inheritance and will never have to work again.

United States Constitution When this sacred eighteenth-century document was written, business as we know it didn't exist, but trade and enterprise did, and the Constitution is at pains to foster them. It gives Congress the power to confer monopolies (patents) to reward inventors; it establishes a national standard of weights and measures; the commerce clause prevents the states from putting tariffs on goods coming from other states or screwing around to erect their own private business preserves. As, step by step, modern business came into existence, the legislatures, national and state, and the courts generally bent over backward to change the rules to encourage business. The grants, subsidies, immunities, and special powers accorded business, which outrage its critics, may not be fair or even needed in the twenty-first century, but being very, very nice to business goes way back, which may or may not impress you.

United States Military Academy at West Point Along with the Rensselaer Polytechnic Institute at Troy, New York, the first college in the United States to instruct its students in science and engineering. Graduates of both institutions helped lay the foundations of industrial America. In 1854, an English visitor to the Point, impressed by the energy of the place, was told by a cadet, "We must get up early, for we have a large territory; we have to cut down the forests, dig canals, and make railroads all over the country." It is not by accident that, both before and after the Civil War, Union Generals such as William T. Sherman popped up all over the exploding railroad industry as both civil engineers and executives.

urban sprawl "I can't define it, but I know it when I see it," said the judge of pornography, and that applies as well to urban sprawl. Everyone agrees that it is unsightly, unecological, and uneconomical, save for the sprawlers, who are, of course, half the population.

usury In the Middle Ages the word meant making a profit by lending money, and it was forbidden. Modern usage defines usury as making too much profit by lending money. How much is too much has never been permanently decided. During periods when interest rates have shot up, states have been known to sic the law on credit card companies or even banks' consumer loan departments for charging too much. Price controls of any kind are a nightmare to enforce, but price controls on money are double nightmares. Slap a ceiling on consumer loan interest rates, and the lenders just vanish, taking their money someplace where they can get their price.

Vail, Theodore Newton (1845–1920) The primary credit for the building of AT&T goes to Vail, whose executive ability, political craftiness, understanding of technology, and ruthlessness were used to build a national telephone system that was the admiration of the world, although the company was often so disliked that the threat of a government takeover sat on its horizon for years.

Vail cut his teeth as an executive in the Post Office Department, where he instituted several important organizational changes saving time and money. There, he absorbed the idea that a communications system should reach everybody, and he went into the phone business under the slogan of "One System, One Policy, Universal Service." When the original Alexander Graham Bell patents expired, so did Vail's monopoly, as thousands of independent phone companies jumped out of the woodwork to challenge his single-system idea. Using Wall Street allies, he kept his smaller competitors from getting the capital needed for expansion. Though his tough guy tactics failed to eliminate the independent and cooperative phone companies munching away at AT&T's business, it did bring the threat of a government attack under the Sherman Antitrust Act. AT&T's bacon was saved in 1913, when Vail, a flaming apostle for "natural monopoly," was able to negotiate the Kingsbury Commitment with the Justice Department. This accorded the corporation a monopoly, natural or unnatural, that would survive for sixty years or more. In a climate when many thought telegraph and telephone should be folded into the Post Office Department, the Kingsbury Commitment was seen by the phone industry as the price all had to pay to continue as private enterprises.

value investing Buying stocks and bonds the same way people buy houses and automobiles, that is, getting your money's worth by not overpaying and by putting your dough into well-run companies. You wouldn't think there would be any other way of buying securities, but it seems that most people can be sold stock in any kind of a company if the seller can come up with a good story, as often as not a fairy story. Value investing takes work and a considerable knowledge about how to determine which is and which is not a good company. As for overpaying, it never occurs to some otherwise sensible people, who are price-conscious about buying vacations, clothes, and washing machines, that even a stock in a good company may be too expensive, so that a buyer will be getting less than he/she is paying for.

variable-rate mortgage The interest rate on this kind of mortgage is subject to bobbing up or down to a limit of 2.5 percent during the life of a mortgage. Customarily the rates may not move more than a half-percent in any twelve-month period. The interest rate movement is tied to the prime rate or some other interest-rate index.

This makes for uncertainty in the monthly house payments and therefore in the budget, but there is a solution for that, too. It's called a variable-maturity mortgage. Under its terms the monthly payments stay the same, while the mortgage's duration grows or shrinks as interest rates rise or fall.

vermin exclusion Not what you think. It's a clause in freight insurance contracts excusing the insurers from paying damages caused by small, sharp rodent teeth owned by animals that often sport long, hairless tails. One of the infinity of contingencies business must attend to.

vertical integration A vertical-integration company is one which may own its own raw material sources, transportation, and other service units it would otherwise have to buy from outside providers. An oil company with its own oil wells, pipelines, refineries, and gas stations would be classified as vertically integrated. Vertical integration, much in vogue in the early twentieth century, gives a corporation all kinds of power and control, but it's often been difficult to make all the parts in the vertical column profitable. The modern corporate style tends toward other forms of organization. At one time, automobile companies strove toward vertical integration to the extent that the Ford Motor Company owned its own steel mill and glass-manufacturing units. By the

1990s automobile manufacturers were fighting with their unions to outsource as many parts as possible. Computer manufacturers, which make almost none of the parts that go into the boxes bearing their logos, are highly unintegrated—or should that be disintegrated?—companies.

vigorish **1.** The house cut of the gambler's winnings. **2.** Extortionate interest on a loan, bearing in mind that the definition of "extortionate" will vary from person to person. Whenever the subject of interest comes up, people get moralistic or weird. Free marketeers define interest as rent on money, and thus it should bob up and down like everything else in the market. In actuality, however, some interest rates are set by custom, by law, and by the action of governments run by economists and businessmen, who think that if they can find the optimum rate and peg money to it, a vast number of good things will follow. Sometimes they do and sometimes they don't.

VIOXX The name of a drug used against rheumatic and rheumatoid type pain, said to have caused thousands of fatal strokes and heart attacks. Newspapers and surviving kin accused its manufacturer, Merck & Company, of selling millions of doses of VIOXX years after they had reason to suspect it was better at killing than curing. These events would have been unthinkable for the company's long-time chief, George Wilhelm Merck (1894—1957), who pioneered bringing academicians into a company research park, where, in his words, scientists were given "the greatest possible latitude and scope in pursuing their investigations, the utmost freedom to follow leads promising scientific results no matter how unrelated to what one would call practical returns." The returns came, in addition to major breakthroughs in the first synthesis of vitamins and human nutrition, the development of antibiotics and cortisone, and five Nobel laureates. Merck epitomized the much-spoken-of responsible citizen business executive, not only in the way he ran his company, but as the head of biological warfare research during the Second World War and in his work with a roster of civic organizations ranging from the National Science Foundation to the Save-the-Redwood League. Happily for him, and tragically for his customers, he did not live to see the MBAs besmirch his and his company's name. Were there more high-minded people running companies back then, whenever back then was, than there are now? Who can say, but whenever a great oak falls, it stings the heart.

vision **1.** The faculty of sight. **2.** A meaningless word used by big-shot business people, politicians, and the shabbier, less literate members of the clergy, all of whom are to be heard on every public occasion urging their auditors to have it. **3.** A hallucination.

waiter, waitress Americans regard serving others as infra dig, and businesspeople have taken note and switched to job titles that give not the slightest hint of what the bearer does. Thus, restaurant persons are staff, and gasoline station attendants are fuel distribution personnel.

Walker, Madame C. J., née Sarah Breedlove (1867–1919) Although hers is the epitome of the rags to riches story, people get antsy about this African-American, orphaned at six on the deaths of sharecropper parents, because the hair treatment products that made her rich were designed to straighten hair. To a later generation, the Walker System is an acceptance of a white standard of attractiveness, so that Walker, despite her many generous good works, her astonishing ascent from poverty, and her business talents, dwells in a shadowland of recognition.

Wall Street   A narrow thoroughfare on the lower tip of the island of Manhattan, .994193 of a mile in length and named for a wooden barrier built in 1653 by the Dutch to keep out Indians, Brits, and other riffraff. It didn't work. Millions of persons, many of questionable origins, have poured into the place, creating a succession of ever larger traffic jams. On September 16, 1920, a terrorist of unknown ethnicity or religion detonated a bomb at one end of the street, killing thirty-three low-echelon wage slaves unlucky enough to be out at noon trying to get a bite to eat. It is also the seat of the New York Stock Exchange.

Walton, Samuel Moore (1918–1992)   The latest in a 150-year-old line of merchants, each of whom found a cheaper, faster, and better way to serve an ever-expanding mass market with an ever-expanding variety of merchandise. If you believe that prosperity is a function of consumer spending, then, by the time of Sam Walton's death, the health of the world economy depended in no small part on the volume of sales being rung up at his Wal-Mart stores.

Born in Kingfisher, Oklahoma, Sam—who once donned a grass skirt and did the hula-hula on the floor of the New York Stock Exchange—created dinosaur-sized "malls without walls" and resurrected the department store after everyone in the industry had declared it dead.

By placing his stores in relation to centrally located warehouses, he gained a significant advantage over the competition. His bag of tricks also included his personnel policies and his ability to extract name-brand merchandise at low prices. At the time of his death, he could lay claim to having been the most successful businessman in the history of his industry, a status that did not deter the minority of captious critics who maintained that his greatest contribution was to litter his native land with ugly buildings, increase traffic congestion and air pollution, and hoodwink the millions into stuffing their lives and the nation's waste disposal facilities with every kind of chintzy, short-lived merchandise that commerce could come up with to dazzle the barbarian consumer hoards, but nobody could beat Sam's prices.

war Always a tonic for the health and power of the state, in America, if not elsewhere, war has on occasion been rather good for business. For those lucky enough not to have been in uniform, World Wars I and II were highly profitable and happily remembered periods. From the Devil's point of view, the desirability of war is merely a question of balancing bodies against bucks.

Wasserman, Lew R. (1913–2002) The man who liberated the movie stars from long-term studio contracts, and thus opened the way for eight-digit contracts. Next, Wasserman took his company, MCA, into the movie production business, and, garnering such power that his company was called "the octopus" by his impotent rivals, he achieved something akin to dictator status in Hollywood. When the Department of Justice chopped a couple of his tentacles off for violating antitrust laws, Wasserman reacted by hurling very large campaign contributions at very needy politicians, thus making the industry the Washington force it remains.

Wasserman was almost as well known in his industry for his despicable treatment of his subordinates as for his business genius. Even for CEOs, who, as a breed, seem prone to cholerically sadistic mistreatment of underlings, he was a standout. The whispered connections to organized crime that attached themselves to this distant and frightening man made him look like a character out of one of his own gangster movies. In the end he lost his empire, living to see it fall into the hands of an undercapitalized French water company. But he died very rich, and isn't that the best revenge?

wasting asset Anything, including old devils, that is being used up and whose value therefore is constantly diminishing. A coal mine, if you happen to own one, or any human being over the age of fifty is a wasting asset, as is a factory, an oil field, or a bond or option that expires at a given future date.

watered stock In general, stock selling for more than the company is worth, like the famous dot-com stocks, whose shares were worth hundreds of millions when the companies issuing them had no assets, no income, and no sane prospects. Wall Street legend traces the beginnings of watering stock to Daniel Drew, the mid-nineteenth-century Wall Street pirate, who, beginning his business career as a cattle drover, is supposed to have induced his animals, which were sold by weight, to drink copious amounts of water so that they would fetch more. In his time he was famous for watering the stock of the Erie Railroad, issuing and selling more and more of it even as the real value of the railroad deteriorated under poor management. Today, stock is watered just as Drew did it, by issuing stock options to executives, by taking on huge amounts of debt, and by any number of other horrid little tricks.

Westinghouse, George (1846–1914) Inventor, engineer, and businessman. A haphazardly educated boy from upstate New York, Westinghouse learned his business growing up in the shop culture of machines and small manufacture. In comparison to Thomas Edison, who concentrated on inventing spectacular consumer products, Westinghouse's specialty was systems for industry.

His first great success was the railroad air brake. There were air brakes before Westinghouse, but they didn't work. Westinghouse's genius was to buy up the useful patents, invent and perfect what was lacking, join the parts as a completed whole, and then sell the air brake to a railroad industry that would have been happy to save its money and take a pass on the invention, except that passengers were getting hives at the thought of being killed in train wrecks. Westinghouse's next great success was his automatic railroad signal and switch system, which got the steam-powered railroads to adopt two new technologies, compressed air and electricity.

Westinghouse is best known for having taken inventions made by Europeans—the most celebrated of whom was the mad, Serbian scientific genius Nikola Tesla—and perfected a workable system of electric generation and transmission, which we see in the high-voltage wires and electrical substations of today's power grid.

By 1889 the Westinghouse company had gone global with more than a half a million employees around the world. Such is the upsy-downsy nature of business that eighteen years later the company was in temporary receivership, and George Westinghouse, while able to hold on to his job, had lost control of his company.

whisper number Another variety of Wall Street bollocks. The unofficial market analysts' guess as to how much money a company will make per share. The whisper number is concocted out of greed, unethical calculations, water cooler conversations, yak-yak on the telephone, well-founded rumors, ill-founded rumors, hopes, winks, fears, shrewd back-of-the-envelope figuring, hints, and blind man's bluff. Companies that exceed their whisper are rewarded by a jump in their stock price; companies that fall below it get coal in their stockings.

whistle blower The mortality and accident rates for this occupation equal those of uranium miners, high-iron construction workers, test pilots, and topless dancers with breast implants. The expression "thankless task" was invented to describe the rewards received by those who blow the whistle on corporate or government hanky-panky. These include being sent to corporate Coventry—generally a small room without windows, phones, or work—being sued by lawyers wearing expensive shoes, being designated deranged, and being accused of alcoholism and/or drug addiction.

white-collar crime A corruption of "white-collar grime," a term originating in the laundry industry, referring to the ground-in dirt on the collars of the white dress shirts of business executives. The existence of white-collar crime is what is called an urban myth. (There are no rural myths.) The nonexistence of white-collar crime is reflected in the fact that official FBI crime statistics contain no such category. Ignore rumors to the contrary and trust your stockbroker.

Women's Bank Around the time American women got to vote in 1920, banks bestirred themselves and opened tellers' windows for their use. Then, in June of 1921, the Women's Bank opened in San Francisco to encourage "economic independence," while offering the same services as the Bank of Italy, its sponsoring institution. All its staff and employees were women, and within two years it had ten thousand customers and a million and a half in deposits, a respectable figure then.

work ethic The quality of breaking one's ass on the job. CEOs and coaches use the term unsparingly, if not exactly as it was meant by its originator, Max Weber. How it made its way from Weber's 1904 book, *Die protestantische Ethik und der Geist des Kapitalismus,* to the board and locker rooms of America is a bit of a puzzle. Weber, whose many works attest to his having a touch of the old work ethic himself, was the first to recognize that modern business was more than an *appetitus divitiarum infinitus*—an unquenchable hunger for riches—and something other than the millennially old swap, barter, and trade mentality of the ancient bazaar and the medieval fair. It was part of a distinct cultural system that gave rise to peoples stamped with certain values, traits, and patterns of behavior. That Weber's *Geist des Kapitalismus,* or spirit of business, is not as naturally part of being human as having a belly button is obvious in the clash between the business civilization created in the Christian West and the world's other civilizations.

working capital Loosely speaking, the money tied up in the day-to-day running of a company, i.e., buying raw materials, paying wages, and carrying unsold inventory, as opposed to the money sunk in buildings, equipment, and so forth. Companies needing to borrow working capital are not necessarily broke, and companies with adequate working capital may be on the verge of going down the toilet.

working late at the office 1. An excuse given to hide an assignation with that new pretty and/or handsome lawyer in legal. **2.** What millions do. Americans and Japanese work longer hours than anybody else but have little or no more to show for it. The standard of living in France, Germany, Sweden, Finland, etc., is about the same, although people in those countries work shorter days and fewer of them. Experts are at a loss to explain these incongruities, although some theorize that Americans and Japanese are dumber and therefore have to work harder to keep up with lazier but smarter people in other countries.

workout and **workout artist** In business the term has nothing to do with squash or aerobics. A workout is an attempt to put a distressed business back on its feet again, and a workout artist is one who makes his living as a doctor of sick and dying companies. There's a certain amount of blue smoke and creative accounting in the workout business, where it sometimes turns out that companies, cured and healthy again, relapse and die after the workout artist has exercised his briefly valuable options and is down the road doing business at a new address.

work shifting Shifting the work to the customer may have begun with the introduction of the shopping cart and the elimination of the clerk fetching the merchandise.

Whether or not the computer and other electronic devices save labor, they have made it possible for companies to shift the work and the cost thereof from themselves to their customers. Airlines have their passengers issue their own tickets under threat of charging them more if they don't, tens of thousands of offices have their phones answered by a machine that makes the caller do the work once done by the switchboard operator, lists of FAQs (frequently asked questions) on a million Web sites substitute for salaried personnel answering customers' questions, and major retailers are training their clientele to bag their own merchandise and check themselves out of their stores. While the rich continue to patronize places where they are attended to by human beings, the masses are content, and some of the few who are not would rather deal with an intransigent computer than a surly, incompetent clerk.

World Trade Organization See **WTO**.

write off Moving something on the books from black to red, from something to nothing. If a factory burns down, management writes it off by reducing its recorded value to zero. If a customer declares bankruptcy, his debts are written off, and what was once on the books as an asset, that is a plus, is now declared worthless. Companies "take write-offs" or confess a loss for a variety of reasons, which can range from the costs incurred in employee layoffs to recognizing that any number of once optimistically valued things on the books are actually so much junk. Many a company that vastly overpaid to acquire another company has later had to admit it was hornswoggled on the deal and has been forced to write off the difference between what the acquired company was really worth and what the hyperthyroid idiot CEO paid for it. (See **nonrecurring charge** and **zombies**.)

WTO or **World Trade Organization** Based in Geneva, Switzerland, and not to be confused with the WTO or World Tourism Organization, based in Madrid, Spain. The WTO is the latest in a progression of endeavors to make buying and selling abroad as effortless as buying and selling at home. With over 130 member nations and more seeking admittance, the WTO is the most comprehensive and effective instrument for promoting and overseeing trade yet devised. It has a real adjudicative authority and, in many ways, is a more effective organization than the United Nations. Nevertheless, it is not even remotely omnipotent. The United States, or the other gorilla-sized commercial powers, can and do occasionally bare their teeth at a WTO ruling, but not often and not indefinitely, since all concerned have too much to lose if the WTO is weakened. With all its faults, flaws, and weaknesses, the WTO is the best thing of its kind in the last two or three centuries, if not ever.

WTO jurisdiction cuts across every human concern—health, labor, food, climate, and daily life. The organization has the power to make a difference in these areas. How much of a difference varies according to politics and ten thousand clashing and competing interests. The WTO's member states have delegated to it limited authority, and that authority is always under challenge from a huge spectrum of groups and interests.

American right-wing suspicions about the threat to national sovereignty represented by organizations such as the WTO have grown in the course of the last four decades. In more recent years, left-liberal sentiment, which once supported globalism of every sort because it is said to break down barriers, encourage diversity, and raise up the not yet developed, has come to have second thoughts due to the fear that international trade at any cost will knock off the environment and drag down working conditions.

yield The generic word, taken from farming, for what you get. Any yield at all is at least OK, and a lot of yield is a lot better. The yield on a stock is its dividend; on a bond the yield is the interest you earn this year or the interest you can expect to get all the years you own the bond. The yield on a piece of real estate is the rent the owner collects, and the yield on a sales tax is what the government takes in.

Your call is very important to us It is not.

youth nation A market segment, a statistical category come to life and turned into a new ethnic group. Business no more intended to suck youth out of the bosom of the family and give it an independent existence than it intended to do away with the family meal (see **breakfast**).

Businesspeople may or may not have consciences but, assuredly, they have no consciousness, no capacity to reckon the side effects of what they are doing, whether it's polluting the Hudson River or San Francisco Bay or bringing forth youth nation. Yet youth nation exists, and it has millions of inhabitants, all of whom dress, eat, consume, and shape their beliefs in accordance with those of their commercially created ethnic group. It is little wonder that parents will squint at their teenage offspring and ask themselves, "Who are these people, when did they move in here, and where in God's name are they from?"

yo-yo (Tagalog word for comeback, or so the devil has been told.) A textbook example of how to launch a fad and make a mint from it. The yo-yo had been around for nigh on three thousand years before Donald Franklin Duncan (1899–1971) got hold of it. You can see pictures of kids on ancient Greek pottery playing with the silly thing. Chinese children of the same vintage had them, too. Duncan gussied the yo-yo up and in 1929 talked a major newspaper chain into a cross-promotion that brought in fifty thousand new subscriptions to the *Chicago Herald-American*—and Duncan was off and running. In each of the next three decades, he sold between 20 and 30 million. What Duncan did for the yo-yo, he next did for the parking meter. Again, he took something, not of his invention, on which he owned no exclusive patent, and sold the hell out of it. By the time he sold his company in 1935, the Duncan Parking Meter Corporation was responsible for 80 percent of the meters around the globe.

yo-yo stock One whose price goes rapidly up and down. Human yo-yos pay financial advisers goodly sums of money to tell them to buy such stocks at the low yo and sell them at the high yo, thus high-ho and off to the brokers we go.

zero-coupon bond A non–interest-paying bond. It is not as bad as it sounds. For example: A one-hundred-dollar zero-coupon bond maturing in ten years might be purchased for twenty-five dollars from the issuer of the bond. If the buyer holds on to it for ten years, she will be paid its face value of one hundred dollars, thereby making seventy-five bucks on the deal.

Since the government taxes the interest on the bond every year to maturity, even though there is no interest paid, zero-coupon bonds are ordinarily bought for tax-exempt accounts; people also buy municipal zero-coupon bonds because they are tax exempt. Since the bonds pay no interest, in the years before maturity they are prone to fluctuate wildly in price, but all kinds of securities have a place in the financial firmament. If you know that you will need a certain sum of money at a future time, say for college tuition, zero-coupon bonds may serve your needs. The above example is the vanilla version of the zero-coupon bond; there are many other, fancier kinds of zeros, which may or may not be nefarious, but are complicated, devious, and tricky. Only people able to figure square roots in their heads should play with them.

zombies Financial institutions and banks of the living dead, propped by government-sanctioned funny bookkeeping but too weak to operate as they should. Prime examples are the Japanese banks that lent money to businessmen who overpaid for New York skyscrapers, foreign factories, and movie studios, then stuck their lenders with billions of bad loans, driving them to insolvency. The Japanese, like the Americans, were afraid to let their banks collapse because of the too big to fail theory, and the Japanese business world found itself populated by zombies.

zone pricing Charging different prices for the same thing in different places. The most famous zone-pricers in our time are the drug companies, who lost the Corporate America Miss Congeniality Contest when it became known that customers in the United States were paying more for drugs than people as close as Canada. While regarded as immoral, unethical, and fattening, the practice contravenes no principle in free market theory, which does not hold that prices, like social and political rights, must be equal. Minority group members, various age groups, the ill, and the handicapped have had to deal with zone pricing of one kind or another within the United States for years, and electronics now makes it possible to vary the price of everything from Coca-Cola to electricity, according to the time of day, the place of purchase, and the intensity of demand. Government keeps trying to limit business's power to set prices as it will, but the resistance is obdurate. Part of the businessperson's art is knowing who the consumer is, how to segment the market, and, therefore, when and how much to change and adjust prices. (See **redlining**.)

zoning The most widespread government intervention in a major field of economic activity. This use of the police powers, which can diminish or augment the value of private property, is, in all probability, the occasion of more corruption of public officials than any other area of government action, including drugs. The first zoning ordinance was passed in New York City in 1916, and within twenty years zoning had been adopted everywhere to protect property values, which often translated into building restrictions that had the effect of excluding lower-income (read minority) people in many districts. In the last generation, the imposition of environmental zoning has extended the regulation of real property to include virtually the entire nation.

How effective and desirable zoning is has long been debated, but in the real world of greasy-thumbed city and county politics, there is no chance of zoning being replaced by a better method.

Zukor, Adolph (1873–1976) Zukor immigrated from his native Hungary at age sixteen, in time to learn enough about American business methods so that he would be ready and able when the industry he was to make his mark in was born. Although he is chiefly associated with Paramount, he gave the whole movie business the form it would have until the coming of television. The studio star system was of Zukor's invention, and it was he who adapted the vertical soup-to-nuts integration practiced in other industries to Hollywood. At his zenith his studio was pumping out two hundred pictures a year, which were distributed by a Zukor company and shown in the hundreds of Zukor-owned or controlled theaters across the country. Ultimately, the Department of Justice, having decided that the movie business was in flagrant violation of the antitrust laws, moved to break up such monopolistic arrangements.

Although the nature of movies makes it impossible for film executives to be as completely unaware of their products' possible side effects as other business executives are, they have come close. Other than a certain personal concern about his own social respectability, Zukor seems to have been about as aware of what his products may or may not have done to warp the simple-minded and twist the impressionable as the coal industry was of what it was doing to the state of West Virginia. It's the old story—businessmen take care of business, and that's all they do. (See also **Wasserman, Lew R.**)

ACKNOWLEDGMENTS

My thanks to Carl Bromley, Ruth Baldwin, Mary Evans, Susan Dooley and Dan Akst. The Devil thanks Alan Greenspan and the Conference Board.

EYNDE

FINIS CORONAT